NOTHING TO FALL BACK ON

NOTHING TO FALL BACK ON

The Life and Times of a Perpetual Optimist

Betsy Carter

HYPERION   NEW YORK

ISBN: 0-7868-6761-2

Hyperion books are available for special promotions and premi-
ums. For details contact Hyperion Special Markets, 77 W. 66th
Street, 11th floor, New York, New York, 10023-6298, or call
212-456-0100.

FIRST EDITION

10   9   8   7   6   5   4   3   2   1

FOR MY MOTHER

"By now you must feel as though God is picking on you—
well if he is, he has found a formidable opponent."

— LETTER FROM A FRIEND

NOTHING TO FALL BACK ON

One

On one of those perfect days in September, when the full summer air and coolness of autumn make you wistful and optimistic at the same time, I got married. It was the second marriage for me, the third for him. I was forty-five, and felt that finally, I had met the man I was meant to be with. He was brooding and handsome with curly black hair and eyes the color of sea urchins. Although his name was Gary, my friends called him "Thank God for Gary." It was supposed to be a joke, but it wasn't, really.

My friends thanked God because Gary was funny and kind; on a good day—say the Jets and Giants had both won—he could be downright ebullient. He was smart and large and could carry you through a crowd if the going got tough. A real catch.

But they thanked God because now I'd be someone else's problem and because they worried that I was not a good catch. Not after the blaze of bad luck I had just run through. They figured that with his physical strength and the sureness of his love, Gary had the power to reverse my misfortunes and beat back the bad karma. And I thought they might be right.

The morning of our wedding, Gary and I played two sets of tennis (I won the first, he won the second). We picked up a lunch of smoked turkey sandwiches, iced tea, and potato chips, then brought it to the beach, where we had a picnic on the sand. It was 2:34 when I looked at my watch. "At two thirty-four every Saturday for the rest of our lives, let's always remember this time and this place and how perfectly happy we were," I said. Gary held out his pinky, a little finger that weighed about a half pound and was covered with hair—if you could call it a pinky. "Pinkies," he said. "Pinkies," I answered. It was a rule left over from my childhood: Never make a wish or swear a promise without sharing pinkies first.

We were getting married at a restaurant that overlooked a harbor; the metal clips clanking against the masts of the small sailboats sounded like bells. Upstairs was a changing room where a few friends had come to help me put on makeup and get dressed. Victoria painted my lips Coral Blush and dabbed concealer on the deep furrow between my eyes, while Lisa read us a story from *The National Enquirer* about a boy who'd raised a family of pigeons in his closet for two years before his parents found out. I pulled a blue garter over my thigh, slipped into my white silk dress, and stepped out onto the balcony. There, a photographer snapped pictures of me staring out at the late afternoon sky.

From my perch, I looked down and watched the guests come in and shake Gary's hand. There was my friend Ron Rosenbaum. He showed up two hours early and paced around the parking lot, not wanting to be the first guest to go inside. Everything about Ron seemed to be stoked by a ferocious brain—his wild red hair, his fierce brown eyes, the way he couldn't stand still—it all kept the engine going. Ron had written personal ads for me in case no one asked me out after my first marriage ended.

He needn't have worried about arriving first. My ex-husband's parents beat him to it. They walked in, smiling and as gracious as the day I married their son. At that wedding, she was still a flirtatious beauty who'd welcomed me into a large family unlike any I had ever known. He had bright blue eyes and was never afraid to tell someone she was wrong or that he loved her. Now a demure silk dress covered her hip replacement. The light in his eyes had dimmed and he had a slight limp—the result of a recent stroke.

Gary was bringing his eighty-nine-year-old mother over to meet them. She was large boned with big ears, and had a loopy smile. She was him without the beard. She hung on Gary's arm as he introduced them, and I wondered what she might say. Weeks earlier she had told me in her broken Viennese English that when she found out at forty-three she was pregnant with Gary, she'd considered having him "destroyed." I hoped that she wouldn't bring that up again today.

At the far end of the bar, my boss was scrutinizing the labels on the wine bottles. Was he thinking about the precarious fate of the magazine I ran? My oldest childhood friend was standing on the deck right beneath me. She held her cardigan close to her chest and looked around uneasily at the room full of people she'd never met. I heard her ask her husband, "Do you think it will rain?" in her familiar high-pitched voice. There wasn't a cloud in the sky, but she always was a little anxious.

When we were eighteen, she made me promise that we would become lesbians together if we weren't married by the time we were thirty.

And there were my dentists, both in dark navy suits. I'd never seen them in anything but white. They were much better looking than I'd ever realized. Come to think of it, I'd never seen either of them in daylight. A few feet to their right was the shrink who once told me that I ought to consider having an exorcism. She was wearing too much makeup and overlarge hoop earrings, and was talking to my dour lawyer, whose eyes kept darting around as she spoke. He was the one who told me on the day that we met how we were destined to become close friends because with my life, I'd always need a lawyer.

When we were putting together the seating plan, Gary and I had decided to put my shrink, my dentists, my lawyer, and my doctor at the same table. Gary had suggested that we drape black cloth over their table and put up a sign that said: "The Dark Years." "The Dark Years" had become our code phrase for the seven years when my luck went haywire and everything I held dear came apart. Let's just say that several years later, when I told Ron how, during a bike trip, a bolt of lightning had hit the roof of the building next to me, causing it to burst into flames, he slapped me on the back and said, "Congratulations! A couple of years ago it would have been *you* that burst into flames!" You get the picture.

So while no one actually said it, I knew everyone there that day saw this wedding as a celebration of survival, an amen to a time they had all been part of, or at least witnessed like horrified rubberneckers. I appreciated how they had stuck by me during those years, and thought how they deserved this party as much as I did. How else to explain why a person with a sound mind would throw a wedding extravaganza more appropriate for a giddy young virgin than a divorced middle-aged career woman. The white roses framing the *chuppah*, the water gently slapping against the nearby sailboats, the sweet sound of Van Morrison singing "Have I told You Lately," would surely put a lump in the throats of even those of my friends who reveled in dark humor.

I walked down the stairs as the band started to play "Long Ago and Far Away" ("I dreamed a dream someday, and now that dream is here beside me."), then watched from the doorway as Gary loped down the aisle—a long winding deck on the bay. I took my father's arm. He was so frail. He was unsure of his steps and leaned on me to help him. I couldn't remember when we'd ever been this physically close for this long a period. The last time I'd walked down the aisle, it was with a jubilant stride and a parent on each arm. My mother whispered in my ear, "Sweetie, you should try and slow down a little." Now my mother was too sick to leave home and the walk seemed stiffer and sadder than I had expected. My sister, Miriam, was waiting for me under the *chuppah*, and we shot each other half smiles, as if to say, "How can it be that we're here again?" Gary and I exchanged our vows, then he stomped on the ceremonial glass so hard that the entire deck shook. Even the rabbi had to laugh. We put our arms around each other and walked back down the aisle, my legs trembling underneath me. All the while, the sunset was a frenzy of reds, violets, and oranges. For me, there's never been another one like it.

We had planned that before we joined the party, Gary and I would have a private moment upstairs in my changing room.

It would be our first time alone as man and wife, and I imagined there would be a passionate kiss and a teary embrace. As Gary walked in and closed the door I heard something strange. How do I put this? I was honking. Suddenly, I was doubled over wheezing and gasping. "I can't . . ." There were no words left, just wild hand motions trying to conjure up the right gesture for "air." "I can't breathe," I finally gasped. From the look on Gary's face, I realized that he wasn't expecting me to have an asthma attack in the middle of our wedding.

Two

My mother used to tell me that I was born happy. "It's your nature," she would say, as if that explained everything. "You inherited *my* family's happy go-lucky attitude," meaning that I carried none of the dark Teutonic baggage from my father's side. "You would lie in your crib for hours smiling and not complaining even when your diaper was reeking," she'd laugh. "You were happy even when you were full of shit." My mother told me that long before I could even speak, my grandmother, the one from the happy-go-lucky side of the family, would stare at me and shake her head. "She's awfully cute, but so dumb," she would say. "Thank God she's a girl." And my father, who from as far back as I can remember, talked about me in the third person, would look at me, then turn to my mother and ask, "Why does she have such a maniacal grin?"

No one ever asked me why I was so determinedly upbeat, but here's what I think. Even in the womb, all my fetal instincts were telling me it was dark out there, that I needed to figure out how I would find my way. Ten years earlier, my parents had to flee Hitler's Germany. They came to this country in 1936: she was twenty-two, he was twenty-six. They had no money and no prospects. Now they were sharing a tiny apartment with a newborn baby and a five-year-old with a bad case of scarlet fever. My mother, once an adored only child, had lost her father two months earlier. It was probably beginning to dawn on her that making a living would be her responsibility. My father, once the heir to a department store fortune, felt demeaned by working as a stock boy or a clerk, and eventually found a way to let whomever he was working for know it. So what choice did I have, really? I had to be cheerful, even downright incandescent sometimes, if I was to stay afloat when the family undertow threatened to suck me under.

I wasn't naive enough to believe that happiness was anybody's birthright, but that fall, when I returned from marrying Gary, it was tempting to think I might be on a lucky streak. For the past five years, I'd been the editor of my own magazine, *New York Woman*. It was an idea I'd had one day while working at *Esquire* as its editorial director. A woman would never be editor of *Esquire*, I'd been told, and after six years there, I felt ready to be in charge of my own magazine. Running *New York Woman* was the most joyful experience in my twenty years of journalism. I started the magazine in 1986, during the swank years for Wall Street and New York. For a long time, *New York Woman* rode the coattails of those swank years—and so did I. There were parties on yachts, sales conferences in Aspen, and black-tie dinners where I got to introduce Mikhail Barishnikov and eat caviar tarts.

The staff of the magazine was a blur of energy that, when you came in close, consisted of ferocious organisms with curly hair ("There are lots of you here," my boss once said to me. "You know, curly brunette Semitic types."), linen jackets, black tights, little boy Ts from J. Crew—and raw, unharnessed ambition.

We developed the intimacy that breeds when any clique of women comes together in a small space for any length of time (which is what we were trying to capture in the first place). Hardly a day went by when there weren't tears over a boyfriend who wouldn't commit or a solemn confession of some extra-marital affair. Then there would follow the reassuring hugs, the murmured words of comfort, and the inevitable lightbulb going off in someone's head signaling that here again, buried in the seeds of one person's heartbreak, was the germ of a perfect story idea. When we managed a break from our day-to-day traumas, there were birthdays to celebrate and anniversaries to mark. No occasion was too small for a party. After I told one of our young staffers that she was getting a raise, she jumped up and down and squealed, "Ooh, I'm so excited. I've never gotten a raise before." Within minutes, we were all sitting around my office munching on popcorn and chocolate chip cookies and lifting champagne glasses to toast the next Nora Ephron.

The magazine was gaining a reputation for sauciness, intelligence, and, some said, a kind of edgy neurosis. This was hardly surprising, since that was pretty much the personality profile of everyone who worked there. We only had one man on the staff, an honest-to-God bar-hopping, womanizing heterosexual. He tried valiantly to hold on to his masculinity by hanging a small basketball hoop above his desk and downing burgers and fries for lunch, but he was no match for the frenzy of estrogen that engulfed him each day. After less than a year with us, he got engaged. After that, it was a matter of weeks before he became preoccupied with china, silverware, and caterers. The hoop came down, the picture of the bride went up, and he started eating oat bran muffins. That was it: We had him.

Every now and then, an emissary from our corporate owners would pay a visit to our offices. It was usually right after we'd run a story about famous bimbos, or about male construction workers who dressed up in silk dresses and sling-backs on weekends. First we'd get a warning phone call from the downtown office telling us that someone was on the way, no doubt aimed at making sure none of us were running naked through the offices when he got there. We'd use the time to wipe the muffin stains off the wall and turn down the strains of the Talking Heads singing "Burning Down the House." Sometimes I would walk through the halls and look at posters advertising the magazine, or fondle the promotional candy bars with our logo spelled out in milk chocolate, and marvel at how something that was once just make-believe in my head had become this flesh-and-blood reality.

The night after I got back from getting married, *New York Woman* had a huge party to celebrate its fifth anniversary. I can still replay it all, like a video running through my mind frame by frame.

I am standing at the podium at Larabelle's, a disco in midtown Manhattan, wearing a dress borrowed from the magazine's fashion closet. It is sleeveless with red sequins and a low-cut V-neck. My face is flushed under the floodlights, and I think of my smile as being a little bit too eager. I am presenting the Life of the City Awards, to "women who have changed New York." A parade of people comes up to the stage. They shake my hand or kiss my cheek. Here's Queen Latifah, Susan Sarandon, Donna Karan, The Guerilla Girls (in full gorilla costume), Wendy Wasserstein—on and on it goes.

When the last Steuben glass trophy is handed out, I look around at the giant blowups of the magazine covers and the sea of faces in the audience, and I feel for all the world like Billy Crystal at the Academy Awards. At this moment I see myself through the eyes of the girl who came to New York City twenty years earlier wanting more than anything to be a journalist. I have gone higher and farther than the girl could have imagined, and now that I've made it to this place, there is no reason to doubt that's where I'll stay.

The rest of the night is a blur except for the end. As the guests start to leave the club, I feel the adrenaline rush of being center stage, of people I've never met before shaking my hand and telling me how they love the magazine. "Don't leave this evening," I want to beg them. "Don't let the party end." The band is playing a hard-driving version of "Born to Be Wild." I am swaying and pumping to the beat by myself on the dance floor. One by one, the staff of *New York Woman* joins me. We are as exuberant and unself-conscious as kids at a band shelter on the Fourth of July.

For one moment, I catch a glimpse of my boss. He is standing behind a pillar, holding on to it with both hands. He is watching us dance; he can't take his eyes off of us. My boss is a spirited and unabashedly lusty man; I expect him to join our bacchanal. But he stays frozen behind the pillar. He is not even smiling. There is something else in his eyes, something far away and cold, almost scary. I wish I hadn't noticed.

Fuck it, I think, this is my night. I turn my back to him and keep on dancing. I've survived in this business and this city for nearly twenty years. What can he possibly do to me?

Three

Even as a little girl, I knew I wanted to be a journalist in New York. It always came out as one word: ajournalistinnewyork. That's what I wrote my career book about in seventh grade. On the day of my graduation from the University of Michigan, I flew to New York with my boyfriend Rob. I was going to get a job on a newspaper; he would get a job with the city and dodge the draft. We barely had enough money to put ourselves up at a rundown YMCA on the West Side of Manhattan, which seemed to come alive at around five in the morning with the clacking of high heels. "I've got a bunch of eager tourists on my floor," I whispered to Rob on the phone one morning. "You wouldn't believe how late they come in."

"Those aren't tourists," he said. "They're hookers."

"Oh."

Welcome to New York.

For the next couple of weeks, I went to every publishing company in town: Time-Life, *Newsweek*, Condé Nast, Fairchild.

It was always the same story: Leave your résumé with personnel and we'll get back to you. No one ever did, because no one *ever* does.

In desperation I turned to the Career Blazers Employment Agency, where I met Marsha, my first real New Yorker. When I told her I wanted a job that wouldn't involve typing, she went "hmmmph" and started patting her bouffant hairdo as if she were touching up a snowman. "Look, honey, journalist, shmirnalist—wherever ya go, they're gonna ask how many words ya type a minute. But I'll do my best."

Several days later, Marsha came back with a couple of prospects, including a position at a newsletter published by McGraw-Hill. "You're going to have to type," she told me, "But they say they'll let ya do some reporting." She told me it was called *Air & Water News*, and was about air pollution and water pollution and "that kinda stuff." The words *Air & Water News* sounded so important, so journalistic. This was the job for me.

On the morning of the interview, I put on a red tartan plaid suit with a tiny miniskirt and white vinyl boots. It seemed professional, yet a bit Goldie Hawn-ish. Perfect for New York City! I walked into the *Air & Water News* offices on Sixth Avenue and Fifty-second Street and met with the editor, a quiet Canadian named Jim Marshall. I tried to think of something to say about air and water pollution, but came up blank. Instead, we talked about a new group he'd just seen, Big Brother and the Holding Company, and I told him about the ladies who came and went at five in the morning at the Y.

Later that afternoon, I called Marsha to see how it went. "Not bad, I don't think," she reported. "He said that anyone who showed up for a job interview dressed the way you did probably had the nerve to do anything. I'll talk to you tomorrow."

I hung up excited and a little confused. Was that good or bad?

The next morning, I called Marsha from the Horn & Hardart's down the street. "Well kiddo, congratulations," she said. "You got the job. Eight thousand dollars a year. You start next Monday."

Unbelievable. I was going to be the editorial assistant of *Air & Water News*! So it wasn't *Time* magazine, but it was a start.

The *Air & Water News* staff was lean. There was Jim, his managing editor, Tom, and me. The newsletter came out once a week on mucous-green paper that was impossible to photocopy. At a subscription price of fifty-two dollars a year, the company didn't want *Air & Water News* wanna-bes getting their issues for free. I had to answer the phone, paste up the newsletter, and walk it down to the main McGraw-Hill headquarters on Forty-second Street each Friday. I went to pollution conferences in Washington and got to wade around the city sewers in thigh-high boots. I visited sewage treatment plants and had two articles printed in *The Congressional Record*—one about how air pollution affected animals in city zoos.

One afternoon, I attended a luncheon at the Hilton Ballroom. When the main course was finished, people came around with large plastic bags and scraped all of the remaining food into them. They brought the bags of garbage up to the stage and ceremoniously dumped them into a machine that made chomping noises, as if it were trying to eat furniture. Finally, the contraption spewed out dung-colored masses of what looked like sod. When we left the luncheon, we each got a briquette of the stuff wrapped in a red ribbon. We had just witnessed the first trash compactor in action.

I was living the life I'd always said I wanted to live. I dropped phrases like *press conference* and *putting the newsletter to bed* as often as I could. I carried a reporter's notebook with me everywhere. Who knew when there would be some breaking news about sludge? I took fiction writing and film courses at the New School and saw *The Fantasticks* twice in one summer. Although I was born in New York City, we had moved to Florida when I was ten. I was old enough to remember snow and subways, and young enough to romanticize the glamour of it, and spend the next ten years yearning to return. The New York of my twenties seems worlds away from the cramped apartment of my childhood—even though I was living in a cramped apartment only ninety blocks away.

And of course there was Rob, my boyfriend from Michigan. Together, we practiced being New Yorkers, walking around Greenwich Village on a Saturday night, going to see *Dr. Strangelove* at the Thalia, eating Chinese food at the Hunan Balcony. Mostly, though, Rob preferred to stay home and watch *Mission: Impossible*, or drink beer with old friends from school. One July morning, we drove to Jones Beach. We sat on a blanket watching young parents with their kids. I could see myself as one of them, at home raising a brood of little Robs. That night, on the way back from the beach, I picked a fight with him over why he wouldn't try any foreign food in New York except Chinese. But I knew the fight wasn't about Moo Shu pork. It was about being trapped in a small apartment every day with a brood of small children.

In ways that neither of us could put a finger on, coming to

New York made us strangers to each other. When we were in Ann Arbor, Rob got it all right. His dark good looks, his low-keyed manner and unshakable midwestern belief in how things ought to be were what that club was all about. There, Rob was the host and I was the visitor. But in New York, everyone was a foreigner. People talked too fast and believed that anything could happen—which was why they came to the city in the first place. I liked how New York tasted and was hungry for more.

New York scared Rob, and for all the right reasons: size, noise, dirt, rudeness. He seemed to get smaller and more timid the longer we were there. And when we fought—which was more than ever—he'd call me hyper, tell me to calm down. But I hadn't come to New York for a rest. One Sunday morning, when I didn't want to hang around the house and read the paper with him, he blurted out something I suspected he'd wanted to say for a long time: "You don't sit still for a moment. Why can't you just be normal?"

The truth was, this was the most normal I'd ever felt.

We fought and broke up, then came together again after three days. It went on like that all summer, until the Labor Day weekend that my mother came to town. I served hamburgers for dinner. I cooked them pretty well around the edges, but the centers hadn't thawed. That was the kind of thing that really ticked Rob off. The three of us hacked away at the meat in silence, until my mother put down her silverware and shoved her horn-rimmed glasses on top of her head. "So, what are you two kids planning to do about this relationship?" she asked. She had a way of starting a conversation in the middle that caught you so off guard you found yourself struggling to catch up to the rest of it.

Rob jumped right in. "It's funny, but we both seem to want different things from our lives," he said. He told her how much I'd changed, then added: "She's so into this journalism thing. Truthfully, I don't know what I want to do with my career, plus everything here is so damned expensive."

My mother tsk-tsked about the high prices of apartments. "The city is a rat race," she said. "It's certainly not for everyone."

Rob shook his head, "You've got that right," he agreed. It was as if they were speaking from a preprepared script but had forgotten to show me my lines.

"I don't mean to be presumptuous," she finally said, although that's exactly what she had in mind. "But it seems to me that you kids aren't planning a future, so maybe you owe it to yourselves to start seeing other people."

Rob lit up. "That's not a bad idea. What do you think, Bets?"

What I thought was, Jesus Christ, she's broken up with another boyfriend of mine.

Four

He turned out the lights and left me sitting alone at the antique oak table "Close your eyes," he said. "Don't open them until I say to."

I sat there studying the afterglow of the candlelight flickering on the inside of my eyelids. Crackling sounds escaped from the kitchen. Then the smells—buttery, earthy, slightly burnt—like nothing I'd ever smelled before.

I heard his footsteps as he came back into the dining room. "Okay, you can open them now." His voice was husky with excitement. "Voilà," he said, extending his offering. "For you, duck à l'orange flambé." I could see the fire reflected in his cornflower-blue eyes. "With Grand Marnier."

"So beautiful," I moaned.

"Pureed butternut squash." His cheeks glowed pink as dahlias. "And wild rice with toasted nuts and morels."

"Mmmm. Heaven."

He poured two glasses of cabernet sauvignon. "To many perfect meals together," he said, clinking his glass against mine.

"And to the perfect chef." I clinked back dreamily.

Even when he wasn't bathed in candlelight, Malcolm had a beautiful face. The saucer eyes, the square jaw, the full pink lips, the wavy dirty-blond hair. It was hard to say if he looked more like Paul Newman or Robert Redford.

We'd only known each other for twenty-seven days and nineteen hours—long enough for my entire world to be upended. The first time I saw him was at a party at Columbia University. At midnight, a man in a white U.S. Navy uniform walked through the front door, not a common sight around Columbia in the late sixties. In that room, dark and gummy with pot smoke, he was luminescent.

"Who the hell is that?" I asked.

"My cousin Malcolm," said Tim, the man I'd been talking to most of the night. "He's in from Washington for the weekend."

I followed Malcolm with my eyes while he went into the bedroom to drop his coat. When he sat down on the couch, I bounced onto the empty space beside him.

"Hi," I said. "Having a good time?"

"Okay, I guess. Just got here."

I gave him a loony smile. Immediately, he excused himself to get some Brie. I watched him cut a perfect triangle of cheese and place it in the center of his cracker. I noticed how he dabbed his lips after sipping some Chianti, and I pasted my eyes to him as he wandered around the apartment. If he talks to someone else, I vowed, I will intervene. When he stopped to scan the bookshelf, I decided to make my move.

"Hi again," I said, with a jump in my voice. "So, what brings you to New York?" (He couldn't walk away from that one without answering.)

His parents were in town from Boston. He loved the theater. He'd spent a lot of time in New York. Before the Navy, he worked as a stringer for *Time* magazine.

Time magazine? My heart nearly fell into my shoes. I told him I was a journalist too. *Air & Water News*. I told him about the sewage plants, the noise pollution conferences. "Really cool stuff," I said, all the while thinking, Oh God, I can't believe I'm saying all this.

Just then, Tim tapped Malcolm on the shoulder and told him he was ready to go. Too bad. I'd planned to say something really groovy about waste management. The two of them left with barely a good-bye.

Not much to go on, but the following morning, I called my mother. "I met the most perfect man last night," I told her. "He's great looking, he's a journalist, he lives in Washington, and he hasn't a clue who I am. I really like him."

"Well, he sounds wonderful," she answered, "but be careful. Don't count your chickens before they're hatched."

Fat chance. The following afternoon, my friend Jill and I went to Chinatown. It was a bone-chilling day in March. As the sun set, it started to sleet, and we ducked into the first open place we could find: Bobo's, a restaurant so tiny that its address was 16½ Pell Street. As we walked into the nearly empty dining room, three people were walking out. Something about the young man wearing the white Navy uniform made my head swivel.

"Oh, my God," I cried. "It's you!" Everyone else—Jill, the waiter, the young man, and the two people with him—started. They searched the room. It's who? Jim Morrison? Jackie Kennedy?

"Hi," I said, staring into those unforgettable eyes. "Don't you remember me? Friday night? Friend of Tim's?"

"Uh, sure. Hi," he said. Not knowing what else to say, he added: "This is a nice place. The food is terrific, especially the sparcribs and the pork dumplings." Out of the corner of my eye I noticed the one who must have been the mother nudge the one who must have been the father out the door.

"Well, it's great to see you again," I continued.

"You, too," he answered. "I'll call you next time I'm in New York."

"Terrific. Want my number?"

"That's okay," he said, shaking his head. "I'll look it up in the phone book."

"No," I insisted. "You'd better write it down." I borrowed a piece of paper from the waiter's ordering pad, wrote down my number, and handed it to him.

"Thank you," he said, stuffing it into his pocket. "Here's my card."

Jill and the waiter stared at me as Malcolm walked out the door. Then the three of us swooped down to study the perfectly embossed script on the card. No address, no phone number. Only the words *Malcolm Neal Carter, Lieutenant Junior Grade.*

The waiter nodded thoughtfully as though he'd just read the words *General Dwight David Eisenhower.* Jill raised her eyebrows. "He's so cute," she said. "I think he likes you."

Ten days later, Malcolm Neal Carter called me. "I'll be in New York next weekend," he said. "Would you like to go out?" Stay cool, I told myself, feeling my face flush and my heart race. Act mysterious.

"Are you kidding?" I said way too loudly. "I'd love to."

We agreed that I'd get some theater tickets and he'd pick the restaurant. I got us orchestra seats for a show in previews; he made reservations at a French restaurant on West Fifty-fifth Street. The show turned out to be *Hair,* the blockbuster of the season. During the standing ovation, he kissed me on the cheek.

The rest of the evening had enough charm to stand up to the best of first date stories. I guessed his sign. He told me stories about seeing Jimi Hendrix at a concert in Monterey, I told him about my piece in *The Congressional Record* on air pollution in zoos. He ordered an artichoke as an appetizer. I did the same—though I had never seen one before. He peeled each leaf away from the stem, scooped up a dollop of vinaigrette, and slid the leaves between his teeth. I ripped off one spiky leaf after another, dunked them into the vinaigrette, popped the whole thing into my mouth and just kept chewing. We both ordered the coq au vin, which Malcolm said was the best in New York.

For dessert, we shared *tarte tatin.* The crust was thin and buttery; the apple slices were perfectly glazed with caramel and capped with a drizzle of crème fraîche. Malcolm sipped his coffee, put a piece of the confection in his mouth, and gazed at me with what appeared to be rapture. "Perfection," he sighed. My heart said he was talking about me; my head said it was the *tarte tatin.*

The date ended with Malcolm kissing me on the forehead and inviting me to Washington two weeks later. "I'll call you," he whispered. "We can discuss the menu." When he phoned later that week, I was hemming a skirt. I held the phone between my shoulder and ear and continued to stitch while we talked. "So, what are you doing?" he asked.

"Oh, I'm hemming a skirt," I said, hoping he'd pick up on how domestic I was.

I heard a little laugh. "Somehow, I can't imagine you sewing," he said.

We talked about the coming weekend. He said he'd take me to the Luray Caverns in Virginia. We'd go hear Roberta Flack at a bar in D.C. And of course, he would cook dinner.

"What's your favorite cookie?" he asked.

Not even my own mother knew the answer to that question. "Pecan Sandies," I said.

I'd been living on frozen egg rolls and unspent determination. Malcolm seemed kind, nurturing. I said good-bye in a love cloud, and stood up to return the phone to its cradle. Something was tugging at my thigh. I had sewn my skirt to my panty hose.

Seventy-eight days and nine hours after we met, Malcolm asked me to marry him. "Of course," I said. I'd never been surer of anything in my life. We agreed that I'd quit my job at *Air & Water News* and move to Washington as soon as possible. One week later, we flew to Miami so that Malcolm could meet my parents. Military men could fly half fare, but they had to wear their uniforms. So Malcolm was in his Navy whites when we stepped off the plane.

My parents were already well into our airport ritual. They both stood at the gate and scanned the crowd. My mother spotted me first, pointing a finger and announcing in a loud voice, "There she is!" as if everyone else at the gate was also waiting for me. Then my father saw me, nodded his head, and started to laugh. We hugged and kissed, and then they both stared at the lieutenant J. G. "So," my father said with mock fanfare, "this must be the famous Malcolm Carter."

My mother straightened her spine and shook Malcolm's hand—I could never predict when she would turn formal. "Hello, Malcolm, it's so nice to finally meet you," she said. Malcolm and my father headed for baggage claim while my mother and I lingered.

"Isn't he cute?"

"Very," she answered, as though that was exactly what she didn't mean.

Through the floor-to-ceiling glass, we could see the wing of a Delta 727 looming like a bat. My mother turned to me, her voice still laced with reserve. "Honey, you know I think you're adorable," she said. "But this boy, this Malcolm, he's awfully good-looking—maybe too good-looking. There are going to be problems."

My mother had always handed down judgments as if she were God's chief of staff. For her, all of mankind was divided into two camps. After meeting a new friend of mine that she liked, she would purse her lips together and say, "Now *that's* a real human being," like the rest of us weren't.

She sized up Malcolm without hesitation. Amazing—they hadn't exchanged a single word, yet I could tell she was already anticipating breaking up with him. Really, I thought. I'm twenty-three years old and getting too old for this.

"How can you be so judgmental?" I asked, close to tears. "You don't even know him and already you're dooming the whole thing. That's an awful thing to do."

Sorrowfully, she shook her head. "I know, I know. Call me horrible, but I have to tell you the truth."

I worried that Malcolm had already been banished into the not-a-human-being camp. If that was so, there was little I could say or do to bring him back. But if my mother's prophecy cast a pall, it was only momentary. By the time we got to the house, she was acting as though I'd brought Walter Cronkite home for a visit. "Malcolm, you're a journalist," she would say. "What do you think will happen in the Mideast?" Or: "Malcolm, you're in the military, what should we do in Vietnam?" Malcolm delivered his opinions as freely as she did, and for the next four days, they discussed her pot roasts and my poor eating habits as if they'd known each other for years. Despite the miles between us, my mother's judgments bound me as close to her as they did when I was a child. She embraced Malcolm as an ally, someone who would make sure that I finished everything on my plate. Even my father allowed as how Malcolm seemed to be a very nice fellow.

If my mother still worried that he was too good-looking, she never mentioned it during the frenzy of wedding planning that went on for the next three months. Somehow she'd convinced my father that the wedding had to take place on the roof of New York's St. Moritz Hotel, overlooking Central Park. My guess is that she didn't consult him about the white rose centerpieces at every table or the filet mignon for 120. Had we been guests at this wedding, she'd have inevitably leaned over at one point and whispered to me that these people must have spent a "pretty penny." But since she was now the comptroller of Florida's largest printing plant, she could be forgiven if for once she wanted people to whisper about how extravagant she was.

For someone whose romantic daydreams had always bordered on pedestrian, I was suddenly verging on storybook.

Sometimes I wondered if this wasn't all happening too fast. Malcolm could be patronizing, even bossy, but I didn't allow myself to get bogged down by second thoughts. Anyway, at this point the wedding would have gone on without me. Every day at least one fondue pot or piece of Waterford crystal arrived in the mail. The dress dominated most conversations. The frenzy of presents and seating plans kept my mind off of what getting married really meant.

When the big night finally came, Miriam and I wound up together in a windowless room where the attendants were meant to help the bride with her gown and makeup. She and I were intimate the way sisters are—we shared the same room until she went to college. But we'd never fixed each other's hair, or played dress up—she didn't care about things like that. It was odd, the feeling of her fingers working the twenty-four mother-of-pearl buttons that ran down my back.

"You look like a real bride," she said, with a question in her voice.

I heard the first few chords of Pachelbel's canon. In a moment, I would take each parent on an arm and walk down the aisle. For the first time since the word *wedding* had become part of my life, I realized that all this fuss was about celebrating two people bound together for life. *For life?* Wasn't that asking an awful lot?

I grabbed the telephone and called the room where Malcolm and his best man were getting ready. "Malcolm," I said. He was chewing on a roast beef sandwich.

"Just remember one thing. This isn't forever."

He said, "Sure. I know what you mean."

Later, after the cake was cut, the dancing had begun

and I'd completely forgotten our conversation on the phone, my grandmother—my father's mother, who, as family lore has it, was the Sally Bowles of Kaiserslautern, my parents' hometown—pulled me aside. "If you ever have an affair," she whispered, "you can use my apartment."

For the next year, Malcolm dressed up in his starched khaki uniform and went off to his job at the Pentagon each morning. I worked a block away from the White House, where I was the editor of *The Shield*, a house organ for a large bank in the Washington area. Eugene McCarthy was running against Lyndon B. Johnson for the Democratic presidential nomination, and even from my windowless cubicle in back of the bank, I could smell change in the air. It was 1968 and I might as well have been selling ham sandwiches on the streets of Tel Aviv.

"Love and Peace" hadn't made it to the bank yet, or at least not to the vice president's office. The vice president was my boss and a dead-ringer for Frank Perdue. Because of the Eugene McCarthy poster that hung in my office and the short skirts I wore to work, he called me the bank renegade. About the skirts, he said, "It's immoral. You sit on the bus in one of those, and all the niggers can look right up your legs." I hadn't heard anyone use that word since I left Florida.

At home, I was about as rebellious as Little Bo Peep. Malcolm created a cocoon of domesticity, a buffer zone that fortified me to do battle in the daytime. Each morning he packed up a lunch for me to take to work, and every afternoon at around four o'clock, he'd call me up to discuss what we should have for dinner. From the moment I walked into the apartment at night, I became enveloped in a garlicky haze of pot roast and mashed potatoes or something that smelled just as delicious. If I tried to help with the cooking, he shooshed me out of the kitchen, claiming my willy-nillyness was too distracting. He took over all the shopping and had the last word on the clothes I bought. He made sure that I got enough sleep at night, and kept track of when I was due to have my teeth cleaned. Malcolm spoke the same language of love that my mother spoke. I came to rely on his opinions and judgment as much as I did hers. Behind every romantic union lies some unspoken deal, and this was ours. He was the strong, paternal figure who took care of a childish and helpless me.

At work, I was anything but helpless. My indignation over my racist boss made me feisty and tenacious; someone who wanted to be heard. Once a year, all the trade journals were required to create a one-page public service ad for the United Fund. I found a photograph of a little black boy and a little white girl holding hands and running through the park. Above their heads I wrote: "Everyone Needs a Friend." And beneath them: "Give to the United Fund."

When I showed the ad to Mr. Perdue, he puffed out his cheeks. "Uh-uh," he said, shaking his head. "Uh-uh. I'm not doing this."

"You're not doing what?" I asked, as if I didn't know.

"I'm not running this photograph," he answered, still shaking his head.

"What's wrong with the photograph?"

"You know darn well what's wrong with the photograph. It's obscene, that's what it is."

"It's not obscene. It's sweet and really makes the point."

"Oh come on, you know exactly what I'm talking about."

"No, I really don't."

"This is totally inappropriate for *The Shield* and we won't run it. That is my final decision."

"I don't think we have much choice here," I said. "I have friends at *The Washington Post.* If you don't run this ad, I'll tell them why you didn't. I don't think that would look very good for *The Shield.*"

I had no friends at *The Washington Post.* Even though I had traded my maiden name Cohn for Carter (ironic, since Malcolm's grandfather changed his family name from Cohen to Carter), I couldn't forget that I seemed to be the only Jew at the bank, and that made me vigilant about filling the role they expected me to play.

So poor Mr. Perdue caved in and ran my ad. It wound up being chosen by the United Fund as one of the five best of the year. The poor guy was forced to fill two tables at a banquet honoring the winners. For days, I overheard him on the phone, hunting down appropriate black employees to bring to the luncheon. "Does he have good table manners?" he grilled each branch manager.

Mr. Perdue and I were not destined to be colleagues for long. That fall, I took a photo of kids playing on the new life-sized rhinoceros at the children's zoo. If the horn of the rhinoceros was oddly placed near a little girl's thighs, I honestly didn't notice. I ran the picture on the cover of the magazine.

After that issue of *The Shield* came off the press, Mr. Perdue summoned me to his office. "This time you've gone too far," he yelled, slamming the door. "You can't pull this stuff over on me." He picked up the magazine and started jabbing his finger at the girl's crotch. "Pornography, that's what this is. Pornography! And another thing, I know you went all out for Eugene McCarthy. Well, let me tell you something, Miss Cohn Carter— you're going to see some big changes in this town, and you're not going to like them."

One month later, Richard Nixon was elected president. Malcolm's tour in the military was up, and we decided to leave Washington and move to Boston so he could work in his stepfather's business. I quit *The Shield* only days, I'm sure, before the old chicken man got around to firing me first.

Five

"Honey, I have something to tell you." We were standing on the roof of our apartment building in New York City on a steamy August day in 1955. My mother was backlit by the ruddy glow of a bowing sun. I could tell from how her words stuck to her tongue that whatever she had to say made her nervous.

"Daddy and I have decided that we're all going to move to Miami." She bit her bottom lip and watched my face.

MIAMI. It wasn't a word that came up often in Washington Heights.

"Daddy will go down in September and find a job. Then you, Miriam, and I will drive down in November," she pressed on.

MIAMIMIAMI. The word danced in my head to the beat of maracas.

"The weather's so warm, you'll never have to wear a coat or boots."

MIAMIMIAMIMIAMI.

"And we won't live in an apartment building. We'll have a backyard."

MIAMIMIAMIMIAMIMIAMIMIAMIMIAMI.

In all of my ten years, no word had ever promised so much or sounded so exotic—so American—as *Miami* did that night.

It was handed to me like an unexpected gift, an extra dip in the pool. I had no idea how much planning had gone into this move, nor how much my parents looked to it as their only salvation. My father had tried his hand at running a grocery story, selling real estate, peddling insurance. He was gone from early morning until after my bedtime. My mother said that he was not a people person, and that was why he had so much trouble holding down a job.

Mostly what I knew of him was what he left behind. One Halloween morning, I woke up to find a scarecrow he'd built from a broom and some rags. When I was at camp, he would send me stick-figure cartoons showing sorry-faced tubes of toothpaste and scowling lightbulbs. Squishing toothpaste from the middle of the tube, then not screwing the cap back on, or leaving lights on all over the house: Those things drove him nuts, because they were flagrant signs of waste—and things he couldn't control. When bleeding ulcers started to fester in his stomach, it was hard for me to keep the toothpaste tubes separate from the grocery store in my ten-year-old head.

Meanwhile, she was putting in her time as the comptroller for Kallen's, a men's clothing store in midtown Manhattan. To hear her tell it, Kallen's was Potsdam and she was Roosevelt, come to make peace: "I told Mr. Lippman straight to his face that I thought this year's raises were way too low and unfair to the boys. He said, 'Coming from you, Norma, I have to take that seriously.' And what do you think that son of a gun did? He raised everyone by eight percent."

She told these stories at dinner, and always seemed hurt when hurrahs didn't follow. My father stared at his chicken while Miriam traced a pattern with her fingernail on the dinette table. I tried to look interested. Like most families, we were divided into teams. I was my mother's ally, so it fell to me to say something encouraging, which usually came out like, "That's nice, Mom," since I didn't actually know what a comptroller was. Some nights my father would slam his monogrammed sterling silver fork to the table. "Ach, Norma," he would say, his words thick with irony. "What would the clothing business in America do without you? She's a genius, your mother. The next Arnold Constable."

My mother was smoking up to two packs a day by then. When she developed a grating, intractable cough, she had us all convinced that she had lung cancer. After all, her mother had just died from it and she'd never smoked a cigarette in her life. My parents were exhausted, she from supporting the family, he from not—and now there was the threat of her illness looming over their heads. Their marriage was already as fragile as a cracked egg. If it was to survive, it needed something more than a night at the Copa, or a weekend in Cape Cod.

Cousins from my mother's side had moved to Miami years earlier. Max, a man with laugh crinkles around his eyes, owned a large meat store there. I only found out years later that Max's meat store was actually a slaughterhouse. Euphemisms got a lot of play in my family. Another cousin, Bernard, was never home when we went visiting because he was away at "the farm." I was thirteen when I learned that "the farm" was really a federal prison in Pensacola where Bernard was doing time for tax evasion.

My parents were funny that way. If they didn't wholly believe the mythology of their lives, they never let on. Maybe they lost too much too fast and had little left but the promise of who they were meant to be. Whatever the reason, they told their stories in carefully couched phrases calculated not to reveal any indignities.

They chose to live in Washington Heights because the park—with its hills and acres of oak trees that spiral up to a surprisingly successful replica of a medieval monastery called The Cloisters—was the closest thing in the new country to their native Black Forest. The fact that they lived on the upper reaches of Manhattan was almost incidental. Except for the hamburgers and Clark Gable movies that crept into their lives, they might as well have been in Dusseldorf. Every Sunday the men would dress in suits and the ladies would wear hats with elaborate quills, and the couples would walk arm in arm through the park. After about an hour of this, they'd swoop down to Nash's pastry shop and fortify themselves with eclairs, Napoleons, and cups of dark coffee.

They never lost their accents. Their sentences were often topsy-turvy, though my mother, in particular, reveled in using American colloquialisms. I tried pushing them into mainstream America as best I could and begged them to become friends with the American grown-ups in our building, the parents of my friends. More than anything, I wanted us to join the Sunday night dinners at the local Chinese restaurant and the annual Fourth of July picnic. But they would have none of it.

My parents disavowed anything German, even refused to teach me the language, yet they were suspicious of anything that wasn't. They filled our small four-room apartment in Washington Heights with the ornate china cabinet, formal headboards and upright desk that they had managed to bring with them to America. The furniture, like the odd formalities they imposed on our lives—a slight nod of the head when they greeted their friends, compulsive attention to good manners—was the glue that kept them bound to who they'd been before. And it was precisely that which kept us apart from where we were now. Until now. Surely MIAMIMIAMI would get us away from the Black Forest.

Through his connections in the produce community, Max knew of an opening at a wholesale grocery store. He was sure he could help my father get the job. My father left for Miami in September. Miriam, my mother, and I would pack up the green Plymouth and drive down to join him two months later.

None of my friends had moved out of the neighborhood yet. Miami was a new city and still had a slightly foreign ring to it. Whenever I said, "We're moving to Miami," people answered with the question, "Oh, you mean Miami Beach?" "No, Miami." In those days, it was more exotic than Atlantic City.

One morning, some of the Seven Santini Brothers showed up and start packing up our dishes. I had taken to wearing my New York Yankees hat to school. I wore it in the tub and hung it on my bedpost at night. As long as I had it on my head, I was still a part of my old life—not someone made different by living 1,500 miles away. I sensed upheaval ahead and felt certain the hat would keep it at bay.

The night before we left, I overheard my mother on the phone to her Aunt Flora. "I don't know if I'm up for this," she said, blowing her nose. "I hope I didn't make a mistake." My mother never doubted herself out loud, and something about how her voice caught made my heart drop. That night I slept in my Yankees hat.

Whatever jab of indecision my mother felt the night before was gone by morning. At 6:30 A.M., she stood in the doorway of our bedroom, lighting a cigarette. "Time to hit the road, kids," she said. By the time we packed up the car, a small group assembled to say good-bye. There were tears and a reckless exchange of promises with people we were certain to never see again. My mother sat in the front seat staring straight ahead. No hugs from her; no invitations to visit us in Miami.

We drove for five days and four nights. Miriam and I sat in the back. My mother was alone in the front with her AAA Triptik spread out in the seat next to her. She cut a swath through the A1A highway with the determination of Patton marching into France. At least Patton didn't have to put up with a ten-year-old and a fifteen-year-old in the backseat.

"No one's ever told you before," Miriam said after I pinched her arm radish-red. "Your real name isn't Betsy. We call you that just to pretend you're normal. Your real name is Bratsy!"

"*Maaa*, that's not true, is it? My real name isn't Bratsy, is it?"

My mother took a drag from her cigarette. "The two of you are driving me crazy." she exhaled. "Cut it out or I'm dropping you in Richmond. You can find new parents there." This went on until we hit Jacksonville on the afternoon of the fourth day.

The hard facts of people's lives are hidden in a place like New York City. Rich neighborhood, poor neighborhood: You never really know how people live inside those monolithic apartment buildings. In Jacksonville, life was more naked. Shacks that looked as if they'd been blown inside out lined the road.

There were no avenues, no parks, no separation of public life from private life. Black people lived in a different part of town. When we drove through it, my mother locked the doors and closed the windows. If this was Florida, I didn't like it one bit. It was too hot. People seemed angry, trapped by where they were. Every place smelled like the inside of an old trunk and besides, I couldn't understand a word anyone said. I pinched Miriam and made her bleed.

When we pulled into an Esso station, I got out of the car and started walking. I heard my mother run up behind me. I walked faster. She grabbed me by the shoulder. "What are you doing? Where are you going?" she asked.

"I hate it here," I said. "I just hate it. I'm moving back to New York and getting a job."

"Oh, honey," she said, hugging me to her. "Miami won't be like this. You'll see. You'll go to the beach, you'll be able to ride your bike to school. We'll live in a private house with a backyard. You're going to love it."

Ride my bike to school! It was enough to get me back into the car. Later that night in the motel room, lying in bed pretending to sleep, I overheard her whisper to Miriam, "She told me she was moving to New York and getting a job." They laughed together. I closed my eyes and thought about how sorry they'd feel when I was gone.

The next day we covered the last page of the Triptik. We drove until evening, until we reached a place where the buildings were flamingo pink and the air was treacly with jasmine. Everywhere, there were palm trees, their rubbery green fronds *shhhhsh-ing* in the breeze. We discovered a tree with a reddish-brown papery bark called a gumbo limbo tree, and kept singing the words "gum-bo-lim-bo-gum-bo-lim-bo." The moon was bigger than I'd ever seen it and everything it touched glowed. This was Miami.

Ralph's Rooms sat at the end of a strip of motels on Biscayne Boulevard. The lime green and bleached white rooming house did anything but glow. My dad had been living in one of Ralph's rooms for the past three months, and now that the family was reunited, we would occupy another. We lived there for a month. The rooms were small and badly lit, and the furniture was dark and heavy. Miriam and I shared a bed. What started out as small-scale bickering in the car ride down escalated into warfare. We were scared and cooped up and could only take it out on each other.

"We've got to get these kids out of here before they kill each other," my mother said one morning, folding over the real estate section of *The Miami Herald*. It was time to hunt for a place to live.

When the real estate agent unlocked the mint green door at 204 NW 32nd Street, I thought to myself that if I could live in a place like this then everything I had ever dreamed of was possible. It was the whole bottom floor of a two-family house plus a backyard. The kitchen, a brilliant work in Formica, was big enough for a table and four chairs. It had six drawers built in, and a window that looked out onto a small backyard. There were big closets with rows of shelves, a living room, a separate dining area, and two bedrooms. "How could anyone have ever moved out of here, it's *soo* beautiful," I said.

My parents walked in and out of the rooms, pulling open closet doors, touching the light switches. The kitchen excited my mother. "I could have a separate drawer for my cigarettes," she said. My father was silent. I watched the veins on the side of his head throb. His eyes got heavy and hooded—the look he always got when the subject was money.

"It's very expensive," he said.

No doubt, he was doing the math. He had taken a job working as a clerk in a wholesale grocery store for $175 a week and my mother had no job at all. He was looking at $95 a month in rent alone. Maybe he was thinking about the promises he and my mother had made each other about starting over again in Miami and how this was his chance to do the right thing as a father and a husband.

"Ach, Rudy, it's the best we've seen yet," my mother said with studied calm. They were standing in the little backyard, almost whispering, but I heard the impatience in her voice. Still, this was one of the few times I saw her defer to him. Miriam and I watched them from the kitchen window. They took notes; she counted things on her fingers. They tapped the trunk of the mango tree and pointed in a direction that probably had something to do with school. There were several more "Ach, Rudy"s and hushed words that I couldn't quite make out. When they came back into the house, he pulled in his stomach and stuck out his chest. "Your mother and I have decided," he said. "This is where we're going to live."

On the first night in our new house, the lights didn't work. We burned candles and stumbled over the packed cartons. My father was edgy—new place, new job, lots of money being thrown at things like doormats and toilet seat covers. Each time he tripped over a leaf from the dining room table or knocked over a stack of records, he said, "Now what?" as if it were one more thing being asked of him.

By eleven o'clock, our hands were filthy from all the unpacking. "This is New York dirt we've moved down to Miami. I wonder if we've moved a new kind of germ here?" I said.

"Just you," said Miriam.

We were so tired and giddy that we couldn't stop laughing at her stupid joke.

That night, I lay in my new bed in my new room. The bed was what they called a "junior single," only a few inches wider than I was. I felt the roughness of my mother's linen sheets on my legs. I thought about how these sheets had traveled from Germany to New York and now to here, and what secrets they must keep.

I sat up in bed and looked out the window. The moon shone like a searchlight. In its light I made out the mango tree in the backyard and a rusted green-and-white lounge chair that the previous tenant left behind. In New York, all I saw when I looked out my bedroom window were garbage cans. Now there was sky and trees and grass in my own backyard. I lay back down on the scratchy sheets and drifted off to sleep thinking that I never wanted to live anywhere but here.

In the morning, the sun was so bright it made everything in the house look like an overexposed photograph. The boxes that the night before had loomed so dark this morning looked like sand castles. I stepped outside, barefoot, in my pajamas. The sun doesn't shine in Miami. It blazes. Houses are pink, frangipanis are a gaudy purple. Coming from the muted blacks and grays of New York City, this was the world in living glorious color, like nothing I'd ever seen or imagined.

Six

The most memorable thing about the year Malcolm and I spent in Boston was leaving. For nine months, I worked in the hushed offices of *The Atlantic Monthly*. It was a serious place with honorable intentions. No one spoke above a whisper. No one dared to enter an editor's office without knocking first and waiting to be admitted. At least it wasn't *The Shield*; no one cared how short I wore my skirts. But the place wasn't raucous the way I envisioned a national magazine would be, even though I didn't know then that laughter, shouting, and the occasional throwing things across the room were all integral to working at a magazine. I felt out of step with the gentility and erudition of the place.

I sat in a pen with the other fact-checkers and copy editors. From our window we could look out onto the pond in Boston Common and watch the giant boats shaped like swans go by. I daydreamed about getting on one of those swanboats and floating away from *The Atlantic Monthly* forever, but of course that was impossible. No one ever left *The Atlantic Monthly*.

My memories of being there are not fun-filled. Every once

in a while, Joyce Carol Oates would rush through the halls and into the fiction editor's office with her latest work. As naturally as rain falls, Joyce Carol Oates wrote. Sometimes we received scraps of legal-sized envelopes, filled on both sides with her urgent handwriting—a short story written while on a bus, another in a doctor's waiting room.

My job was to read unsolicited articles and copyedit manuscripts, a job that required a great deal of concentration and attention to detail, talents I didn't have in abundance. Nine months after I arrived at *The Atlantic Monthly*, I was given a piece to work on about the Army Corps of Engineers. The writer was a meticulous reporter and the piece was dense with numbers and factual detail. Somewhere around the third paragraph, I picked up my pen and started doodling on the notepad by the phone. After an hour, I hadn't made a dent in the Army Corps of Engineers, but I had filled page after page with drawings of penguins, ducks, and curly-haired girls with nooses around their necks.

This went on for another three days. I had already missed my deadline and had promised the copy chief she'd have it by that afternoon. By eleven o'clock, I had to keep reminding myself to inhale and exhale. "I can't do this, I can't do this," kept beat with my pounding heart. "I've got to get out of here."

Impulse is like a lob at the net. You either jump up and slam a winner, or you lose the point. This one came at me high and slow, and before I could give it a second thought, I was standing in the managing editor's office. "Michael, I don't think I can work here anymore," I said. "It's too quiet, and I'm not doing a very good job anyway. What I really want to do is go to New York and be a reporter."

Michael was flawlessly credentialed. As I talked, he twirled his mustache. He banged his teeth with the eraser tip of his pencil and after a pause long enough to sing the "Hallelujah" chorus, he finally spoke: "For several years I worked at *Newsweek* in New York. It was a difficult place." Pause. "It was a very manic place. Mondays and Tuesdays we'd sit there with nothing to do. Wednesdays and Thursdays we'd start to get busy, and by the time Fridays rolled around, the place was a hubbub. People were frantic. They worked all night. Lots of drinking. I found it to be a very unpleasant experience. Unhealthy really." He stared at me with surprise, as if he'd just noticed I was there. "You know," he said, brightening, "I think you'd fit in perfectly." Michael offered to send my résumé to the chief of correspondents.

For the rest of the afternoon, I couldn't quiet the rhetorical conversation playing in my head:

"What if Malcolm doesn't want to move to New York?"

"I'll move by myself."

"Don't be silly. You don't even go to the grocery store by yourself."

"This is different. How can I pass up the chance to work at *Newsweek*?"

"Great, but what would you do when you came home from work at night?"

"I'd work every night. That's what you've got to do at those places."

"That's ridiculous. Besides, you'd miss him."

"Oh, shut up."

Malcolm and I had moved to Boston so that he could help out his stepfather with his photo franchise business. But like me, Malcolm had dreamed about being a journalist, and had even been one, during that time he was a stringer for *Time* magazine in San Francisco during the Summer of Love in 1967. That night, when I told him about the conversation I'd had with Michael, Malcolm smiled. "I'd move to New York in a minute," he said. "We've been here nine months. I really don't like the photo franchise business. Let's start sending out our résumés."

"You think we could really do that?" I asked.

"It's as good a time as any," he answered.

The next morning, I came to work with a freshly typed résumé and handed it to Michael.

On a Saturday afternoon, three weeks after my conversation with Michael, Malcolm and I were home in Boston. Malcolm was in the kitchen making linguine and clams for dinner, and I was lying on the couch reading *Love Story*. Jenny Cavilleri had just learned she had leukemia, but it didn't stop her from getting off some smart-ass one-liners. Her pluckiness in the face of imminent death made me cry so hard, I was sucking in my breath and heaving. When the phone rang, I picked up the receiver and blew my nose before I said hello. Malcolm noticed as my voice quavered and my words got more formal. I could see him wipe his hands on a towel and come toward me. "Who is it?" he whispered.

"*Newsweek*," I mouthed slowly, pointing at the receiver. "Next Thursday at three—that would be perfect," I said—"*interview*." I stretched my lips, still pointing at the receiver— "Thank you. See you then."

I hung up and did a little dance in place, jumping from one foot to the other punching the air with my fists. "There's a job opening to be the media researcher. That was the chief of correspondents. He said Michael gave me a great recommendation." I couldn't tell if I was out of breath from my little jig or from excitement.

Malcolm hugged me hard. He said, "I'm so excited for you." But I heard something wistful in his voice. Of course, I thought. He wants an interview at *Newsweek*, too! He had been so supportive about moving to New York, I felt rotten every time I remembered my first impulse: that I'd go without him if I had to. It is the only rationalization I can come up with for the highly irrational thing I did next.

"I have a great idea. Come to New York with me," I said, trying to sound as snappy as Jenny Cavilleri. "We'll talk to the chief of correspondents together!"

"You sure that's a good plan?"

"I know it is," I answered. "Wouldn't it be fabulous if we both got jobs in New York at the same time?"

"That would be something, wouldn't it?" he said. We headed off to our closet to choose my interview outfit. I grabbed a black-and-white checked short skirt; he matched it with a black sweater and black platform shoes. "It looks professional," I announced. He beamed back.

On the following Thursday morning, Malcolm and I sat before Rod Gander, the chief of correspondents at *Newsweek* magazine. Rod had a benign smile and a firm handshake that made you feel like yes sir, he was on your side. Rod, Malcolm, and I—we were in this together, and Malcolm and I listened to his every word. When Rod picked up his pen and wrote on his legal pad, we took it as evidence that things were going well. And when he put down the pen, dropped his chin into his palm, and shook his head, we were sure he was about to tell us what day to show up for work. "I've been doing this job for twenty-five years," he said, "but this is the first time I've ever conducted a his and her interview. It's pretty amazing."

Back home in Boston, Malcolm and I kept replaying that meeting. Was that a good thing that he said, "It's pretty amazing"? One month later, we were still puzzled over why we hadn't heard a word back.

Interviews aren't my strong suit. Before I went to *The Shield*, I interviewed for a job as an editorial assistant at *National Geographic*. In between my first interview there and my second, I stepped on a broken Coke bottle while walking barefoot at an outdoor rock concert. The glass cut a deep gash that damaged the tendon and required twelve stitches. The inevitable infection set in, my foot doubled in size, and my toes were purple and dangled out of the white bandage that held them.

When I hobbled back to *National Geographic* the next week, the white-haired man with the gnarly hands who had interviewed me earlier seemed not to notice the crutches and the foot throbbing in front of him. We discussed the importance of fact checking at a magazine such as *National Geographic*, and I told him of my ambition to be a reporter. He told me of his love for dolphins. I noticed that my heart was racing and my breath was coming out in jerky puffs. My arms were getting blotchy, with welts the size of potholders.

"The bottleneck is particularly interesting. They're the most vocal, and use hundreds of clicking noises to communicate." My neck was hot and itchy. Did he even notice that my face was the color of a plum? He squeezed his eyes shut, trying to come up with the exact number of words in a dolphin's vocabulary.

"One hundred. Maybe even more . . ."

"Umm, excuse me." I tried to sound relaxed. "I'm taking a lot of penicillin. Maybe it's an allergic reaction." Not enough air for full sentences. "Hospital nearby?"

"Certainly, dear," he said, as though I'd asked for the key to the ladies' room. He called in his secretary. As she led me away, he thanked me for coming and told me how much he'd enjoyed our chat. I never heard from him again.

But we finally did hear back from *Newsweek*. When the telegram came at 10:30 one Tuesday morning in January, Jerry Jeff Walker was singing "He spoke with tears of fifteen years how his dog and he, traveled about . . . Mr. Bojangles . . . Mr Bojangles . . . dance." I was crouched like a dog underneath the bathroom sink, snuggling up to the radiator because it was the only warm spot in the drafty apartment. It was four months after our duet at *Newsweek*. Since then, we'd moved from Boston to New York, where Malcolm got a job as a reporter at the Associated Press and I got fired from my brief stint as a salesgirl at Brentano's bookstore. The transition was difficult. Malcolm expected that I would fill my jobless days with domestic chores, which never seemed to happen. I told him he was picky. He told me I was short-tempered. We were both right. I ripped open the telegram.

BABETTE UNABLE TO REACH YOU BY TELEPHONE WOULD APPRECIATE YOUR CALLING ME FRIDAY AT NEWSWEEK JOEL RICH SENIOR EDITOR NEWSWEEK MAGAZINE

Two things were strange about this. Babette is my given first name, but nobody, including my family, ever called me anything but Betsy. And who sends telegrams to someone twenty blocks across town? But there was no doubting this—I'd gotten a telegram from *Newsweek*.

This time I showed up for the interview alone. I was dressed properly and no one had to take me to the emergency room. It was the same job I'd interviewed for earlier. I didn't question why it took four months for them to get back to me and when they asked if I could show up for work the next week, I said I thought I could. That night I cooked Malcolm's favorite dinner: pot roast with kasha and roasted carrots. "The pot roast is slightly underdone," he said, "but at least you tried."

I shared a small office with Hugh, the media writer. Hugh was a nervous man in his mid-thirties. His eyes darted and his shirt was always untucked. He rubbed his hands through his hair, and pieces of it stuck up like someone who'd stuck his finger in the socket.

As Hugh's researcher, it was my job to do the reporting for the stories he wrote. In the early part of the week, I went out on interviews or did them on the phone. By Thursday night, I typed up my notes into comprehensive reports that we called files. The files from domestic bureaus were pink, except those from Washington, which were green. Files from bureaus overseas were blue. On Friday mornings, Hugh had stacks of blue, green, and pink sheets of paper on his desk. He wrote all day Friday, and that night, he submitted his story to the editors. Fridays were when Hugh was at his most agitated.

We sat together in our windowless office late into the night. Sometimes, usually after the sun set, Hugh wept. Often he cursed his fate. "Christ, I hate writing," he would say, whipping up his hair. "Why can't I be a secretary?" Hugh acted out his anxiety so unself-consciously that I wondered if he knew I was there. When he called his ex-wife and yelled sharply into the phone, I hunched over my work and pretended that I wasn't listening—particularly when he slammed the phone down and shouted at me, "She's quite a bitch, isn't she?"

Because I was new to this job and gave myself over to it with total abandon, I didn't think I could say no to Hugh— even when, one Tuesday evening, he asked me to go with him on a blind date. "I'm scared," he said. "Okay, then," I answered. "I'll come with you."

We went to a Hungarian restaurant on the Upper West Side. Heidi was a broad-faced brunette who told complicated anecdotes about the pulmonary clinic where she worked as a receptionist. I told her all about my new job as a researcher at *Newsweek*. We got along quite well. Hugh played with his roast pork and cabbage and didn't say a word. Hugh never heard from Heidi again. I kept ducking her calls.

After three weeks at the job, I got to know Hugh's friends and family very well. Whenever any of them called the person would drop their voice and, in a tone reserved for the insane or elderly, ask: "How is he today?" Hugh was high-strung and we knew we each had to do our best to calm him down.

Late one Thursday afternoon at the end of my first month, the phone rang and Hugh picked it up. "Oh, that butcher," he cried. "I can't believe this! And all those times I complained about her whining."

The more he shouted, the more strenuously I stabbed at my typewriter. It was my first big story—*The New York Times* had leaked secret documents that revealed how policy in Vietnam was really formulated—and I had helped dig up some inside information about the Pentagon guy who leaked them. Hugh was sobbing. "I can't stand it," he said, slamming the phone into its cradle. He dropped his head onto the desk, his hair spilling around him like potato peels.

"Oh, God, oh, God," he keened. "Oh, God," he yelled again, only this time he stood up, turned toward me and smashed his fist into the wall above my head.

Maybe he wanted my attention.

I tried to sound comforting. "I can't help but notice that something is terribly wrong," I said.

Slowly, he choked out the words: "My mother just died."

Part of me was not surprised: We'd been building to a crisis of this pitch since the moment I got here. The other part of me was horrified. Here we were, it was Thursday afternoon, the biggest media story of the year had broken, and the writer's mother just died.

"Oh my God! That's awful," I said. "I'm so sorry. What can I do for you?"

"I guess I'd better get up to Ossining," he said. "I'll get the bus. Do you have any money on you?"

"Sure," I said, grabbing my wallet. "Here, take it." I dumped all my bills and change on his desk.

"Thanks," he said, blowing his nose. "Can you do me another favor?"

"Anything."

"I guess I won't be able to write my story tomorrow night," he said. "Will you tell Joel?" He counted my bills and put them into his wallet.

"Absolutely."

Slowly, sadly, Hugh got up from his desk, put on his blue blazer, and headed toward the door. On the way out, he grasped my shoulder. "Thanks Bets," he said, "you're a real friend."

I sat at my desk, stunned. I had stared into the wild eyes of fate—Hugh's mother, the about-to-be released secrets from Vietnam. But now was not the time to ruminate. There was work to be done.

I called Hugh's closest friends and told them the sorry news. Then I went into Joel's office. Joel was lying on the floor, his feet propped up on his attaché case, reading manuscripts, "Excuse me," I said, "I hate to bother you, but something awful has happened."

Joel kept reading, but I continued: "Hugh's mother died."

Nothing. "So I thought I'd collect some money and send some flowers up to Ossining." In order to get up, Joel had to roll over onto his stomach, crouch on all fours, and slowly pull himself up by holding on to his desk. He still hadn't met my eye, and I was betting he wished I wasn't watching this maneuver. Finally, he was upright. "Slipped disk," he said, reaching into his pocket and handing me a twenty. "I guess Tony will have to write that story."

"Thanks," I said, backing out the door. "Feel better."

As discreetly as the angel of death, I swooped into all of the offices on the twelfth floor and delivered the news about Hugh's mother. I came away with a haul of over $200. Before I left for the day, I called the funeral parlor in Ossining to find out where Edith Tompkins would be buried.

"I work with her son," I whispered into the phone. "We want to send flowers."

"Just a moment please," said the man on the other end. Through the muffled sound of someone putting his hand over the receiver, I heard him shout: "Anyone here working on Edith Tompkins?"

A few moments later, he returned. "Nope," he said. "She's not here." Odd, I thought. Oh well, they probably hadn't moved her body out of the house yet. So I called the Ossining florist and placed an order for a $200 funeral bouquet to be delivered to the Tompkins home first thing the next morning.

As I dictated the note—"so sorry for your loss. Your friends and colleagues at *Newsweek*,"—the florist broke in. "Who died?" she asked.

"Mrs. Tompkins. Edith. Hugh's mother."

"Edith Tompkins? Dead?"

"Oh, yes," I said, "Passed away early this afternoon."

"Well, I'll be damned."

That night, Malcolm prepared a roasted chicken. I sat on the stool next to him. "It's odd," I said, cutting up broccoli florets, "Hugh never mentioned that his mother was sick. Who do you suppose he was calling, 'that butcher?' "

"Don't know," he answered, taking my hand that was holding the knife. "You'll chop faster if you let your wrist do the work . . . like this."

Ever since I started working at the magazine, I had been bringing home nightly stories about the people who worked there: the beautiful woman editor who wore suede pants, then sat on the floor in them during meetings; the brilliant sports editor who went to the track all day, then turned out perfect copy at night; the senior editor who kept a piano in his office and played Chopin during deadlines. Malcolm hardly responded. Maybe he feared I was so captivated by this new world, that somebody in it would gradually supplant him as my mentor. That night particularly, he didn't seem one bit interested in Edith Tompkins's untimely demise.

The next morning, the phone was ringing as I walked into the office.

"Hello, this is the Ossining Florist Shop," said my friend from yesterday. "There's been a terrible mistake. Edith Tompkins is alive. I saw her in the beauty parlor this morning."

"Impossible," I insisted. "Her son left here yesterday afternoon in tears. He said his mother had died. Maybe Mr. Tompkins had another wife before Edith." I felt the panic rise in my voice.

"I don't think so."

"Maybe Edith had a sister." I was flailing.

"No siree."

All I could think was that I was the fucking media researcher at *Newsweek* magazine. Surely I could get to the bottom of this.

"I'll call you back," I said, then hung up. I felt nauseous. The phone rang again. It was John, Hugh's best friend.

"Betsy," he said, straining to sound normal. "I'm here in Ossining with Hugh. Wow, you reached so many people. Fantastic. Just fantastic. The house is filled with flowers. Beautiful. Lots of Hugh's friends are up here now. Hugh's so grateful."

"How is he?" I asked, lowering my voice.

"He's, uhh, he's okay. Umm, there's something you should know. I don't quite know how to say this, but . . . well . . .

Hugh's mother didn't really die. Well, actually, his cat Ella died. But he was so embarrassed about the way he carried on in front of you, that he told you his mother died."

I was so startled, all I could do was repeat John's words.

"Hugh's mother didn't really die?

"His cat died?

"He was so embarrassed about how he carried on in front of me that he told me his mother died?"

John answered each question in a dull monotone. "No, she didn't." "Yes, it did." "Yes he did."

There was no question about one thing: Hugh did not plan to return to *Newsweek*.

I was left holding $200 of my coworkers' money. I went into Joel's office. This time he was writing up his expense account, stapling restaurant receipts onto a sheet of paper.

"I'm so sorry to interrupt," I said. "This is a little awkward. But you see, it turns out Hugh's mother really didn't die. His cat died. So, here's your twenty back."

I placed the bill at the edge of Joel's teak desk. His eyes never met mine; it was if I were not even there at all. As he reached for his phone, he crinkled his nose, flicked his free hand, and said, "Babette, I don't know what you're talking about. Keep the money."

Retracing my footsteps of the day before, I gave Tony back five dollars; Ann Ray, ten dollars; Jeanie ten dollars; and on and on. The Hugh story became a permanent anecdote around the magazine. That's how people got to know me, as the girl who collected $200 for a dead cat.

Seven

On the first morning of our first day in the new house, I set out under the fiery Miami sun determined to make friends. Half a block into my mission, I saw a duck. Behind the duck there were four black paws, two pale legs, and four Radio Flyer wagon wheels. The legs belonged to a skinny girl, about my age. She had short straight hair, an overbite, and pointy features.

"Hiya. You're new here," she said. "Ahm Lou Ann Brown. We live down the street. This is Poke the duck. The dog is Grackle and the little thing in the wagon is mah sister Janie."

The words lolled around her mouth like jawbreakers. Ann became "Ayenn," down became "dowenn," and little, "leyall." "Hello, I'm Betsy Cohn," I answered, "We just moved here."

Lou Ann knew that.

"We heard y'all were from New York. My parents said you'd probably be Jewshhh."

"Yeah, we are," I said. It hadn't occurred to me yet that everyone wasn't. "Are you?"

Lou Ann squinted, then turned to the duck as if to ask, Did you hear that?

"Well, hardly," she answered. "We're Baptists. Everyone around here's a Baptist. You wanna ride bikes?" That's about how long it took for us to become best friends.

Lou Ann had such bad asthma that each time she breathed out, she whistled. Even at ten, she had a slight stoop from the sheer effort of taking in air. Every week she visited a chiropractor.

"What does he do?" I asked.

"You know, he makes adjustments and tells me to drink goat's milk," she said.

I had no idea what she was talking about. She had two brothers, a little sister, and Poke and Grackle. Her parents were from a small town in South Carolina, and the entire Brown family was steeped in the bigotry and chauvinism of the deep South in the 1950s.

Lou Ann was the oldest girl child, which is why the task of babysitting Janie, cleaning the house, and folding the family's daily bundle of laundry fell to her. I became her helper, and spent most of my hours after school in the Brown living room separating the darks and the whites. It felt strange to be on such intimate terms with Mr. Brown's underpants and Mrs. Brown's brassieres when in person, the two of them were the scariest people I had ever met.

One afternoon, while Lou Ann and I were drying dishes, Mrs. Brown told a story about what happened to her that morning in the supermarket. "I am mindin' my own business when this nigger right next to me pulls the apple juice from the middle of the pile. And all around me, these cans of apple juice are falling down and rolling around like there was no tomorrow. God, how stupid can you be?"

It was the second time I'd ever heard the word *nigger* said out loud. The first had been a couple of weeks earlier at school. I was pitching in a softball game, and had taken my frizzy hair out of its ponytail. One of the boys in the outfield yelled to his teammates, "The pitcher has nigger hair! The pitcher has nigger hair!"

I asked Mrs. Brown, "How come you dislike Negro people so much?" She looked at me as if I had just said, "Why doesn't Mr. Brown fold his own dopey boxer shorts?"

"We don't like them because they're stupid and they smell bad," she answered in a singsong voice that said what a stupid question that was. Mrs. Brown could snap like that. When we were alone with her, she'd yell at us for doing a sloppy job of vacuuming or not folding the hospital corners on Janie's bed, then get all playful, grabbing Grackle's paws and pretending to cha-cha with him to "Jamaica Farewell." But the minute Mr. Brown walked in, Mrs. Brown would stop laughing and everything would get real quiet. She never took her eyes off him.

Even though Mr. Brown had lived in Miami for twenty years, he had the pallor of someone who wintered in Fargo. He had large bony hands and a hair-trigger temper. One afternoon, after Mr. Brown sanded and polished the floor on a new room he was adding to their house, eight-year-old Curtis accidentally stepped on his dad's fresh work. Mr. Brown's face turned gray. Slowly, as though he savored each word, he said: "Curtis Brown, now I am going to have to whip you. Bring me my belt."

Curtis handed his father the belt and followed behind him. Once inside the bedroom, Mr. Brown closed the door. The sounds of leather against flesh cracked through the walls. Curtis screamed. Then quiet. Again, ugly smacking sounds. More cries. I ran out of the Brown house, sick to my stomach.

Beatings, it seemed, were a big family event in this neighborhood. Tony, the girl who lived upstairs from us in the duplex, got hit with a belt several times a month. Even in my elementary school, bad boys (never girls) got hauled into the principal's office. At the spot on the wall where people keep pictures of their family, the principal, Mr. Woodruff, hung a thick wooden paddle with holes in it. It was a reminder to all who entered Mr. Woodruff's office that he had the power to take a boy's pants down, make him stand spread-eagled with his hands against the wall, and give him a whacking commensurate with that day's offense. Cutting class. Sassing the teacher. Smoking outside. The next time you saw that boy, his eyes were glassy and you knew his rear end was mottled with welts. Funny stuff went on in this Miami.

When you are ten years old, whatever is going on in your own home seems normal. You don't talk to anybody about it, and you don't question whether it's right or wrong or whether that's the way everyone else treats one another. It's just how things are in your family. But the kinds of things I saw at the Browns' or heard coming from my neighbors upstairs gave me a queasy feeling in my stomach. The people who hurt Curtis and Tony and the boys in school seemed to enjoy how terrified and helpless they made these kids feel.

I couldn't even distance myself from them by assuming these things happened to other people. Watching Mr. Brown's face get pinched when Curtis stepped on his new floor, I saw my father slamming an angry fist through the bathroom door because Miriam had used all the hot water, leaving none for his bath. I remembered the game he used to play with me, chasing me with heavy monster steps as I ran as fast as I could screaming, "*Maa, Maa.*" But usually this happened when she wasn't home.

"You're a baa sheep," he'd laugh. I'd dive onto the thick quilt on their bed and hide my face in a pillow. He'd yank the pillow away and catch my nose between his thumb and forefinger. The rest of his hand covered my mouth so I couldn't breathe. I'd try kicking, but my legs were too short to reach him. That dream, where you're sinking under water and can't catch your breath? That's what it felt like. When I'd get really dizzy, he'd let me go. "Okay, *baa* sheep," he'd say. "Now you can run to your *maa.*"

Thirty years later, when I developed chronic asthma, it felt like a giant hand covering my face. I thought of Lou Ann's crouching and how she would suck in air as though she was afraid each breath would be her last.

If Lou Ann was my first Southerner, I was her first Jew. In fact, I was a lot of people's first Jew. Our neighborhood was full of southerners from Tennessee, the Carolinas, Georgia, most of whom came to this town for the cheap real estate and booming job markets in construction and tourism. This was a neighborhood of Southern Baptists whose devotion and connection to their Lord was all-encompassing. No meal commenced without grace, no school day began without "The Lord's Prayer."

Although I tried unsuccessfully to bring grace home, no one could stop me from reciting, "Our Father, who art in heaven . . ." in my fifth grade class. I was trying desperately to soften the stigma of being the first Cohn or anything like it to ever attend Kensington Park Elementary School. One day, tall, cute Tommy Ford, his eyes as narrow as mail slits, asked me what kind of name Cohn was.

"It's Jewish," I said. "I'm Jewish."

"You're Jewshh?" He pronounced it as if to get rid of the word as fast as he could.

"Yeah, of course I am," I said.

"Do you have those horns, you know, those devil horns and tails Jews have?" he asked.

"What do you mean?"

"Well, that's what I've always heard."

I took Tommy's hand and rubbed it all over my head. "No horns," I said. "See?" He smiled, relieved or embarrassed. I couldn't tell.

Around that time, I had my first sleepover at Lou Ann's. We'd had another labor-intensive day of folding the Brown laundry, feeding Janie, and scrubbing two bathrooms before falling asleep on the foldout couch in the living room. Since the front door opened right into the living room, the first thing Mr. and Mrs. Brown saw later that night when they returned home was four entangled skinny legs. Although their whispering woke me up, I thought it best not to be alone with them, so I kept my eyes shut and pretended to be asleep.

"My Lord, what a sight they are," Mrs. Brown said with a smile in her voice.

I thought I heard Mr. Brown shudder. Then he said gravely, "A Jew and a Baptist together in one bed. Look at them. You'd never guess how much hatred there was in this world."

Eight

When I started working at *Newsweek*, it was trendy to wear polyester shirts with virtual story treatments on them —I had one with a scientist peering under a microscope, his charts and graphs behind him, a mouse in a cage next to him. Malcolm wore velvet bell bottoms and sideburns down to his chin. He worked the night shift at the Associated Press, and got home at six in the morning. At *Newsweek*, the pace was manic and the hours more erratic as the week stretched out.

The chaos was about more than just the vagaries of closing a news magazine. It was the early seventies. The Vietnam War had divided the country across generational lines. There were National Guard troops on campuses and weekly battles between hard hats and longhairs at peace demonstrations. Mr. Perdue's old friend Richard Nixon was glowering as his presidency collapsed around Watergate. And it all seemed to be happening inside the *Newsweek* newsroom on Madison Avenue. My research on the Pentagon papers—the story that sent poor Hugh into retirement—was typical: four days of research and reporting turned into a twelve-page pink file, dropped on top of piles of blue and green files from other reporters, boiled down by the writer to an eighteen-inch story—if it was deemed to be worth that much by his senior editor and the three top editors who read it next. Hours could pass as top editors pondered stories and the fate of the nation over veal piccata and twelve-year-old scotch. The researchers and writers left behind spent their time drinking the cheaper stuff at their desks and flirting endlessly with one another. The cocktail of weighty stories and the undercurrent of sexual energy made work feel like where you wanted to be even if you got home at three in the morning on Saturday and had to be back seven hours later.

Home by contrast seemed a much duller, if safer, place to be. When I came downstairs most mornings, Malcolm had a cup of raspberry tea and freshly squeezed orange juice waiting for me. The kitchen was warm and sun-filled, and if it was the right season, there would be a bowl of newly picked zinnias in the middle of the table. Often there was the smell of baking bread. An infant swaddled in a flannel layette could not feel as safe and coddled as I did there.

Malcolm and I spent our days off in a small house that we bought in upstate New York. The house, on a pond, was one of two identical split-levels built by Joe Rinaldo and his brother. Joe was in the carpet business, which explained the plaid wall-to-wall in the basement.

We put Laura Ashley periwinkle-and-rose paper on the walls and bought an antique cupboard and oak dining table. Malcolm had a flower garden, and managed to coax asparagus, corn, lettuce, and squash from the half acre around the house. While he gardened and cooked, I rode my bike or swam in the pond. This was how our marriage was meant to be. It was idyllic, yet when I was there, I missed the definition I got from being at *Newsweek*.

Tuesday mornings, when I held the magazine in my hands and studied its crisp pages, I forgot the long hours I'd worked the week before all that and felt reassured that I was a part of something as important as *Newsweek*. My expectations of what it would be like to be a journalist in New York paled beside the real thing.

Of course, I was just a researcher, but all the young women were. The men were the writers, and we were their acolytes, there to pick up their lunches, take their phone messages, and do all the grunt work so that they could spin their magic at the end of the week. In this man's world, there was also a sense of sexual entitlement. Lines were crossed all the time. One Saturday afternoon, I was at the copy desk making last minute changes on a story. A senior writer—a man I'd barely ever talked to—walked by, leaned over, and kissed the back of my neck. It was a soft enough kiss to make me start sweating.

I took a trip to the front lines of the sexual revolution when I was assigned to report a story about *Penthouse* editor Bob Guccione. He had me wait with him at his cardiologist, then invited me to watch as he photographed naked women through lenses dripping with Vaseline. His sad baby-blue eyes were pink around the edges because he slept about three hours every other night. He wore lots of leather and had the sated look of a man who'd had a little too much of everything. When he left me alone in his suite at the Drake Hotel, I searched under his bed, thinking I'd find some bizarre sex toys. I didn't. Later it dawned on me that he was the kind of guy who would want people to think he kept weird sexual aids under his bed.

Guccione was sexy in the way men who wear black leather and chains on their bare chests are sexy, which is to say he was obvious. He got a kick out of being a porn peddler amidst the self-important New York media crowd—particularly because his magazine was making more money than most—and he oozed the confidence of a man pulling off his own joke.

He also gave me one of the best reporting tips I ever got. After he mentioned that journalism was the only class he'd ever failed in high school, I interrupted: "So you flunked because you were bored and thought you were smarter than the teacher?"

"You know," he said, "you'd get much better interviews if you didn't always answer your own questions. And, for the record, you can say it was because I looked up the teacher's dress."

I spent a week with Guccione. On our last night together, we went to the bar at the Drake. At several minutes past midnight, Natalie Cole was winding down her act. As I made shuffling movements to leave, Guccione pulled a twenty-dollar bill out of his wallet and slammed it onto the table. "Twenty dollars says you don't go home tonight," he said. I picked up the twenty and stuck it down my shirt.

"You lose," I said, and walked out. By then, we'd both exhausted our roles, and I'm sure he was as relieved as I was when I left.

I loved the game of getting people to tell me what I wanted to know, and flirted with the possibility that maybe I was good at it. I also flirted with what flirting could do for me, and I was sorely naive about the sexual power of young women. Marrying

Malcolm put sex in a safety zone. Sex with him was fine; I assumed that after being married for five years, fine was as good as it got. But away from home, I tested what my sexual power could do, and pushed it as far as I could.

There was a man.

It started with funny notes he left on my desk, then escalated into sweet letters with very clear intent. There was a picnic in Central Park, a kiss, a weekend away, and six years of sharing bottles of Ruffino wine at lunch or drinks after work, then sneaking off to my apartment or a nearby hotel. The sex was exciting and I was consumed with thinking about when we would make love next. Because he was the kind of man who gave me a beautiful copper box from India; entwined his leg with mine under the table at a restaurant; laughed at the coy white robe I wore the first night we slept together—he called it my christening gown—he was also the kind of man who always had women around him. There was something in the air between him and these other women, and I never knew quite what it was. I was a married woman having an affair with a guy who flirted with other women. I couldn't make accusations, yet I was always one step away from feeling humiliated. The odd thing about it was that when I was with him, I forgot all that. I forgot that I was married and I never felt guilty.

During a visit home, my mother noticed the deep circles under my eyes. "Are you working too hard?" she asked.

"Nah," I said breezily, "I'm just having a good time."

She narrowed her eyes and exhaled. "I see that," she said. A puff of smoke landed on my cheek. I could tell she suspected what was going on.

The way I was living my life was wearing me out, and I

wished I could be sustained by things less ephemeral and exhausting. The paradox was that without the comfort and acceptance that I got from Malcolm, I would never have the nerve to live the sexy and precarious other life I'd created.

Things would be different when we had children—I was sure that was true. We talked about how I'd teach them to swim and play tennis and he'd teach them to cook. "I hope they have your blue eyes," I said.

"That would be nice," he agreed.

I thought how lucky a kid would be to have him as a father. We were casually sloppy about birth control, but nothing happened. We chose not to mind. We were in our late twenties: He had his career; I had mine. Children would come later. We cheered each other on professionally, and spent way too much time apart during the week. After work, on the days that ended when the sun went down, I went to the Cowboy, a bar across the street, with my *Newsweek* friends. Malcolm chalked that up to what he called my late adolescence. It was a lot of time wasted, he thought, but if he suspected some of that was also time wasted with another man, he never let on.

By Sunday nights, I looked forward to the week the same way I used to anticipate a date. In that way, *Newsweek* wasn't that much different from seventh grade, only this time I got to hang around with the cool kids. Pete Axthelm was the sports columnist and leader of the pack. He was a large man who carried his weight in front of him and walked as though at any moment he might tip over backward. Once four of us followed him down Madison Avenue mimicking his gait. We must have looked like a troupe of Charlie Chaplin players passing through town. Pete had a great eye for the pretentious and ridiculous, but also understood the passion that pushed athletes to a state of grace. He loved the track and gambling; they were his life. His job was really just a hobby.

Nearly every night, Pete led a group over to the Cowboy. I hung around them long enough to become part of their bantering and in-jokes. I knew the details of all their sex lives, and was privy to the lascivious things they said about women—who got drunk and did it in a cab; who didn't wear underwear to work. They created lurid scenarios around all the interviews I did with men, and made unrelenting fun of my awkward attempts to climb the *Newsweek* ladder. Some nights we stayed at the Cowboy until eight, other times I didn't get home until one or two in the morning.

Axthelm gave everyone and everything nicknames. He, of course, was Ax. Women with curly hair had jinglets, and if you told a story that went on too long, you were doing a blurto. He decided that Malcolm's elegant primness deserved the name Virgil. Two stern researchers earned the name Sunshine Girls. Another young researcher won the name Balcony after he jumped off a second-floor porch at a party when he saw his married lover dancing with her husband.

Because my job was to write reports for the media writer that were supposed to be concise but descriptive, and because I dreaded Ax's denouncing my stories as blurtos, I practiced telling well-rounded anecdotes. Often I exaggerated to make myself out to be a hapless bystander of outrageous events. But often things really happened that way. When I interviewed a well-known TV talk show host at the elegant "21" restaurant, he kept referring in a foghorn voice to one of my colleagues as "that miserable little bitch." I watched a lot of bad public access tapings—naked men massaging naked women with spaghetti—as the new cable television industry tested the boundaries of the FCC. But I also got to interview classy people like Barbara Walters, who'd been hired by ABC for a million a year, and angry ones like Harry Reasoner, who hid his jealousy by publicly worrying over the fluff Barbara would bring to a serious news show.

After three years, I finally got promoted from media researcher to media reporter. My job was to cover television, radio, magazines, and newspapers. Research always brought me back to that room at *The Atlantic Monthly* where I was forever being called to task for the tiny errors that somehow slipped by me. Once, at *Newsweek*, after I had some eye surgery, Malcolm called up my boss to say that one eye was bandaged and I'd be out for a day or two. "She's a bad enough researcher with two eyes," my boss said. "Tell her to take her time."

But reporting appealed to the side of me that needed to know everything about anyone I met. I was not afraid to ask hard questions. My smart mouth, as my father called it, was finally paying off. As the reporter on the burgeoning disco trend, I spent until dawn at a sprawling club in Queens called The Enchanted Garden. The evening began when one of the owners, a twitchy man in a navy blue suit, picked me up at a coffee shop in Greenwich Village. He brought along his mother. "Why are you wearing a suit?" I asked him as the three of us crowded into a booth.

"Because I was meeting a lady from *Newsweek*," he answered. "I didn't realize it would be you."

The Enchanted Garden was like Timothy Leary's idea of a bar mitzvah. Exotic birds flew freely around the dance floor until early in the morning, when they gave out from lack of oxygen. For an Arabian nights party, the owners brought in some camels, llamas, and a snake charmer; for Island of Paradise nights, they hauled in palm trees, a seventy-pound roasted pig, a harem of hula girls, and a fire dancer. The Enchanted Garden featured prominently in our "Disco Whirl" cover story, and the magazine hit the newsstand the same week that the young entrepreneur, whose name was Steve Rubell, and his partner opened their club in Manhattan: Studio 54.

In what I can only describe as a touching act of loyalty, Rubell credited *Newsweek* and me with his success in New York, which meant that anytime I wanted, I could go to Studio 54 and move to the front of the line. The place was exhaustingly hip and loud. You felt as if anything could happen, and between the sex and drugs and strobes and famous people, it did. Malcolm and I spent one New Year's Eve there watching Grace Jones descend naked from a swing onto the dance floor at midnight. Rubell set the stakes higher and higher, and for thirty months, he managed to outdo himself. Each time I saw him, he seemed more frantic, more jazzed up. He talked nonstop and he developed a tic, blinking his eyes repeatedly, as if he were trying hard to keep them open.

Years later, when Rubell was in prison for tax evasion, he called me and told me how scared he was. After his release, he phoned to tell me how wonderful it felt to walk through Central Park breathing real air. When he died in 1989, there were pictures in the papers of him and Liza Minnelli, Bianca Jagger, and Halston—a sampling of the fancy people who hung out at Studio 54. The public image was left intact: an exuberant hyper creature whose energy created a fantasy world for the rich and famous, and the wanna-bes as well. But he was also a gracious man who wore a suit and brought his mother along for his first interview with a national magazine.

I spent a couple of days with a young television evangelist named Jim Bakker and his wife, Tammy Faye, at their PTL Club in Charlotte, North Carolina. Bakker was a television natural and the fastest rising star among a growing breed of hotshot Holy Rollers. He easily moved himself to tears, and people were forever falling onto their knees and being born again at his feet. Once, he dumped piles of Latin American phone books on the floor and asked the audience to pray for all the names in the books. On my last morning there, a quartet was playing "Jesus Came Down." Bakker was shouting that we should all accept Jesus in our hearts, and as always, half the audience was rocking back and forth, waving their arms in the air with tears pouring down their cheeks. I thought I heard a voice within me. I felt certain that it was Jesus in my head, urging me to open my heart and sing out praises for the Lord. It was not my first run-in with Jesus—but more about that later.

Being a reporter for *Newsweek* meant everyone returned your call. It also meant that you could get thrown into any story—some of them quite scary. When Son of Sam was terrorizing young women in a Queens neighborhood, I interviewed the parents of the murdered girls. I covered a riot in a Brooklyn prison. When I was reporting stories like that, I became my mother: cool and efficient. It's not that I didn't get scared—I did. But I learned to keep going despite how scared I was. My longtime boss, Harry Waters, one of the great *Newsweek* writers, used to call me a chameleon. "I never know who you're going to be," he'd say, "Suzanne Somers or Rocky Marciano." I didn't, either.

Talk about chameleons—the first time I saw the comedian Andy Kaufman, he was singing along to the Mighty Mouse record on *Saturday Night Live*. I was mesmerized. I wanted to know everything about him, what was real and what wasn't, and got an assignment from our sister publication, *The Washington Post*, to cover his performance at Carnegie Hall. I interviewed him at Hicks Ice Cream Parlor, where he ordered four scoops, butterscotch sauce, hot fudge, and lots of whipped cream. When the sundae came, he bowed his head, said a silent grace, then excused himself so he could go to the men's room and wash his hands. "Please tell your readers if they ever meet me in a restaurant, not to shake my hand until I'm finished eating," he said. "Otherwise I'll have to get up and wash my hands again."

All the while we talked, he kept that goggle-eyed expression you can still see in *Taxi* reruns, and he never broke from the monotone of a seven-year-old in a school play. He told me how he once read all of *The Great Gatsby* to a nightclub audience in Indiana. "I wanted to see how far I could go before getting booed off the stage," he said. No one left until he finished reading the book early the next morning.

On the night before his show, he walked me back to the *Newsweek* building. I was about to wish him luck and say good night when I remembered that he'd promised he would pick a woman from the audience and wrestle her onstage. "Oh, and one more thing," I added. "About that wrestling thing. You're not really going to pick a stranger. She's going to be a plant, right?"

He fixed me with a cow-eyed stare. I thought that I'd hurt his feelings. I wasn't prepared for what happened next. He reached toward me with both hands, putting one arm around my neck in a headlock and using the other to flip me over and lay me flat on the sidewalk. Just then, one of the magazine's top editors, a man who usually ignored me, walked out of the building. Without so much as a blink, he stepped over my body, nodded slightly, and said "Good night, Betsy."

Something about his nonchalance, the way I just didn't seem to matter, stuck with me. One afternoon soon after, Ax took me to the races at Belmont Park. I bet all the money I had on a horse named Gigi, a chestnut-brown beauty. Sure enough, she rounded the final turn with force and promise until, a couple of lengths from the finish line, she just toppled over on her side. Turned out she died of a heart attack. As they hauled her off in a horse ambulance, Ax told me I was a blight, and that I was never to come to the track with him again, even if he begged me.

A familiar sense of uneasiness came over me.

Just before we headed to the Cowboy one evening soon after that, I yelled something down the hall to one of the sports reporters. The education editor, a man who looked like Omar Sharif and was well thought of by the top editors, came out of his office, folded his arms, and stood in front of me. "Betsy," he asked, "did you come to *Newsweek* to be the mascot of the sports department?" At that moment I suddenly saw myself the way he did. I wasn't cute or funny. I'd become what Ax called "a blackboard scratcher," shrill and irritating. It made my skin crawl. Maybe it was time to leave.

That fall, Malcolm and I went to Nova Scotia for two weeks. It was rugged and unspoiled and we took our time meandering through it. Early on the Sunday morning of the last day, we headed down an empty road toward Halifax in our rented Volkswagen bug. The air was still thick with dew, which made the empty roads slippery. "This is like driving in a cloud," I said to Malcolm. "Put on your shoulder harness." He snapped his cumbersome pre-seat-belt apparatus into place just as the wheels slipped out from under us. The car flew across the highway, like a planchette over a Ouija board. Then we hit a tree and flipped over. Twice.

I never took my eyes off Malcolm. If I watched him, I bargained, nothing would happen to him.

Malcolm had recently bought a rock polisher, and for the past couple of weeks, I'd been kept awake at night by the rumbling of what sounded like waves crashing in a bottle. The bag of stones he'd collected on this trip flew in all directions. I thought, please let me live to hear that stupid rock polisher grind again.

We hung upside down in a crush of metal; neither of us spoke. I heard footsteps coming toward the car. A large male head with red cheeks peered in through what was left of the front windshield. I thought he said, "Oh, Lord," but maybe I made that up because he was wearing a priest's collar. I know I heard him yell, "Someone help me get this girl out of here, she's in shock." I remember thinking, I've died and gone to heaven, and everyone is Catholic. What am I going to do? I also remember thinking what a great story this would make if I ever got back to *Newsweek*. Miraculously, Malcolm and I were okay. I just damaged a muscle in my leg and Malcolm was bruised. But I was left with a sense that there wasn't an endless supply of time in my life left to waste.

73

The week after we came back from Nova Scotia, in early fall 1977, I learned that Rupert Murdoch had decided to add some American properties to his international media empire, including the *New York Post* and *New York* magazine. The editors decided to put together a cover story on the Australian press baron, and I was one of the reporters. That week, I tracked Murdoch all over New York. I bribed his doorman, showed up at his health club. When I turned up at a Broadway show he was attending, Murdoch backed away, pointed a finger at me, and said to the person next to him, "There she is again, that woman from *Newsweek*." Two nights later, after an evening press conference, a reporter from *The Wall Street Journal* and I found our way into his lawyer's office, where we turned on the lights, sat on his plush gray carpet, and pulled the garbage can from under his desk.

I was struck by the comic book clarity of this sight—a thirty-three-year-old woman, on her hands and knees, foraging around in someone else's trash. Matched up with my frantic double life at home and at the Cowboy, it was the final piece of the puzzle. It was time to grow up and move on.

In March 1979, two young men from Knoxville, Tennessee, came to New York and bought *Esquire* magazine, a forty-seven-year old media institution that had lived a long time on its literary legacy of Hemingway and Fitzgerald. Truth was, it seemed doubtful that the magazine would ever see its fiftieth birthday.

Phillip Moffitt and Christopher Whittle were outsiders. They had unlined baby faces and slow East Tennessee drawls. They were full of enthusiasm at their press conference, strutting around like little kids about to pee in their pants. They were perfectly versed in *Esquire's* history and bursting with ideas about its future direction. I went back to *Newsweek* pretty certain about what was going to happen. "These guys are really smart," I said to my editor. "They're going to make it. But they're messing with an institution, and they're going to get creamed by the New York press."

I took Moffitt, the editor-in-chief, to lunch at the Palm, a popular Manhattan steak house where the portions of meat are the size of your head. He turned out to be an interviewer's nightmare. Each time I asked him a question, he squinted through his tiny brown eyes and said nothing. Or he said something like, "This is neither the time nor place to answer that question." At one point, I scribbled into my notebook: "This is the worst interview I have ever done."

Frustrated and out of questions, I resorted to pissing him off so badly he had to say something. "So what is your story anyway?" I asked. "Are there a bunch of people in Knoxville sitting around in bright orange robes waiting for you to come back?"

He ignored my question but started talking about himself. I learned about his hardscrabble background in Tennessee, how his parents mortgaged their house so he could start his small publishing business, how he was president of his class at the University of Tennessee (Chris managed his campaign).

When we finished eating, Phillip got quiet again and stared off into space. I wound up staring at him staring. Finally, he pointed his index finger toward the ceiling. "There's a star out there that you're not touching," he said.

I paid the bill and went back to the office to write my story. No one I knew talked like that, but there was something about that untouched star that stayed with me. Phillip turned out to be an eerily intuitive man who would meet people for the briefest amount of time and notice things about them most of us wouldn't mention—if we noticed them at all. Over the next few months, we met for occasional lunches or drinks. He always ordered filet of sole and hot water with lemon afterward ("Tea with lemon, no tea," he'd tell the waiter). Then he'd offer up some insight. "You have this Mary Tyler Moore thing going," he said once. "It's not working for you anymore. You're more real than that."

It was seductive to have someone try to pin me down this way, but it was also maddening. He'd begin a sentence: "I've been thinking about your relationship with your mother," then refuse to finish it. Keeping his eyes focused in the area of my forehead, he'd shake his head and wave his hand back and forth in front of his face: "I can't say more now." And that would be the end of that.

Right before Thanksgiving of that year, Phillip and I had a drink after work. "I think you'd be a very good editor," he said out of nowhere. "You've outgrown this *Newsweek* thing. It isn't who you are anymore. It's time for you to move on." When he followed that sentence with this one: "How would you like to come to work at *Esquire*?" I thought to myself: No more sports department mascot, no more Cowboy. Something inside shouted at me to grab it. "Yes," I said.

Then I went home and threw up.

Nine

By the time we moved to Miami in the mid-fifties, Miriam was in her second year at the High School of Music and Art. She wanted to be an artist, and being at that school with other promising kids was the biggest thing that had ever happened to her. Her first oil portrait was of a white man standing with his arm draped around the shoulders of a black man.

At Miami High School, Miriam dug in her heels by refusing to be like the other kids. She wouldn't comb her hair in a flip or wear the shirtwaist dresses that were the rage. She worked for the school newspaper and dated the son of a Lutheran minister, a boy who was as reserved and out of place as she was. At home, she continued to paint and daydream about returning north to study art at college.

The move had completely the opposite effect on me. Fitting in was my life's work, and Miami represented my greatest challenge. I took on the natural coloring of ten-year-old girls at Kensington Park Elementary School, squishing my feet into pointy Capezio shoes and wearing madras shirts with button-down collars. The more difficult fitting in became, the harder I worked at it. I knew I was making progress when Jeanette Cole invited me to a party at her house. Jeanette Cole wore spaghetti-strap dresses and had long blond hair that fell over one eye. Her boyfriend Jeff had a silky pompadour. His black Ivy League pants hung low on his hips. Sometimes Jeanette, Jeff, and I rode our bikes home from school together. There was a row of houses under construction that we passed. The houses had foundations and the rooms were partitioned off with plywood walls. Jeff figured out that the workmen left the site at 3:00, which meant that by 3:15, he and Jeanette could go into a skeletal bedroom and make out. My job was to mind our bikes and stand guard outside.

I guessed that Jeanette inviting me to her party was my reward for a job well done. When I got to her house that Saturday night I noticed the neat row of lounge chairs lined up in the backyard. "Swim party?" I asked.

"Oh, silly," she laughed. "Make-out party. Haven't you ever been to one?"

The answer was no. I was ten years old and had only kissed two boys at camp. Neither involved furniture. That night, Danny Lincoln and I lay in the lounge chair together and hugged each other for a long time. Then he stuck his tongue in my mouth and waggled it around. I stuck my tongue back into his mouth. He rubbed my shoulders; I ran my fingers across the downy part of the back of his neck. We took a break to eat potato chips and dip, then went back to the lounge chair for more kissing. When I came home later that night, my mother asked me how the party was. "It was fun," I said. "There were all kinds of games and stuff. I did very well."

Three weeks later, I came home with a baton. I made the family sit on the couch as I threw it in the air and caught it with one hand while marching in place. They stared at me as though Billy Graham had just crashed through the living room ceiling. "Is this really interesting to you?" Miriam asked.

Then, in the way my father had of talking about me in the third person, he said to my mother, "She's become so American."

In our family, anything American was regarded with a mixture of awe and suspicion. That included me. Although Miriam was born in this country, she found as much comfort in my family's formalities as I did in ignoring them. Every day for the first seven years of her life, she would go to our grandmother's house for lunch (minute steak and peas) and then again after school, where they would sing together and Omi would tell stories. Omi taught Miriam German, and even now, when Miriam speaks English, she uses German syntax. "For dinner, what do you want?" is how she might construct a sentence. She also has the maddening habit of never saying anything directly. Instead, she'll say things like, "I think going to the movies might not be a bad idea." Miriam's eyes still cloud up whenever she talks about Omi.

Omi died when I was three. She stayed with us during the last months of her life, and I remember crawling into bed with her. She had smooth, slender fingers and would give me round butterscotch candies—the thick ones that didn't have the hole in the middle. There was nothing scary about her, even though she was so sick. When I was older and told my mother how I remembered the rummy taste of those candies, she'd get annoyed and say, "That's ridiculous. Your Omi never ate candy."

By that time, Omi's legacy in our home had reached sainthood. Maybe she didn't eat sweets, but every time I eat one of those butterscotch candies, I think of a kind lady with soft hands in a white quilted bed jacket.

From the beginning, my mother said I was the sunshine in her life: She picked me. Miriam was creative and tempestuous, like my father. Together they knew that however sunny my mother thought I was, I had my dark side, and they were hell bent on exposing it. In crowds they'd loom over me, squiggle their fingers in my face and say, "Betsy, do you know where you are? You are in *giant* land."

"*Maaa*," I'd yell. "*Maaa*, they're teasing me."

On cue, my defender would step in. "Ach, Rudy, leave the child alone."

Being my mother's ally set me apart from my father in an uncompromising way. If she was the competent one who judged him for what she felt was his ineffectiveness, I was her clone. If he was furious at her for making him feel demeaned, well, it was a lot easier for him to take it out on her little emissary

My mother was my safe place. On Friday nights, I'd sit on her lap; Miriam sat at the foot of her chair. While we'd watch *Mama* and *Our Miss Brooks,* my mother would smoke at least a half a pack of Pall Malls. The smell of her breath as she blew smoke out of the side of her mouth, the warmth and curves of her body as I molded my body into hers, were my touchstones. That was where I belonged. Since then, I've had two husbands, lived in twelve houses, and worked at eight magazines. I've always tried to make each of them my place, but it's never been that simple.

. . .

Lou Ann's mother—now, there was a model American mom. Every six weeks, Lou Ann helped give her a home permanent. She twisted Mrs. Brown's brown hair around skinny pink rollers, then glopped on permanent solution that smelled like cow urine. After half an hour, Lou Ann combed out her mother's curls. I thought she looked beautiful.

For months, I begged my mother to perm her straight brown hair. "That's not for me," she insisted. If Mrs. Brown bought a tube of Tickled Pink lipstick at Walgreen's, I saved up $1.25 to buy my mother the same thing. Most days I came home from Lou Ann's house brimming with news of her mother's latest accomplishments. "She baked the best thing I ever tasted," I reported one night. "It was a tall orange chiffon cake, with white orange frosting and bits of orange peel in it." My mother's idea of baking came from German recipes—yeast cakes, *Linzer tortes*, spice cookies; nothing as showy or sweet as orange chiffon cake.

One of the best things about Mrs. Brown was that she was always home. My mother worked since I was born, so it was a big deal when, shortly after we got settled in our new house, she announced to the family that since my father had found a job in a wholesale grocer's, she was going to take the year off. By the time we moved to Miami, she later told me, she was exhausted from supporting the family.

My mother was also meant to have unblemished hands. Theirs was the last wedding in the splendid Kaiserslautern synagogue with its stained-glass windows, and she was marrying into one of the most prominent Jewish families in town. Three months later, the Nazis burned the synagogue to the ground, and a month after that, on Columbus Day 1936, my parents came to Washington Heights, where they wound up running a small grocery store. Stocking produce and managing the deli counter was alien to my father, so it fell to my mother, with her innate practicality, to keep the place running. "We got out in the nick of time," they'd say about escaping from Germany. And later, when they talked about leaving New York and moving to Miami, they'd use the same words.

Now, during that first year in Miami, my mother got to lie out on a lawn chair and read while munching on one of the oversized bars of Nestlé Crunch she'd stashed away in the kitchen drawers. That's how I'd find her when I came home from school.

Just before the end of fifth grade, I got chosen to be a Patrol Girl—a lieutenant—for the next year. I couldn't wait to tell her. That afternoon, I rode my bike right into the backyard. Her chair was empty. I ran inside, where she greeted me with a Cheshire cat smile. "I have a surprise for you," she said. "Come here."

She took my hand and led me into the kitchen. There, sitting on the counter like a queen on her throne, was the glorious orange chiffon cake of my dreams—orange peel shreds and all.

"It's beautiful," I cried. "I can't believe this."

My mother had crossed all boundaries: She had become a stay-at-home mom baking her daughter's favorite cake, an American mother who made chiffon desserts in the middle of the week. My mommy had defied every aesthetic bone in her body and baked this gaudy American cake just for me.

I cut a wedge and took a bite. The combination of sweet icing and acidic orange rinds exploded in my mouth.

"This is the greatest moment of my childhood," I said.

And in her typical idiomatic English, she answered: "I'm so happy you like it. I feel like a million dollars."

Right before Thanksgiving, our sixth-grade class at Kensington Park auditioned to be part of the Christmas Carol Concert at the Orange Bowl. Our music teacher, Mrs. McGee, said that singing at the Orange Bowl would put Kensington Park right on the map. Mrs. McGee had a pitch pipe that looked like a rotary phone dial. Every day for the next three weeks, she stood in front of the class, blowing into the pipe and waving her hands excitedly as we sang, "O Little Town of Bethlehem," and "Away in a Manger." I joined in with gusto. Two weeks later the results were in. Kensington Park Elementary school was on the map.

"I'm going to sing in the Orange Bowl!" I shouted, running through the house one afternoon in early December. "I'm going to sing in the Orange Bowl!" My mother had just come in from the backyard. Her halter top hung loosely around her neck, and the smell of baked Coppertone mingled with my own sweaty excitement as I threw my arms around her.

"You're going to sing in the Orange Bowl?" She seemed confused.

"Yeah, Christmas carols on Christmas Eve."

"You're not exactly Peggy Lee," she said.

"Mom, I'm not singing alone. There are going to be two hundred other kids."

"Oh, honey," she said, her voice melting into triumph, "I'm so proud of you."

This was yet another victory for our gene pool, more validation that the Cohn sisters were, in fact, the exceptional gifted girls she'd always suspected they were. My father wasn't quite as thrilled. By singing about Jesus, in public no less, I would be committing a grave act of betrayal against him.

He was an atheist in Germany, but became a devout Jew after coming to America. As an act of gratitude, he even took on the middle name of Moses. We lit Sabbath candles every Friday night. Each time he came into the house, he kissed the mezuzah on the door, and every year on Yom Kippur, he observed the day-long fast with stubborn determination. "It was very easy this time," he'd say at sunset, tearing off a piece of challah with a shaky hand.

To him, Christmas carols and singing about Jesus were personal affronts. To me they were the only way I knew how to show him I wasn't scared of him, that he wasn't going to make me be like he was. For the next two weeks, I carried on as though I was the choir master at Saint Patrick's Cathedral. Every day, I put on the record of Christmas carols I'd bought at Burdine's, and in a penetrating alto, sang along. One night, Miriam and my mother were out shopping; my father was resting in his room. I was working on, "O Come All Ye Faithful"

"Oh come let us adore him, oh come let us adore him
Oh come let us adore him, Christ the Lord."

Just as I got to the "Christ" part, he shouted: *"No Christ in this house. I won't have it!"*

I turned the volume even higher for the next cut:

"Away in a manger, no crib for a bed
The little Lord Jesus lay down his sweet head . . ."

"I said No Jesus, dammit!"

Wearing nothing but a pair of boxer shorts, he stormed into the living room, grabbed the arm of the hi-fi, and deliberately scratched it across the disc. It made an awful sound. My record was ruined. I wanted to do something back to him that was as mean and hideous as slashing my beautiful Christmas carols.

"You're such a jerk," I shouted, running up behind him. "It's only a stupid song. How am I supposed to sing in the Orange Bowl if I can't even practice in my own house?" Then I did the one thing I knew was forbidden: I reached for his boxer shorts and yanked them down below his knees. With one hand, he pulled his shorts up above his waist. With the other, he took me by the wrist and twisted it until I fell on the floor. He pushed me onto my back, where I lay kicking wildly, trying to keep him off of me. Still, he managed to straddle me: At five feet six and 125 pounds, what he lacked in size, he made up with fury. His short stubby fingers curled into a fist. He punched my face, my arms, my stomach—anywhere he could reach. "You won't play that crap in this house anymore," he shouted.

It hurt like getting hit in the face with a volleyball. I howled more from helplessness and outrage than I did from actual pain; still, I never forgave him the intended brutality of that night. When I told my mother what happened (I left out the part about pulling down his shorts), her face got tight and she clasped her hands together. She shook her head without saying anything. That day I learned two lessons. My mother chose her battles against my father carefully, and they weren't necessarily mine. And if I wanted to have anything more to do with Jesus, then I was going to have to sneak around to do it.

By the summer of sixth grade, I fell in with a pack of Lou Ann's Baptist friends. Sometimes I went with them on Sundays to the white Baptist church on Flagler Street and sat in the oak pews listening to their hymns. I stared at the picture of Jesus hanging over the pulpit. His eyes were limpid blue, his mouth was round and soft, and with that androgynous pageboy—well, he looked, as my mother would say, "like a real human being"; like someone you could talk to, who would never raise a hand. I knew he was off limits for Jewish girls, but I also knew that looking at him made me feel I had worms in my stomach and a secret in my heart. Inside this dark, cool place, I was part of something central to my friends' lives.

As we left the church one June afternoon, a bunch of kids gathered in front of a large poster hanging in the vestibule. Lou Ann's eyes lit up. "C'mon, do it with me," she said, grabbing my arm and pulling me toward the sign.

"Free, enroll now. Starts June 26," it said. All I had to do was sign my name and show up Mondays, Wednesdays, and Fridays at 10:00 A.M.

It is was simple as that. And for the next two months, unbeknownst to any of the Cohns on NW Thirty-second Street, I became a regular at the Flagler Baptist Bible School. We sat alphabetically, which put me in the front row between Margaret Fay Bagley and Billy Crowder. We began each morning with the Lord's Prayer. We read Bible stories or sang, depending how the spirit moved us.

"Jesus loves me, This I know. For the Bible tells me so."

If Mrs. Morris, the red-haired teacher with the shoe-shaped face, thought it was odd that I was a regular, she never let on.

I didn't invite my parents to the graduation ceremony when the two-month course was over, though I did sit on the dais with the other graduates and sing "Just a Closer Walk with Thee." When they called my name, people clapped as Mrs. Morris handed me my blue certificate with Jesus' face embossed on it and the words *Flagler Baptist Bible School* above it in blue ink.

As part of my religious training, I made a garbage can out of four pieces of plywood laced together with lanyard material. Several weeks after my graduation, my mother noticed the square pail under my desk. "This is new," she said, picking it up and turning it upside down. Then she saw the stamp that read "Flagler Baptist Church" and my name penciled beneath it.

"Where did you get this?" she asked. I thought of saying that Mr. and Mrs. Brown gave it to me for folding their clothes, but I knew she wouldn't buy that. Instead, I just told her the truth.

"All the kids were going. It sounded like fun, and besides, I thought it would be educational!"

She ran her middle finger over her pressed lips. "I've got to hand it to you, you've got gumption," she said.

There was begrudging pride in her words. At the risk of raising a southern Baptist, my mother encouraged whatever it was that allowed me to sneak off to Bible school in the first place. Sometimes I thought she saw in me what she might have been like as a young girl growing up in America. We agreed not to tell my father.

Ten

I was to begin work at *Esquire* during the first week of 1980, but not before being interviewed by the executive editor, Byron Dobell. Byron was a legend in New York publishing, having edited *Life, New York,* and *Esquire* and brought along writers like Tom Wolfe and Gay Talese. I was nervous as I headed up to the *Esquire* offices on lower Park Avenue late one December afternoon. His assistant told me that he was in a closed-door conference, and asked me to please wait at the desk next to hers. For the next fifteen minutes, I thumbed through old issues of the magazine and conjured up images of how this great man would look.

Whatever I'd anticipated—someone in a waistcoat and dapper mustache, perhaps—Byron wasn't it. He ambled out of his office, his head leading his body. His shirt hung over his pants, and his pants waded far below his hips. He seemed so aggravated and distracted that I apologized immediately: "I'm sorry to take your time," I said.

"I'm very busy," he answered, wiping his glasses with his shirt. "I don't have much time to talk to you, but I'm sure you're terrific. Phillip says you're marvelous." He said it so curtly that I didn't take it as a compliment. Had he already written me off? Was he doing this just out of obligation to Phillip?

"What more can I say?" He pointed me toward a couch in the office. I took that to mean sit. "We work very hard here. This is probably the longest conversation you and I will ever have."

There was a long pause. I took that to mean our interview was over. As I got up to leave, I saw him glance down at my bag and the enormous book sticking out of it. His mouth, which moments before had been slack, suddenly broke into a lopsided grin.

"So, what are you reading?" he asked, as if he already knew. "Wait, let me guess." He snapped his fingers. "You're reading, umm, *The Magic Mountain*." I nodded my head.

"Hah," he shouted, like a *Jeopardy* contestant on a roll. "I'll bet I know everything about you. Lemme see, your parents are German Jews. . . . You live in Washington Heights. . . . You probably live in Castle Village on Cabrini Boulevard. . . ."

It was all true. For the past five years, Malcolm and I had been living in a complex of buildings designed to look like medieval castles. There were five of them, redbrick buildings that overlooked the Hudson River on the New York side. Coming over the George Washington Bridge from New Jersey, they were the first things you saw looking north.

"Amazing, eh?" he said, raising his eyebrows.

I managed a smile. He clasped his hands together, then cackled as though he just got the joke. "Okay. You're brilliant. You'll be perfect here." He was still giggling as he led me out the door.

. . .

Leaving *Newsweek* turned out to be wrenching. During my last weeks there, my vision got blurry and I stopped sleeping and eating. "Anxiety attack," my doctor said when I described my symptoms. "It's hard to leave a place after nine years."

Malcolm was still working at the Associated Press. We'd been in New York for ten years and had gotten used to the peculiar rhythms of our work lives. I had a reputation as a good reporter at *Newsweek*, and my job was safe as long as I stayed in character. In exchange for being a mascot, I got to feel as though I were part of a large messy family. When I told Ax I was leaving, he said, "Betso, you've got me, you've got the Cowboy. You've even got Virgil. Why do you need to go off to *Esquire?*"

I needed to go to *Esquire* to get away from who I'd become. I needed to go because Malcolm was tired of hearing my stories about *Newsweek* and I was sick of telling them. And I needed to go because until Phillip offered me the job as senior editor, it never occurred to me that I could ever be any kind of editor at all.

Phillip announced my arrival at *Esquire* by sending out a memo. In it he mentioned my experience as a reporter, then added that I was his friend and that people should extend me a warm welcome. No one extended anything the first morning there, not even a hello. At noon, I got into the elevator with a clutch of my new colleagues who were going out to lunch together. They didn't invite me; they didn't even speak to me. We stood silently, floor after agonizing floor, until I came up with what I thought was a clever way to break the ice. Turning to one of the editors who was wearing a red baseball jacket with the letter P on it, I asked brightly, "So, what does the P stand for?"

"It stands for Purim, you twit," he shot back. The rest of the group looked down at the floor, trying to conceal their smirks.

Suddenly, it was the first day of fifth grade at Kensington Park Elementary School. It was so silent in that elevator, I could hear myself sweat. After what seemed like nine or ten days, the doors opened, and I stumbled off to the nearest coffee shop, where I slumped into a booth and ordered scrambled eggs. Anything more solid surely would have me sick to my stomach.

Maybe I'd made a terrible mistake. Maybe, as my mother often said, I had "bitten off more than I could chew." Then I remembered that I came to *Esquire* because I was tired of who I had become at *Newsweek*. But now that I was actually at *Esquire*, I couldn't go back, but I couldn't seem to go forward, either.

The part of the office where I was supposed to sit was under construction when I arrived. My temporary desk was boxed in on four sides. It was an embarrassingly naked metaphor for how I felt there. As part of my initiation during my first few months, I was given the most difficult writers to edit—the ones no one else wanted to deal with. One of them, a grizzled bully with a walleye and a combustible temper, often called me at home. "I can't believe you haven't read my piece yet," he would yell. "I'm an important part of this magazine, I won't be treated like this." Late one afternoon, he sat with me in my isolation booth as we went over his latest story. Every time I suggested a change, he slammed down his pencil and shouted, "That's bullshit," or, "What the fuck do you mean by that?"

I couldn't stand how cornered I felt and without thinking, I lashed back at him. "You know something, you're not a good enough writer to be this kind of a prima donna."

I watched the anger roll into his face as he searched for words to hurl back at me. "If you were a guy, I'd beat the shit out of you," he said.

"Go ahead, then," I yelled.

Byron heard the commotion through the plywood wall and ran in to see what was going on. He had his right hand curled around a glass paperweight. "What's all this noise?" he asked. "This is a magazine, not some Second Avenue bar."

"A Second Avenue bar beats the shit out of this place," roared the bully, grabbing his jacket and briefcase.

As he skulked off, Byron opened his palm and held the paperweight in front of me. "My dear," he said, with mock chivalry. "I was prepared to use this in order to protect you from that cretin. What a schmuck." He laughed his cackly laugh and I laughed with him, knowing I'd come through a part of my initiation.

I'd already survived a run-in with Richard, our unctuous financial columnist. Each day at lunchtime he played squash and, afterward, hung his soggy jock strap on the radiator in his office. One day Phillip said to me, "Tell Richard not to hang his jock strap in the office." There's no way to say that without just saying it, so I did. Every afternoon after that, there it was, the same old jock strap slung over the radiator like a letter sweater. Welcome to the world of men's magazines.

Now there was only one more hurdle. One big hurdle: the Wednesday morning editorial meetings.

Every week on that morning, we gathered in a windowless conference room on oversized chairs to discuss new ideas for the magazine. Phillip sat at the head of the table. Richard sat next to him, and usually kicked off the meetings by telling us about his recent lunch with Henry Kissinger (or some other name worth dropping) and "Henry's" epiphanies about the Chilean economy. "I'm assuming you're all up to date on that situation," he said, pursing his lips and knowing full well that most of us hadn't a clue what he was talking about. A friend told me that he was at a cocktail party one night where Richard regaled them with stories about *Esquire* and how naive we all were. "He made it sound as though the rest of you were washing fruit while he was running the deli."

Andre sat on Phillip's other side. Until coming to the magazine, Andre sold men's clothing at the store in Chelsea where Phillip bought his suits. Andre kept a clothing diary for Phillip, itemizing the suits he'd bought by color and style. That was enough for Phillip; Andre was now our fashion editor. Andre didn't talk a lot at these meetings, though he did take copious notes.

Often Phillip picked up the conversation and rerouted it in a direction none of us could have anticipated. During a discussion about neckties, he took off his shoes and stared at his feet so hard it is as if he were seeing them for the first time. "I think I've done it," he announced with pleasure. "I have made my feet wider." A look of horror swept over our managing editor's face.

Byron provided instant feedback at these meetings. When

he heard an idea he liked, he'd jump to his feet and bellow, "That's brilliant!" Then he'd march back and forth, staring at the floor. "Brilliant. Absolutely brilliant," he'd say, shaking his head. "Why didn't I think of that?"

In the early days, I sat in these meetings silently. All I could think about was how smart these people were, and that the minute I opened my mouth, they would see what a poseur I was. I watched them closely and wondered if I could catch something in their expressions that verified my worst fears, that they were thinking: She's not one of us; she'll never be one of us. I was careful never to wear silk on Wednesdays, knowing that I would sweat right through it. Once I worked myself up into presenting an idea for a special issue called "Red, White, and Jewish," a celebration of Jews in America. The words were barely out of my mouth when Byron leaped out of his chair and began pacing. "That's brilliant, simply brilliant!" he shouted.

I was elated.

Then he continued: "I've never heard of a single idea guaranteed to sink a fifty-year-old magazine faster than this one. Marvelous!" Phillip smiled across the table at me and said, "That's what I like about you Betsy. You're not afraid to make a fool of yourself."

I was always making a fool of myself, as far as my friend in the Purim jacket was concerned. It seemed that every time I brought up an idea, he would shake his head and look vaguely disgusted. It was hard to go on, feeling his disapproval, and usually I trailed off not quite finishing my thought. "That's really wrongheaded," he'd say, or, "This isn't a woman's magazine, you know."

One afternoon, after he had decimated me in yet another story meeting, I worked up my courage and asked Purim to have a drink with me after work.

"Can't. Gotta go to Bloomingdale's to buy a lamp," he said.

Gracious, but direct.

"How about if I go with you?"

"Oh, Christ." He made a disapproving face and shook his head.

"Okay then, I'll come." That afternoon, I followed him through linens and home furnishings and into lighting fixtures.

"Exactly what is it about me that drives you nuts?" I whispered, as he stopped at a brass table lamp, and ran his hand over the peach-colored shade. "Do I remind you of your mother or your sister or someone you can't stand?"

He flipped over the price tag on a black halogen.

"Do you feel competitive with me? Do you think I'm after your job?" My whispers were getting louder and more urgent.

He flicked on the switch of a Tiffany knockoff.

"Do you think it's wrong for a woman to be at *Esquire*?"

He stopped at a Kovack's gooseneck; I could tell he liked it. "Should I talk less at story meetings?"

"Look," he said, turning to me for the first time, "just let me buy a goddamn lamp in peace. Then we can have a drink and discuss, in detail, all the things about you that drive me crazy."

Oh, great.

We went to a crowded bistro near Bloomingdale's and squeezed into a corner table. Purim wasted no time in getting to the point. "I don't dislike you as much as you think I do," he said, licking Myer's rum off his twizzler stick. "I can't be the first person who's ever told you this, but you can be very annoying."

I tried to look interested.

"Like tonight, you followed me around like a gnat." He used his hand to make the motion of a flapping mouth. " 'What is it about me you don't like?' " He mimicked me with a nasally high-pitched whine. " 'Do I remind you of your sister? Do you feel competitive with me?' You just don't quit."

This was becoming unbearable. Part of me wanted to get up and leave, but part of me wanted to wrestle this to the ground. "I was just trying to get your attention," I said.

"God, that's the other thing about you . . ."

Thinking she was about to eavesdrop on a divorce, the woman at the next table arched her back and stared at the plate of guacamole in front of her.

"You're so perky-perky-perky. Yecch, it's disgusting." He actually shuddered when he said it, like a dog after a bath.

I started laughing. "Is that it?" I asked.

"Well, God knows, I could go on," he said. "But how about we order some dinner first?" He almost smiled. The woman at the next table looked disappointed.

I asked him why he wore so much cashmere; he told me I dressed too Miami. "Too bad you're so mean," I said. "You really are very smart." We talked for three hours—summer camp, allergies, the usual stuff. He was funny and secretly sentimental. That night, we became old friends. And like old friends, we never stopped bickering. Things got easier after that. Purim still picked on me at meetings, but now I had figured out how to pick back.

· · ·

Once he stopped being my nemesis, I started learning from him. When we were trying to figure out how to celebrate *Esquire*'s fiftieth anniversary, I watched a perfect idea spring full-blown from his head. "We'll do an issue on fifty who made a difference," he said. "We'll get fifty great writers to write on fifty people who most changed the world in the past fifty years." It won a coveted National Magazine Award a year later, and has been copied ever since. Purim taught me about not hitting ideas dead on, but rather looking at a story sideways and coming up with a surprising, sometimes counterintuitive angle. When Barbra Streisand was filming *Yentl,* a movie about a Jewish girl in a ghetto posing as a boy, I proposed that we send the Yiddish novelist Isaac Bashevis Singer out to Los Angeles to do a profile about her. Purim liked that idea but thought that Chaim Potok (known for his novels about contemporary religious Jews) would be a better match. Potok agreed, and he and Streisand became so close, he ended up being an adviser on the film.

Working on this story brought me closer to April, our art director. A pale wraithlike woman, she wore bangs down to her eyebrows and dramatic slashes of red lipstick. On cold days, she dressed in blue jeans with a plaid flannel lining. Lately she'd taken to wearing a babushka to work. "What's with the babushka?" I asked as we pored over the Streisand photographs.

She looked at the stills from *Yentl,* then looked back at me. "I'm having a religious experience," she said flatly.

Coming to work was starting to be fun. Phillip put me in charge of the fashion department and I looked forward to the male models coming in for auditions, rolling up their pants, showing Andre and me their legs so we could decide if they were good enough for our fashion shoot on bathing suits. I was also the liaison between the art and editorial departments, which meant I got to spend a lot of time watching the designers play with different typefaces and photographs in order to best convey the emotional sense of the story they were working on. I loved the smell of burnt wax they used for pasting up pages; and the list they kept on their bulletin board called "Dead Yet?"—people who nobody could believe were still alive. Whenever one of them died, there was an elaborate ritual of crossing him off the list with a bright red slash through his name. Every now and then a writer like Richard Ford or Geoffrey Wolfe strolled into the office and just hung out. Gay Talese, perfectly turned out in a three-piece hand-tailored suit, stood in line with us at the coffee wagon one afternoon, bought a tuna sandwich for $2.95 and tipped the guy five dollars. Ron Rosenbaum, dressed in baggy khakis and the latest, most garish style of running shoes, trudged in every couple of weeks with a legal pad under his arm, always prepared to chase down a story or jot down half sentences and new theories while he was sitting there talking to you. Ron wrote many of his pieces in coffee shops, and never turned in a story without apple pie smudges or coffee rings every couple of pages. Phillip said to me one day after I'd been there about six months, "You'd show up here even if I didn't pay you." He was probably right.

Once a month we had funny, though excruciating, meetings where we wrote the lines that ran on the cover. We agonized over a single verb and had philosophical debates about which line—"How a Man's Body Ages," "The Aging Male Body," or "Men and Their Bodies"?—most perfectly conveyed the story inside. Someone always came up with a reason why a particular line wouldn't work. April didn't like how the letter M looked on the page. Phillip thought the word *bodies* would make people uncomfortable. Andre felt men didn't want to be reminded that they were getting older. Richard reminded us that we ran the word *male* on the cover two issues ago. Magazine editors actually believe readers notice things like that. We spent one afternoon in Phillip's office trying to write lines for an issue with Roy Scheider on the cover. After six hours, here's what we came up with: "Teachers, Hispanics, and Engineers." We ran these words in large type across Scheider's face without even mentioning the actor's name. It wasn't one of our best-selling issues.

We developed deep relationships with the people who wrote for us. "My writer," we'd say when talking about them, as if in claiming them we could somehow own their words. Since most of the magazine's editors had been writers—and some remained convinced they were better at it than those who were actually doing it—there was a lot of rewriting and subsequent soap operas over whose words were actually printed. We all developed ad-hoc therapy strategies to extract the goods from "our writers." One of our editors sat with his writer from early evening late into the night watching him put words on paper. "It was the only way I can get the story out of him," he explained. I moved on from the confront-them-until-they're-ready-to-punch-you method to asking as many questions as I could, then letting the writer do the rewriting himself.

Esquire was the kind of magazine that let you pluck a trend out of the air and set it on its ear. It had a more oblique way of interpreting the culture than *Newsweek* did, and I loved the zaniness it allowed. During the time when every writer we knew was getting a lot of money for developing screenplays, we decided to do a story called "Is Anyone in America *Not* Writing a Screenplay?" We hired Zippy, a chimpanzee, to pose for the cover photograph wearing a black turtleneck and horn-rimmed glasses. He was seated at a typewriter with a bunch of "how-to" screenwriting books stacked up behind him. Zippy became a character throughout the piece, and I was one of the editors who helped create that character using photos and captions.

Shortly after the Zippy cover, I was invited to talk about our annual "Dubious Achievement" awards on *Midday Live with Bill Boggs*. We got to talking about magazine covers. Boggs remarked on how clever it was for us to put a chimpanzee on the cover instead of the usual celebrity.

"Is Zippy a male or female?" he asked.

"Male."

"Ah yes. And what does Zippy do when he's not posing for the cover of *Esquire*?"

"He hosts a midday talk show," I heard myself say.

The audience became silent. Soon after, I left the stage and went back into the green room. A gentleman in a blue blazer and a wire in his ear came over to me. "Here," he said, placing a silver dollar in my hand. "You've earned this."

After that, I got invited to talk about *Esquire* on other talk shows, but never Bill Boggs's.

Read this," my friend John Walsh said one night, dropping a column from *The Philadelphia Daily News* into my lap. What I read was audacious and brave and made me laugh. The writer, Pete Dexter, had created a world where people were on the verge of violence, and acted on their most outrageous impulses. It was strong stuff, though I only believed some of it. I called Pete at the paper and asked him if he'd like to write for the magazine. "Well, hell, yeah. That sounds interesting," he said. "Jeez. What's your name again?"

The following week he came to New York. We started talking about the writer Norman Maclean. All I knew about Norman Maclean was that he was eighty years old and a former Shakespeare professor. As far as I could tell, the only thing he had in common with Pete Dexter was a gift for storytelling. Maclean had written an astonishing first book, *A River Runs Through It*, that was becoming a cult classic, which made him a natural for *Esquire*. Whoever we sent to profile Maclean would need to get the maleness and tenderness of *A River Runs Through It*, and be able to draw out the author, and for this Dexter seemed perfect. Dexter had read the book and said he would like to hang out with the writer at his cabin in Seely, Montana. Maclean agreed. Dexter would visit him over Christmas vacation. I don't think that an investment banker closing a two-hundred-million-dollar deal could have felt more triumphant than I did making a match like that.

The next time I saw Dexter was at John Walsh's wedding. He was dancing with his wife and had a scarf between his teeth. He set the scarf on fire and kept on dancing with the burning cloth dangling from his lips. Watching him, I started to think that more of the stuff he wrote might be truer than I thought. The scarf embers were still clinging to his jacket when he came over and said to me, "You're what's-her-name from *Esquire*. You know, you're the only editor I've ever worked with who hasn't become a friend." Although I didn't say it out loud, I thought to myself that this guy seemed like a hurricane, maybe it was fine if we didn't become friends.

One day, a colleague who had just had her first baby asked me if Malcolm and I would ever have kids. My answer slipped out unexpectedly. "I'd have to compete with the kid if we did."

She looked startled. "Whoa," she said. "I'm not even going to get near that one."

My answer, a blurto if ever there was one, wasn't even true anymore. I wasn't the helpless child I was in my early twenties. I was in my mid-thirties, and doing pretty well in the career of my choice. Malcolm still cooked, and though we sometimes fell back into our old roles for comfort, the truth was that we'd both moved on from that and become more self-contained. Malcolm now worked long hours at a national magazine. On the weekends he was consumed by his passions for gardening and cooking. I no longer went to bars at night and I stopped seeing the man I'd been involved with. *Esquire* was not as consuming as *Newsweek.* The hours were more regular and I didn't populate our home life with characters from work. This was a natural time for us to have children. I tried to get pregnant, with no success. Those were the days when in vitro and fertility clinics were in their infancy, so our sperm and eggs were on their own. Then, a year later, when I was thirty-six, a doctor discovered fibroids the size of a small handbag on my uterus. They always talk about these things in terms of fruit. I preferred to think of my fruit being discreetly contained in a leather bag. I was in the middle of a cover-line meeting at *Esquire* when my assistant interrupted to tell me that my doctor was on the phone. The doctor had news that would finally settle the question of whether or not Malcolm and I would have children. "You should see the surgeon as soon as you can," he advised.

I hung up and, on shaky legs, walked back into the cover-line meeting. Afterward, when I called Malcolm, I couldn't bring myself to use the word *hysterectomy*. In fact, it took years for me to ever say that word out loud. Malcolm was good at medical crises and was kind and unflappable when they happened. This time, he was speechless. Later that week, he forgot to show up for the meeting with the surgeon.

There was a part of me that wasn't surprised when my tomboy body balked at such a womanly thing as childbearing, but there was another part of me that grieved for the freckle-faced blue-eyed little girl I'd have taught to swim and ride a bike. Malcolm, I don't think, ever considered that he wouldn't have children. For a nurturing man who loved having acolytes, what could be more natural? He never said anything to make me feel this way, but I knew I had profoundly let him down.

After the hysterectomy, my parents came to visit me in the hospital. My father sat on my bed. He pressed his lips together in an attempt to smile, but tears were running down his cheeks. "I can't stand seeing her like this," he said, turning to my mother, who was seated next to him. I never knew he felt that way.

For a long time after the surgery, Malcolm and I didn't talk about children at all. When we finally did, we agreed that we'd look into adoption. It took another year and a half for us to register with an agency. In the meantime, Malcolm's cooking and gardening became more elaborate. He fussed over his snap-dragons and duck terrines and sorrel soup. One day, after get-ting a tour of Malcolm's vegetable garden, a friend visiting from Hartford dropped the comment: "Well, at least Malcolm has somewhere to sow his seeds."

It was a very cruel remark made even more so by the un-thinkable suggestion that neatly planted rows of asparagus could double for children. Malcolm's interest in cooking and garden-ing bordered on obsession; it pulled us apart, I thought, but then again, I envied him for having things he cared about that much. It underscored how lonely I felt—that I had nothing of my own.

Even the house we were living in felt like wearing someone else's hand-me-downs. The former owners, Joe Rinaldo and his wife, Connie, were present in the rhododendron bushes that blossomed early each spring. Their old coffee stains were still in our kitchen sink. The Rinaldos were even underfoot in the beige broadloom in the living room, and the gray-and-blue shag in the bedroom—all reminders of how Joe made his living. So when Joe died five years after we'd bought his house, it was as if a member of the family had passed.

Joe was a quiet, forceful man whose veins bulged around his temples whenever Connie got emotional. During the closing, Connie had sat in a corner of the lawyer's office and cried her eyes out. Red in the face, Joe took her arm and said, "The Cart-ers will let us visit whenever we want." When the Rinaldos came up a couple of months later, Malcolm walked them through his new perennial garden. All the while Connie dabbed her eyes and blew her nose. I couldn't imagine how she was coping with Joe's death.

We went to Joe's wake in Bay Ridge, the far reaches of

Brooklyn. As we got closer, I noticed one limo after another pulling up to the funeral parlor. "Looks like the Academy Awards," I said to Malcolm.

For a quiet guy, Joe drew a big crowd. Inside, the room overflowed with people; the smell of roses choked the air. As we walked through the back door, I caught a glimpse of Connie in the front row. A posse of women holding handkerchiefs surrounded her. She must have seen us come in, because, seconds later, a bloodcurdling scream filled the room. "Oh, my God," she shouted. "It's the Carters!" All eyes were on us as Connie collapsed into a tangle of arms. I sensed hundreds of people reaching for their guns.

"Go on," Malcolm whispered, pushing me toward Connie, "tell her how sorry we are, how much we liked Joe." I tentatively made my way to the front of the parlor as the women pressed smelling salts under Connie's nose. When I finally got there, I put my arm around her heaving body and told her how sad we were for her loss. Connie clutched me to her bosom and held me there in a tight grip. "Go to him," she urged. "Talk to him. Tell him what you've done to the house."

Talk to whom? I looked around. Oh, my God, she meant Joe! Connie took my hand and led me to the open casket. "Joe!" she shouted, as though she were trying to rouse him from a nap. "Joe! The Carters are here! Betsy has some things to tell you!"

Joe was the first dead person I had ever seen.

I stared at his sallow cheeks and his crisp white shirt and noted that the nails on his smooth hands seemed to have been recently buffed. Connie jabbed me in the ribs. "Go on," she insisted, "tell him everything." I started talking slowly in a dull monotone.

"We-screened-in-the-porch-we-planted-marigolds-on-the-
side-of-the-house-we-built-a-stone-wall-above-the-garage-we-
put-Laura-Ashley-wallpaper-in-the-bedroom."

I could have stopped there, but no, I felt the need to tell
Joe every detail of every change we'd made. Somewhere around
"We-caulked-the-tub," a heavyset man in a gray suit took me by
the arm and moved me away. Malcolm later said I looked so
pale, he thought I was going to keel over on top of poor Joe.

For the next three years, the ghost of Joe Rinaldo haunted
the house in ways that made me feel he hadn't quite settled yet.
Several days after the wake, a seagull crashed through the picture window in the living room and flew through the house
dropping bird shit everywhere.

"Tell me that that his beak and white hair don't remind you
of Joe," Malcolm said as he tried to snare the gull with a bed-
sheet. One year later, on the anniversary of Joe's death, a white
cat showed up at our back door. Neither of us believed in
ghosts, yet we called the cat Spooky. And two years after Joe's
death, the pipes in the bathroom burst and saturated all of the
carpets. The smell of soaked wool was still there when we
moved out of the house six months later.

Finding the next house was like falling in love for real. It
was a small log house that overlooked the Hudson River. From
the bedroom window, we watched the boat traffic on the river.
Because the walls were made of log, the house had an orange
glow where the light hit the curved wood. Outside, the colors
changed like a kaleidoscope as the sun's reflection moved across
the Catskills.

We filled the house with mementos of our trips: rugs from
Mexico, blankets from Guatemala, wind chimes from Italy,

masks from Africa. Upstairs, we kept all of our record albums—including soundtracks from nearly every Broadway show ever produced—our childhood photos, and slides from all the years of our marriage.

Of course, Malcolm's garden was perfectly coiffed and co-ordinated. There was always color from the bursts of crocuses and daffodils in April to the last gasp of chrysanthemums in October. On cold nights we built a fire and put on the Wood-stock rock station. Malcolm cooked dinner while I read or played the guitar. Sometimes I danced to the radio, watching my image in the picture window as the sun set on the Hudson behind it like a double exposure. At those times, I felt part of this cozy intimate family. Malcolm and I shared the joke that I had married the perfect wife.

Real life doesn't come with captions. Day to day I showed up with my little bag of tricks that had always worked before, but inevitably the day came when they stopped working. Years later I looked back at a particular time and remembered, yes, that's when it all shifted. The tricks stopped working, luck got flaky. I had been at *Esquire* nearly two years when I started hearing footsteps. All the things that had once seemed in place slowly started to fall apart.

In the winter of that year at *Esquire*, I developed a piercing cough. One morning, after a particularly noisy attack, Phillip came over to my desk and asked me if I'd come there to die. Finally, when my fever hit 101.3, I saw a doctor. He diagnosed pleurisy and prescribed several days of bed rest. Malcolm re-minded me that pleurisy was what most heroines succumb to in operas. We both thought that was pretty funny. He prepared three kinds of soup and froze them so I would have something to eat when he went to see his father in San Francisco.

At seven o'clock on the morning that he was due home, the telephone rang. It was Malcolm, calling from the phone booth at our corner. "Everything's fine," he began nervously. "I didn't want to scare you, though. I've been in a slight accident. I look awful. I was waiting with my dad at the Social Security office, and some psychopath came at me out of nowhere from across the room and punched me in the face." I could tell he was fighting off tears.

When he walked through the front door, I could see that his right cheek was caved in and his right eye was swollen shut. His face was pulpy and purple and red. In an attempt to hide his bruises on the airplane, he wore his stepmother's large straw hat and a scarf tied around the bottom of his face, which made him look even more grotesque. The disguise called as much attention to him as the wound, and I wondered why he even bothered.

All I knew about what happened in San Francisco was what he told me. He was with his father, when out of the blue some guy ran across the crowded office and punched him in the face. There were no words, there was no warning: All he remembered was a blow to the face before falling to the floor. "Did you give him a strange look, make an inadvertent gesture?" I asked.

"Nothing like that," he swore. "Absolutely nothing."

In time I would have let the whole thing pass had my sister not kept picking at it like last week's nail polish. She could be like a ferret that way, nudging and scratching and never letting up. "What *really* happened that time in San Francisco?" she kept asking me long after Malcolm's face healed.

"I don't know," I'd answer.

"But what do you *really* think happened in San Francisco?"

"I don't know. I honestly don't know."

Miriam is a small woman with delicate elflike features. She has a habit of turning her head and looking sidelong out of the corners of her eyes. She says it's because of a weak muscle in her eyes, but it has the effect of her always seeming one step removed from whatever is in front of her. When she works on her otherworldly collages, she can stand in front of the canvas for hours at a time, applying paint, then stepping back to consider her strokes. It's as if she's always looking at one thing two different ways. She sees things that I never see and some that aren't there at all. She's the one who's always put italics into our lives: *"Do you* really *think we're moving to Miami for Daddy's job?" "Don't you think it's odd that they sent you to overnight camp when you were only four years old?"*

Nearly a year after Malcolm's episode in the Social Security office, she brought it up again. "What more do you know about what happened with Malcolm in San Francisco?" she asked resolutely.

"Jesus Christ," I snapped. "Will you drop it already!"

Miriam had always thought that Malcolm was too good to be true and often said things like, *"He cooks, he gardens, he gives you presents. He's the perfect man, isn't he?"* Definitely, she was not going to let it drop.

She stared at me squarely in the face. This time, *both* her eyes met mine: "Well don't you think you ought to find out?" she asked. Something in her voice made me certain that I didn't.

Eleven

Gumption was one of my mother's favorite words, and as much a part of my genetic code as the crook in her nose and my father's curly hair. It's what it took for my parents to smuggle five hundred dollars out of Germany and live on it for their first few months in America. My mother's aunt Flora had it in abundance when she came to Germany in 1936, after my parents' marriage, to get dozens of her relatives out of Hitler's Germany. Flora, who was German-born but living in America, came to Germany, and met with the American consul. As shrewd as she was attractive, she brought the officer a present. "This is from America," she said, handing him a wrapped package. "It's what everybody there is talking about." It was a brand-new copy of *Gone With the Wind*. That day she signed affidavits for more than 100 people, including my parents, promising to support them financially should they become a burden to the American government. Only when I was much older did I realize exactly how much nerve all of that took.

My father got lost in the subway shortly after they arrived in America. They were waiting for a train at the Times Square station. When the train arrived and the doors opened, those in the subway car pushed their way out, while the crowd on the platform shoved their way in; it was like getting caught in a strong current. Once inside, my mother felt the closing doors catch the bottom of her coat. She looked around for my father but he wasn't there. The doors had snapped shut before he could step into the car.

I could picture him standing alone staring at empty tracks in the dirty light of the station. He spoke no English, so the signs he saw—"Queens Local," "Bronx Express"—must have seemed meaningless. He felt like a beggar, approaching strangers with an ingratiating smile, asking for directions. "Washington Heights please." He made sure to keep smiling. "Washington Heights please."

My father was a short man with a gap between his two front teeth and the quizzical eyes of a child. All he had going for him was that he looked helpless and not like some marauding lunatic with a knife hidden in his jacket. Some people gave him incomprehensible instructions in that loud talking-to-strangers voice. Others pointed this way and that. He would nod his head and pretend to understand, then wait for them to be out of sight so he could ask the next person. If he wanted to shout that he had lived in a sixteen-room mansion in Kaiserslautern, that his family owned the first automobile in the town, who could have blamed him? Instead he was quiet and grateful for any help he could get. Finally, a lady with a German accent and a fox-rimmed collar on her coat ("The fox had a face like Wally Cox," he said later) said, "Go where I go," and led him to the train back to Washington Heights.

He never forgot the humiliation of being a helpless foreigner, though as the years passed, the story took on the gilding of all family mythology. "When I came home, I was greeted like a war hero," he would say. "And why not? I had conquered the subways of New York."

It struck me as a horrible story. How awful to be such an outsider at the mercy of strangers. No wonder that wherever my parents went in America, the tonnage from their past followed. When you are forced out of your home, you never give up trying to fit pieces of the old into the new. Our apartment in New York, and later, our little house in Miami, was filled with testaments to their grander days. A tarnished little silver bell sat on top of the mahogany desk in the living room. My grandmother had used it to ring for the servants. We ate our Chef Boyardee dinners with large pieces of heavy silverware bearing my grandparents' initials. Spilling over from one room to the next were rivers of Persian carpets, whose graceful teal petals and rich maroon rosettes were bleached mercilessly by the Miami sun. To look at the priceless pieces of porcelain in our china cabinet or the five-piece sterling silver tea set my mother used for company, you'd think we were on the fringes of European royalty. The truth was that, like many immigrant families with two young children and no cash reserves, we were barely scraping by. Yet with their German formality and genteel customs, we lived a kind of Jekyll-and-Hyde existence.

We moved to a slightly larger one-family house when I was twelve and we hauled all that stuff with us. Though the new house was only twenty blocks from Lou Ann's family and the Flagler Baptist Church, it might as well have been a continent away. Lou Ann and I saw each other only one time after that, three years later when we were both in high school. She showed me the ring she wore on a chain around her neck, and told me that she and Diego would be married as soon as she graduated. I asked about her family. Her older brother had joined the Marines. "Janie and Curtis are growin' up too fast, and Mama and Daddy are real good," she said, thrusting her head, gulping for air.

Our new house had jalousied windows, a Florida room with a faux marble terrazzo floor, and a backyard big enough for a swing set, a lemon tree, and a tiny cement patio. Outside, the style was classic Miami circa 1957. Inside, the place screamed Kaiserslautern, 1932. My high school duplicated the paradox of my home. The oldest high school in the city, Miami High was built when Spanish architecture was the rage. It was an ornate formal structure with potted palms on indoor patios, a giant bust of the Cuban poet José Marti in the courtyard, and brown Cuban tile that made it look more like an old Havana hotel than a public high school.

Of course, the Miami High of 1960 had little to do with its 1929 facade. It was high school, after all; it just had more places than most to sneak off and smoke cigarettes. This was where we tried out different versions of ourselves and then held grudges against the people who didn't buy them. I found my niche there by acting kooky. If fitting in meant the other kids would notice me for my outrageous behavior or silly gestures, then that's what I would do. I let the air out of people's tires while they were at parties and set my cooking partner's books afire by hiding them in the stove. I was flunking sewing until the day Mrs. Ball, my sewing teacher, approached me with a proposition.

"Well Miss Beh-tsy, it seems that you have skills other than being a homemaker," she said one day after class. "You know and I know that if you don't pass sewing, you don't graduate from high school. Am I right about that?"

"Yes ma'am."

"And I feel certain that you don't want to be left behind, now, do you?"

"No ma'am."

"Well then, I have a little prop-o-sition for you."

Mrs. Ball had been asked to prepare a skit for the PTA. "Writing is to me what sewing is to you. I haven't the vaguest notion how to do it. So I'll tell you what. If you write my play for me, I will give you a B in sewing. What do you think of that?"

What I thought was what a person on death row thinks when the governor calls with a last-minute reprieve.

"Mrs. Ball," I said, "you've got yourself a deal."

On the following Tuesday, Mrs. Ball waited for me after class. "Do you have it?" she asked.

"I have it," I answered, "but first I have something I'd like you to read." I handed her a folded piece of paper with a hand-written note on it that said:

> DEAR MRS. BALL,
>   *The grade I want I will not say, but I'll give you a hint, it starts with an A.*
>
>   BETSY COHN

She folded the message, put it in her pocket and said, "I'll take the play please." When I got my report card that term, there, filling the box marked *Home Economics*, was the letter A. "I don't know whether to punish you or feel proud," my mother said when I told her how I got the grade.

I spent most Saturday nights "wrapping" houses with my friend Sherry Lee. The idea was to go to someone's home when no one was there, wind rolls of toilet paper around the palm trees, bushes and shrubs, then hope that it would rain right after the job was done. That would leave shreds of toilet paper clinging to those yards like Miami snow. One night, we got caught. What the cops saw as they pulled up to a dark empty house were two girls tiptoeing around a sumac bush carrying bulges the size of cannonballs under their sweatshirts. Of course they assumed we'd just robbed the place. We insisted we were only playing a trick on the kid who lived in the house, but the cops weren't buying it.

Because we were only fifteen, because we were girls and because there was only toilet paper under those sweatshirts, they put Sherry Lee and me in the backseat of their car and drove us home. My mother was the first to see the squad car pull into the driveway. Her heart was in her throat, she said later: "I thought for sure they were coming to tell me you were dead." When she heard what we'd done, all the relief in her curdled into anger: "This is not how we behave. Who do you think you are?" It was the same iciness I had heard in her voice the summer before, when the owner of the camp I was attending sent a letter home. He enumerated his grievances against me, including leading my bunk into the woods at 2:00 A.M., causing one of my bunkmates to trip and break her leg. "Please do not send her back here next summer," the letter concluded.

"You are not a rich girl from a rich family," my mother said when she read that letter. "I save all year to send you to camp. I won't have you throw it back in my face that way."

But being antic was the only way Sherry Lee and I could figure out how to make it through high school. Sherry Lee came from a family of multiple divorces. She never lived in one place too long: Sometimes she stayed with a grandmother, other times with a first cousin. It wasn't that nobody wanted her, it was just that nobody had time to care for a child, what with all the legal battles and emotional crises going on in their lives. Sherry Lee turned her story into a sitcom. In her complicated, funny anecdotes, her parents became caricatures of grown-ups and she the hapless butt of all the jokes. One of her front teeth was askew. When she laughed, the tooth was what you saw, that and her hawk-brown eyes, which she kept fixed on you to make sure that you were laughing with her. I knew how she felt; still we kept trying.

Each fall, the fraternities and sororities held rush parties: Everyone was invited, even though you could tell before your first bite into a brownie who would make it and who wouldn't. I could think of nothing greater than to be invited to join Honoria.

"Honey, don't count on anything," my mother said whenever I brought the subject up—which was every day. The girls in Honoria were the cheerleaders and part of the homecoming queen's court. They got pinned to the boys in the Wheel club who played on the football team and had names like Bud and D. V. God, I was dying to be part of Honoria.

On the morning of the day that I believed could change my life forever, I sat in homeroom doodling in my notebook. That way, I figured, no one would notice how much I cared. Also, if Dee Dee Dent walked over to me and placed a blue-and-white ribbon around my neck with a big blue cardboard H, I could act surprised and whoop and hug her and say, "Oh Dee Dee, I am so excited, I can't believe this." When Dee Dee walked in that morning, I kept scribbling and looking down at the floor to see where her pointy little flats would take her. Up the aisle, one desk over, Dee Dee stopped in front of Joanie Goldsmith's desk; Dee Dee, all crisped up in her white blouse with the big blue H monogram and her spit curls falling on her forehead just so. She placed the sacred ribbons around Joanie's head. Joanie cried as they walked out of the room with their arms around each other. I kept doodling as though I hadn't even noticed that I'd been passed over. Four doors down, in her homeroom, Sherry Lee had also been passed over for the sorority of her dreams, Little Women.

Sherry Lee and I went to Feder's drugstore after school that day and ordered two cherry Cokes and a plate of French fries. We talked about how dumb the new pledges were. "Dumb as toads," she said. "Dumb as bologna," I said. "Dumb as spit," she said. "Dumb as doody," I said. Soon we were laughing so hard, we forgot about Honoria and Little Women, at least for a while.

A couple of weeks later, I was reading *Mad* magazine and came across one of those little tags that ran upside the pages. "Taxation without representation is Poo-bah," it said. *Poo-bah.* I'd never heard that word before and it struck me so funny, I called Sherry Lee. "So if no one will let us in their club, let's start our own. We'll call it the Poo-bah club." We got some of our other friends who had been rejected by the other clubs to join. We developed a secret language and handshake and I became Princess Poo-bah. The club had no function, and our meetings had no purpose. Every two months we chose new members and made them go through a pledging ritual of collecting 500 empty gum wrappers. As we walked through the halls, we flashed our handshake—a rapid drying motion with the right hand. It was the perfect form of rebellion: a safe way of thumbing our noses at the snobs who'd ignored us. We even tapped some of our favorite teachers, who would write things on our term papers like, "Nice Job, Poo-bah."

The Poo-bah club became a cool antidote to the elite sororities and fraternities. In the perverse logic of high school, being Princess Poo-bah proved to be exactly the entrée I needed. It's funny how a little status can change everything. My grades got better, and I tuned down the act. I got chosen to be the model for the all-American girl in our yearbook. ("Can you imagine that?" my father said to my mother when I told them.) But some things never changed. I still spent most of my Saturday nights with Sherry Lee and hours on the phone with my new friend, Roberto, a Cuban boy from a wealthy well-known family in Havana that was among the first wave of Cubans who ran from Castro to Miami in the early sixties. Roberto had a large round head with dark, woeful eyes. "Hello my friend," he said to everyone he met. He was polite and careful not to show off how smart he was. Roberto became a Poo-bah, and one of the more loyal ones at that. First thing every morning, he called to wake me up. " 'Ello my leetle princess," he said in a mock French accent. "Eeets another beeautiful day in the land of Poo-bahs. You must rise and you must shine."

On the night of our senior prom, Sherry Lee and I rode our bikes to across the street from where the prom was being held. As we watched the couples walk into the lobby, we made fun of the girls' dresses, their wrist corsages, and how funny the boys looked in their pleated cummerbunds. Poo-bahs notwithstanding, neither of us had been invited; we were still outsiders.

My plans for the fall were to go to the University of Florida. Anything else was out of the question. "We can't afford to send you out of state," my father said.

When he left the room, my mother beckoned me closer to her. "If anything should happen to me, your father will tell you he can't afford your tuition," she said in a gravelly whisper. "That's not true. I've tucked away money for you." It was like that every summer before I went to camp. She'd always assure me, "Even if I'm not here anymore, there's enough money in the bank to get you through the summer." I grew up fearing that my mother was always on the verge of being abducted— whenever I drove the car, she'd lie down in the backseat and cover her eyes. The signs were there.

On graduation day, the valedictorian of our class got up before nearly two thousand people and gave his speech. At the end of his talk, as the audience applauded, he stepped away from the podium and stood center-stage. Then he very deliberately lifted his right hand and shook it up and down. It was the wild jerk-off motion of the Poo-bah handshake.

The moment I set foot onto the University of Florida, I felt as though I was sinking.

Actually, I was.

Gainesville was built on a swamp. All around it, giant oak trees dug their claws into the earth and held on for dear life. Beneath them, the ground was ever so slowly being slurped up by the marshlands of Alachua County. Not a place to be if you're eighteen and don't have a firm grip on yourself. It was an intensely social place, more sororities and fraternities. I didn't fit in, couldn't find my place. Sherry Lee got a boyfriend and Roberto joined a fraternity. I didn't make new friends. Every vestige of Princess Poo-bah vanished, there was nothing antic about me. My roommate Carla, drank a quart of Listerine every morning. "It's a real pick me up," she said urging me to try it. Something told me if I started sipping mouthwash, it wouldn't stop there.

Convinced I would run out of money, I took to having dinner from the snack machine down the hall—six peanut butter crackers a night, alone at my desk, which was where I found myself spending all my time, as if studying would give purpose to my depression. By the end of freshman year, my weight dropped from 103 to 87, though my grades were terrific.

Miriam had recently married and she and her new husband, Armand, were living in Ann Arbor, where he taught math. My mother was the one who suggested I go there for summer school. "I've squirreled away the money, it would be a good change of pace for you."

The kids in Ann Arbor seemed more familiar to me than the ones in Florida. I studied Chaucer and worked for the newspaper. I fell in love with a cute boy named Peter Aichen. On Sunday mornings, I went to Miriam and Armand's house and ate scrambled eggs on the blue-and-white plates Miriam brought from home. During the week, I'd picture us sitting together in their kitchen, and it made me feel safer than I had in months. That was the happiest summer of my life. When it was time to return to Florida, I swore I'd get myself into Michigan the following year, whatever it took.

The moment I got back to Gainesville, the person I'd been that summer walked flat out on me. All my life I worked so hard *not* to disappear. Now Gainesville was threatening to swallow me up in its boggy gunk. I lost more weight, and wore the same faded sweatshirt and jeans every day. I must have looked exactly how I felt: parched and neglected—not exactly a look that would turn a guy's head. Unless, of course, the guy was someone who found solace in the frail and vulnerable. Someone like Dr. Bill.

I met Bill at an off-campus party during my sophomore year. There was lots of wine and Dave Brubeck on the stereo and at some point, I became aware that a stocky man with glasses and nails bitten to just short of bleeding was sending me snaky smiles from across the room. His name was Bill. He was thirteen years older than I, and studying to be a psychiatrist. He quoted Lawrence Ferlinghetti and talked about Coltrane. That night, we kissed. Then the letters started coming, thick with Bill's insights. He wrote about me in the third person, things like, "She has legs as skinny as cue sticks. . . . I am worried that I will smother her with my darkness."

I don't know about the legs, but he was dead on about the darkness. Less than a week after we met, I got a frantic call from his roommate, Hans. "Bill is *verry, verry* sick," he said. "He calls for you." Hans picked me up in his beige VW; his face looked stricken. "It's not good," he said. "He does not take food. He does not get up from the couch. It is beside me."

When we got to the apartment, Hans nudged me upstairs.

Bill was lying on the couch. "I'm so glad you could come," he said with a slight nod to Hans. "I needed to see you." Hans stood up. "So I go now," he said, shaking my hand.

I felt Bill's head with the back of my hand. "You feel pretty cool," I said. "Can I make you some tea or consommé?"

"You know what would really make me feel better?" he asked. "I would love to take a hot bath."

"Sure, a hot bath sounds great," I answered. "I'll get it ready for you."

I went into the bathroom. As I knelt by the tub adjusting the water knobs, I heard him come up behind me. "This is nice of you," he said, closing the bathroom door. Then he took hold of my arm: "You'll take the bath with me, won't you?"

"Hmm, I don't want to do that," I said.

"Well, I think you're going to." His voice sounded raw.

Until that moment, I had done every form of heavy petting I could without going all the way. But this was the first time a man had ever asked me to commit an act of personal hygiene with him. It made my legs go liquid.

"I'll sit here and keep you company," I offered.

"No, I want you in there with me." He took me by the wrist and squeezed it hard enough for me to understand that he meant it. I took off my clothes and got into the tub with him. It was amazing how the innocent pleasure of taking a bath suddenly seemed as creepy as stepping into a swamp. His penis bobbed up and down in the water like a mackerel.

I never told anyone, not even my mother, how Bill tried to force it inside me and how, frozen by fear and humiliation, I just sat there. What would anyone have said but that I had gotten into the bath with him in the first place, so what did I expect? There was no way to explain that Bill terrified me, yet I wanted to please him, and somewhere in between, I ended up nearly getting raped in a bathtub by a man I barely knew. Flattered and repelled by his intensity, I stayed all tangled up with Bill for way too long.

Sadism, it seemed, was a real turn-on for Bill. He showed up at my classes and invented reasons for my teachers to let me out of class so I could be with him; he sat waiting at my dorm for me for hours. He was always close by, making me feel smothered and safe at the same time. Once, way past my curfew, he locked us in his car in the middle of the woods and said he wouldn't take me back to my dorm until I swore I would marry him. Finally, in desperation, I lied and said I would. He made me put it into writing. It felt as if no one had ever loved me this way before, though I wasn't sure if I liked it.

After several months, I was more determined than ever to get away from this man and back to Ann Arbor. When the letter came in March, telling me that I'd been accepted to Michigan, I cried with relief. I waited until the long-distance rates dropped, called home at 9:01 P.M., and read the letter to my mother.

That summer, I came home and worked at a local newspaper. Bill took a job at the Miami Veteran's Hospital. I tried hiding my excitement about Michigan from him, but he could hear it in my voice. He became more intense and shrill. Didn't I understand that we would probably end up seeing other people and eventually breaking up? Of course I did. One night I showed my sister a bundle of Bill's letters. "He really likes you," she said, skimming the first few. By the time she finished the whole batch, she bunched her eyes together and squinted. "This guy is nuts," she said. "Do you have to keep going out with him?"

Late one afternoon, my mother got a call from a man at the admissions board at the University of Michigan verifying that I would not be coming there next semester.

"I'm afraid you've made a terrible mistake," she said. "My daughter will absolutely be there in the fall." After nearly half an hour on the phone, they figured out that someone who said he was my father had called them up to say that I was withdrawing my application. It turned out it was Bill, pretending to be my father.

"Can you get him over here tonight?" my mother said furiously. "I want to speak to him, and I don't want you in the room."

Our house was built so that if you stood on your tiptoes in the bathtub, you could look through the window into the Florida room. That night, when Bill came over, I positioned myself in the tub, staring straight at the rattan chair where my mother always sat. Lighting one Pall Mall after another, she talked through clouds of smoke. "What's your thesis about?" she asked. "Tell me, what is it about psychiatry that interests you so?"

Her English was precise. An avid reader, she prided herself on having a huge vocabulary and almost no trace of German in her accent. She loved to tell us how, when she met someone new, that person would look puzzled, then say, "You have a slight accent. Are you from England?" She also knew how to ask questions in such a way that the person being interviewed felt as if she were hanging on his every word. And like her hero, Edward R. Murrow, she used her cigarette to punctuate a question or inhale an answer.

I craned my neck from my lookout in the bathtub to see what would come next.

"Isn't it wonderful that Betsy got into Michigan?" she asked, starting to circle.

Bill walked right into her trap. "Your daughter has a beautiful mind," he said.

My mother pounced.

"I know that," she said, tapping her cigarette for emphasis, "and I intend to keep it that way." She told him she knew about the Michigan episode. "I don't want you to ever try and see my daughter again," she said in her most brittle voice. "You have acted inappropriately and you've really upset all of us. If you ever come around here again, I promise you, I will call the police."

I watched his face go limp and his shoulders slump. "But I love her," he said like a scolded child.

"So do I," said my mother, ending the conversation.

Bill left looking like a raccoon caught in the garbage. I stood in the bathtub, dumbstruck. I felt ridiculous and relieved.

It took years to exorcise the demons that Bill left behind—a fact, I'm sure, that would have pleased him. I never saw him again—except maybe once, twelve years later, on a night when I was walking home from *Newsweek*. He was a block away, a stocky man with black eyeglasses. It could have been the way he held his head, as if ready to defend himself, or that his fingernails were bitten to the quick, but something about that man made me run into Central Park. At night. That's how much I didn't want to see him.

Twelve

There is a moment when you stop letting life just happen to you. Mine came at 10:15 on a cold morning in 1983. I was in the back seat of a taxicab on my way to *Esquire* after an appointment at the dentist. Smudges of snow lined the streets as the cab dipped into the tunnel under Park Avenue. Engrossed in a *New York Times* story about David Bowie, I barely noticed the light go from sunshine-white to chapel-gray. Something—the instant dimness, a jerky turn of the wheel, I don't know what—made my heart race. The cab rushed into the darkness. There was a wall of something solid, something not moving in front of us. A stalled Chevy. Did the driver see what I saw? Shouldn't he slam on the brakes? Why couldn't I find the words to warn him?

In slow, horrifying, motion, every second took on its own entity. Hold on, hold on . . . but there was nothing to hold on to. The world was going sideways. I was hurtled forward. *Launched* was more like it. Shrieking tires, grinding metal. My body slammed into the partition in front of me. I heard the sound of a belly flop from the high dive. I didn't scream. I watched. And then there was silence; as terrifying as the commotion that preceded it. There was blood. I saw a hand I recognized as my own, shaking. My teeth. They'd come undone. This had to be a dream, like dreams I'd had so often. I'm getting up to speak in front of a crowd and all my teeth fall out. I'm opening the front door to greet a date; all my teeth fall out. I thought about rocks rumbling around in Malcolm's polisher, about my parents and what they'd suffered and that this is what that must feel like. A voice, in an accent I can only describe as frantic, broke the black silence. "Get out of my cab! You get out. Now."

Loose teeth rattled around my mouth. My face felt like pieces of a puzzle forced into the wrong places. Inexplicably, the driver was kicking me out of his taxi. I gave myself directions. Reach into your bag. Get your notebook. Write down his license number. Get out of the cab. I leaned against the snowy bank of the tunnel. My maroon beret sat lopsided on my head. Blood trickled from my mouth. People in passing cars noticed but only one person stopped. Another cabby. He took me to the Emergency Room at New York University Hospital. I gave him a lot of money; I have no idea how much. The admitting nurse looked at my face and made a clicking sound with her tongue. She shook her head. "We don't do oral surgery here," she said, and handed me some towels. "You need to go to Bellevue."

I pointed to the phone on her desk. "Call my husband?" I mumbled.

"Sure honey."

I tried to sound calm when Malcolm picked up the phone. "Been in an accident, my teeth." Couldn't cry now. If I did, I wouldn't stop. "Going to Bellevue."

On the street, people made arcs around me the way they do when a homeless person walks by. No one asked if something was wrong or if they could help. I don't remember how I walked the ten blocks to Bellevue or how long it took. I was shivering, I know that. And I was startled by the thought, No teeth to chatter.

Malcolm was waiting in the emergency room when I got there. "Holy cow," he said when he saw me, then put his arms around me. If he felt revolted or horrified, he never let on. He'd already called my dentist. My dentist had called an oral surgeon. We'd go to his office now. Oh God, another cab. Malcolm held me in the backseat and, for sixty blocks, recited the recipes he would make up for me in the blender. The surgeon was waiting for me at the door. He cleaned up my mouth and took X rays, then ran down my list of injuries. Most of my teeth had been knocked out; the rest were broken or cracked. My lip, as he put it, was filleted; the inside of my mouth was cut up, my jaw was broken. He'd have to do immediate surgery. Malcolm snuggled in the dentist chair next to me. "You're going to come out of this looking like Jacqueline Bisset," were the last words I heard before the Valium and Demerol blasted me out of my head.

For the next three hours, I floated in and out. The nurses argued over who would go to lunch. "No one leaves until this is over," the surgeon ordered. My dentist came by and stared into my mouth. "Goddammit," he said, "this is the worst I've seen." He was angry. Why was he so angry? Then the drugs snatched me away again.

I woke up stapled and stitched. The pain was so excruciating, I've lost the words to describe it. When I tried to speak, my tongue wouldn't move the right way; it couldn't find any of the regular places to settle. I could only imagine what I looked like. Malcolm was sitting next to me on a cot in the doctor's office. "Look, I have a present for you." While I was in surgery, he had run to Bloomingdale's and bought a Calvin Klein makeup kit. I ran my hand over the red plastic cover and studied the different palettes of lipsticks and eyeshadows inside. Was he kidding? Right now I had no face. Where would I put all this stuff?

"This is to remind you that you're going to be beautiful again," he said.

Malcolm. Sweet Malcolm. I wished I could smile.

Friends and family came to see me the next morning. One friend came to hug me, then pulled back. "I'm sorry," she said, then ran from the room and didn't come back.

When I called my mother, she cried and said, "Oh, how I loved your teeth." "Mom, that's not helpful right now," I answered.

My father-in-law walked in and headed straight for the brandy. Miriam brought some clips she'd photocopied about Ann-Margret, and a Montgomery Clift biography. It turned out Ann-Margret had broken her jaw falling off a stage in Las Vegas. For months her husband had to make her pizza in the blender. Oregano, pepperoni, he didn't leave out a thing. "Now she's as pretty as ever," said Miriam.

Montgomery Clift smashed up his face in a car accident; Elizabeth Taylor was the first to find him. Miriam told me he got some of his finest roles after the accident. I tried to conjure up some connection between me and Ann-Margret and Montgomery Clift. Nothing came.

That afternoon, I got up the nerve to look at myself in the

mirror. My face was black-and-blue and swollen. My eyes looked like tiny mussels peering out of their shells. Where my mouth used to be was a black hole of stitches, stubs of teeth, and purple wounds. Whatever face I'd had was gone. I couldn't even remember what I looked like twenty-four hours earlier. When I'd asked the surgeon how I'd look when this was all over, he'd stared off into space and said, "Right now it's hard to tell." I didn't feel angry or repelled or even scared as I studied my battered image. Curious, maybe. A voice, more Walter Cronkite's than my own, filled my head. "Your looks were never the thing. You'll be fine." I'd already paid the price for not being beautiful in high school. This couldn't be any worse than that.

Now I didn't just feel different. I had different written all over me. All I wanted to do was grab on to the edges of normal life and crawl back into the mainstream. But I had to remember that things were broken. A kiss, a smile, a whistle—things I once took for granted were gone. I became someone people looked away from, or pretended not to notice at all.

The dentist fixed me up with some temporary teeth that could pass, from a distance. I could talk, except for some lisping and slurring. One week after the crash, I went back to *Esquire*. Working at magazines is the perfect antidote to personal crises. They flow on a schedule and create their own logic. Deadlines supersede tragedy; there are events that must be attended.

On the Tuesday I returned, there was a luncheon scheduled at the Four Seasons restaurant, where we were introducing "The *Esquire* Collection," a new fashion supplement I was editing, to the industry. This is a group you dress up for. You're careful about your makeup, and match your panty hose to your shoes. If your hemline is off, or you're wearing too much eyeliner, someone will notice. If you have a swollen face and a mouth full of stitches, it probably won't get past them either.

"Somebody else should host this lunch," I said to Phillip that morning.

"Why?" he asked.

"Well, look at me. I'm not exactly the face of fashion."

"It'll be fine. Besides, you're the editor of 'The Collection,' " he said, as if that were the only point. Then he fixed me with a hard stare as if to say, "You know this is about more than 'The Collection.' "

I went to the ladies' room and combed my hair.

That afternoon, I walked into a room filled with about a hundred people. I kept my head down. When it came time for me to speak, I walked toward the podium and watched my hands shake. I looked at the faces before me. There were lots of late-winter ski-tans. Some people looked bored, but no one seemed particularly horrified by the sight of my face. My friend Gene was right: "You're an editor," he'd said. "People assume you're smart. You could get up there and say, 'Jack and Jill went up the hill,' and they would think, Isn't she deep?" Remembering that made me want to laugh. I spoke about how our readers trusted us to tell them what to wear and how to wear it. No one seemed to hear that my S's sshhed and my R's were mushy— or that my face was literally askew. Afterward, one of the women in the audience, someone I knew only slightly, told me, "My God, you've lost so much weight, you look terrific." Later that week, Phillip promoted me to executive editor.

I'm not sure when the teeth jokes started, maybe right after the Four Seasons luncheon. Purim gave me a beautiful antique box with an old Massachusetts home painted on the outside. Inside was tooth powder from India, bubble-gum-flavored toothpaste, a striped toothbrush, a toothbrush in the shape of a stork, and licorice-flavored floss. If it weren't for the twice-a-week dentist appointments that went on for the following year; or the reconstructive surgery that resulted in a new face every couple of months; or the fact that I looked haunted and skeletal (despite Malcolm's blended fruits and chopped chicken liver), I could have believed that nothing ever happened.

Three weeks after the crash, a frail old man limped into the office. He leaned on his cane and took each step with great effort. His dark brown eyes looked as if they'd seen things they shouldn't have. I was not hallucinating. As the figure came closer, I recognized it as Pete Dexter, come back as a ghost. He sat down in a chair next to my desk. "What the hell happened to you?" he asked. I told him about the cab accident, then mentioned he didn't look so great himself. He told me he'd written a column about a young boy who'd OD'd, and the kid's brother and a gang of his friends tried to kill him. They'd come awfully close.

There wasn't much to say after that. He handed me his finished piece on Norman Maclean and wished me luck with my next surgery. I wished him luck with his and said that I hoped both of us looked better the next time we saw each other. Later, when I read his piece on Maclean, Pete's words struck me as honest to the core. They were funny and compassionate, even eloquent, without a hint of pretension. After that, we spoke nearly every day.

The face I ended up with bore some resemblance to mine, though it was more thin-lipped and angular than the original. The first time my mother saw it, she sucked in her breath and said, "The cuteness is gone." She was right

Now I had to figure out what was left.

I faced that cabdriver in a courtroom four years later. The trial lasted three days. The cabdriver, a Russian immigrant whose demeanor was layered with ageless misery, fidgeted with the sleeves of his cheap sports jacket as he testified, "She not hurt like she says. I give her tissues. My cab was ruined." My dentist took the stand. In each hand he held a replica of my mouth: one from before the accident, one from after. He traced every crack and break with his finger, taking time to explain the work and time that had gone into the reconstruction. When he finished, he pointed to the pieces of my jaw and teeth lined up on the table in front of him. "So you can see, Betsy's mouth was totally and utterly destroyed."

There it was: my mouth, splayed out on a table like so many pieces of Mr. Potato Head. The jury looked at me, then back at robo-mouth. "Look vulnerable," my lawyer had instructed earlier. Funny that he had to tell me that. Up until now, looking vulnerable was how I got by. Now, for maybe the first time in my life, I felt anything but. I'd been hit in the face and had been waiting four years to strike back.

On the third day, I took the stand. I wore no makeup, a

black pleated skirt, and a plain white cotton blouse. "The simpler you look, the better," the lawyer had said. I gave my testimony. Then the cabdriver's lawyer had a go at me. "You weren't really hurt in that cab, were you?" he asked, pacing in front of me.

"Yes, I really was. It took me a year to get back to normal."

"Isn't it true you needed plastic surgery anyway?"

"Absolutely not."

"Wasn't this your chance to get someone else to foot the bill?" He punched his finger a few inches from my face.

"No, it wasn't."

"You walked away with minor cuts and scratches." Jab.

"I walked away with all my teeth knocked out."

"You work in the magazine business. Correct?"

I caught a whiff of his Paco Rabanne.

"Yes."

"What do you do?"

"I think up story ideas. I assign them to writers. I edit the stories."

"You make up stories? Stories like this one?" The jabs came faster; the Paco Rabanne caught in my throat.

"I didn't make up this accident."

In his final remarks, he turned to the jury: "She exaggerated her injuries so she could have the plastic surgery she needed anyway. This isn't about injury; this is purely and unequivocally about money. That's all it is," he said, stepping next to me, nearly poking me in the eye.

I heard my voice, nervous but firm, asking the judge to stop him from pointing his finger in my face.

"Please move away from the defendant and refrain from

making hostile gestures toward her." The judge sounded irritated.

It took the jury less than half an hour to deliberate. They awarded me enough money to put a down payment on a condo for my parents, and to build a pool at our house upstate. As we walked out of the courthouse, my legs buckled underneath me. I couldn't stand up. My lawyer and Malcolm helped me into a cab and we rode uptown to Greenwich Village. The lawyer insisted that I buy myself a victory present. "Get something that will always remind you of how you made that shyster lawyer eat shit," he said. I ended up with a three-foot-high wooden frog. He is carrying a palm-leaf parasol over his head and wearing a goofy, toothless grin. It seemed to me then, and still does, that it was the perfect way to go.

Thirteen

Sometimes now, when I go to look up a word in my dictionary, a crumbled piece of leaf will float to my feet and I'll remember my first fall at the University of Michigan. I was no longer sinking in Bill or the swamps of Gainesville and was as far from the bubble gum palette of Miami as you could get. I collected bags full of orange and red leaves that autumn and pressed them between the pages of my dictionary. I spent hours alone in my room listening to Prokofiev and Beethoven and writing awful poetry. The world seemed perfect.

I had a single room with just enough room for a desk, bed, and a used hi-fi set from Armand. Next door, Janet and Tanya lived in a large double filled with Gund stuffed animals and funny hats. While I wrote, I could hear them dancing to Motown albums. Sometimes they sat on their bunk beds and sang along.

Early one morning, I woke up with the beginning of a poem in my head:

My Biggest Fear is Nothing, That's what I Fear to Be
A Big and Empty Hollowness within the Soul of Me . . .

I wrote feverishly for hours at a time with the "Rites of Spring" urging me forward, and only lay down my pen when Peter Aichen (rhymes with "breakin' ") came back into my life. We went canoeing on Lake Huron. He kissed me in the Pretzel Bell tavern. He brought me home to meet his parents, and several days after the visit, told me how much his parents liked me. He squinted up his face and used a mock high-pitched voice when he repeated what his mother said: "She's not as cute as other girls you've dated, but she has lovely manners. She's the kind of girl you should marry, Peter." His chocolate-brown eyes went frosty. I didn't hear from him for several weeks. Then came a letter, a short note really, written in a hasty hand. "My head says yes, my heart says no."

Peter wanted to break up with me. In between tears, I tried to compose an offhand response. "Let me know if your head and heart ever get together," was the best I could do. That Sunday, when I went to breakfast at Miriam and Armand's, my voice was wobbly. Armand, whose logic could run to chilling, had no patience for my cow-eyed pining. "Don't be so foolish," he said. "This is the best thing that ever happened to you. If you'd have married Peter Aichen, you'd be nothing more than a decorative ornament on some lawyer's arm." Maybe he was right. Hadn't I spent hours hacking away at poems about the horrors of nothingness? And besides, what kind of a guy would tell his girlfriend that his mother thought he'd had cuter girlfriends? My grief knew bounds.

Every day since I'd been in Ann Arbor, I'd pored over the student newspaper, *The Michigan Daily*, memorizing each byline. Often I'd walk by there, an old redbrick structure that had since been dwarfed by all the newer buildings around it. I'd never let go of my dream to be a journalist in New York, and whenever I'd pass this fairy-tale-looking place, I'd imagine the people inside it doing exactly what I wanted to do. Of course, my mother urged me on with each phone call. "Just go there and tell them you want to join the paper. What's the worst that can happen? They'll kick you out?" Well, yeah.

Finally I screwed up the courage. Because the paper was printed in the basement of its offices, the smell of printer's ink hit me like a surprise party the moment I opened the door to the building. Upstairs, a small corridor divided the large city room where reporters and ad salespeople sat from the glassed-in office where the top editors worked. The editors all had a prison pallor. They wore clothes that they'd likely worn the day before—and the day before that. This was what real journalists looked like, important people with a mission. I wanted to get as close to them as I could. "I'd like to work for the *Daily*," I said to a woman with tight jeans and long black hair. "What do I have to do?"

Her name was Judy and I recognized her byline, she was the features editor. She was beautiful and her silky black hair bounced when she talked.

"See Clarence," she said, handing me off to the managing editor, who was jabbing away at his typewriter with two fingers. Clarence shuddered when Judy mentioned his name. He looked up at me. "I'd like to write for the paper," I said as fast as I could.

"Yeah, sure," he said, eager to get back to his work. "What do you want to write?"

"Oh, you know, features, something humorous."

He told me to write a sample story and bring it back by the end of the week.

It was 1966. The war in Vietnam was escalating, and in Ann Arbor, the peace movement was seething. The *Daily* was the showcase of the most fervid antiwar writing on campus. I worked all week on a piece about fashion on campus—something about evolution, survival of the fittest—and brought it to Clarence a week later.

"This is, umm, different," he said, arching his eyebrows. He ran my piece, and let me write some more. I wrote features and movie reviews and eventually a column called "In a Nutshell" filled with personal anecdotes: a trip to my grandmother's house, the hilarity of finding mice in my apartment.

Amid the moral angst all around me, my writing was chipper and (I noticed later) often ungrammatical. The other editors went on protest marches; made pornographic films; uncovered local scandals; dated an entire rock band. They regarded me with polite indifference. One reader wrote to the paper about my column: "In a *Daily* which relegates hard news to a Hot Line, it seems ironic to find reams of space given to the effusions of a juvenile femme savant, however much she adorns the office."

But I wouldn't be stopped. Shortly after a column I'd written about how my bangs caught fire in a cooking accident appeared, a professor wrote to the editor of the *Daily*: "She doesn't exist. You've made her up! You've created a caricature of the self-absorbed dross that is taking up valuable space on our college campuses. Kudos to you."

My columns as parody? Brilliant! Too bad it never occurred

to me when I wrote them. I hoped that my column could do for me at the newspaper what the Poo-bah club did for me in high school, but this time the ploy wasn't working. I still felt marginal. Every time I answered the phone and said, *"Michigan Daily,"* or washed the smudges of black ink off my hands, I felt as if I were performing a ritual for some sacred club that I couldn't quite be a part of.

As I left the offices late one night, I saw two of the executive editors walking ten paces ahead of me. They didn't notice me behind them, but I could hear as they started to dish about everyone at the paper. I held my breath when they got to me. "She's lively, but totally irrelevant," said one. The other nodded. Then they moved on to the next person. That was that.

"She doesn't exist. You've made her up!"

I felt my face burn with shame, but it didn't surprise me. I guess I knew that's what they thought. (What was it about lively girls anyway? Why did people always equate peppiness with stupidity? Even the words—*perky, chipper*—are dopey.) I hated that Peter and all those people at the *Daily* made me feel like such an outsider, and with grim determination, I turned out "In a Nutshell" once a week until graduation.

Early in the fall of my senior year, Rob Casey showed up at the back door of the house I was sharing with four other girls. He was looking for my roommate Carol, and something about the way he spoke made me happy that Carol wasn't home. I invited Rob in for a beer. He told me how he and Carol were in the same Latin class and that he lived in a fraternity house four blocks down the road. "Jeez, I thought fraternities went out with the Eisenhower administration," I said.

Rob shot me a sidelong glance, as if to say, "Are you making fun of me?" His eyes flashed the color of pennies.

"I mean, it must be great to have that feeling of camaraderie you get from living with friends."

Rob shrugged. I noticed the size of his palms. His bear-paw hands were reassuring. When he asked me out for that Saturday night, I said yes.

On the night of the date, Rob pulled up in a '62 Bel Aire. His hair was still wet from a shower, and when he leaned over to say, "Hey, how are you?" his breath was minty from toothpaste. The inside of his car smelled like Old Spice and the Ann Arbor autumn. There was something steady and welcoming about Rob; this was not a guy who would hold a girl hostage in the woods until she promised to marry him.

We went to a party at Rob's fraternity house. Rob was the president, and I could see why. He met your eyes as you talked, and considered what you had to say. Dating Rob was about as cool as wearing a Lilly Pulitzer dress to a protest march. But when I was with him, I didn't have to pretend I understood Paul Krassner or that I felt intellectually aligned with Herbert Marcuse. And because I wrote for the *Michigan Daily*, the boys in his frat house thought I was smart and hip and downright relevant.

Sometimes, on Sunday mornings, I went to church with him. He sang in that barrel-toned voice of his, shards of green sparkling in his eyes. Many of the hymns were those I'd learned in Bible school, and I'd sing along. Rob and I, as American as peanut butter and jelly. I loved to hear stories about the Casey family reunions and their summer cabin at Ishpeming, in the Upper Peninsula of Michigan. Rob had an uncomplicated clarity about himself and his family. He laughed about how his father called women's breasts "jugs" and his mother sent him Care packages of oatmeal raisin cookies and her own canned preserves every other week. They did things as a family and had annual rituals.

At home, Thanksgiving was an ordeal that my family tried to ignore. Sometimes there was a token barbecued chicken or baked potato, but my parents refused to embrace cranberry sauce or pumpkin pie. We were such a small family—each of us so locked in our own worlds that we had few collective memories. Sometimes on Thursdays after dinner, my mother and I would go to Burdine's department store, then split a Dairy Queen on the way home. Every night, while Miriam washed and I dried the dishes, we'd harmonize songs from *South Pacific* or sing duets from camp. When I was eleven, the four of us piled into our humpbacked Plymouth and took a three-day car trip north to Cypress Gardens. That was about it for family cere-monies.

In Rob's house, they'd start talking about Thanksgiving weeks before Halloween. Who was going to make the rhubarb pies, should they have cornbread or oyster stuffing? These were the kinds of things, I thought, that held a family together. Every July Fourth, all the Caseys would gather up in Ishpeming, build a campfire, cook the trout they'd caught that day, then drive twenty minutes to Marquette for the annual fireworks.

Before I even met Rob's family, I was infatuated with the Casey lore. So I was excited when Rob invited me home to Muskegon for Christmas. "I've got to warn you"—he smiled uneasily—"they don't know many Jews, and they're very conservative."

"How conservative can they be?" I wondered.

"Reeeally conservative," he answered quickly.

"You're going to *Muskegon*, Michigan?" my father said. The words sat uncomfortably in his mouth. "Why do you want to spend your vacation in Muskegon, Michigan?"

"Honey, are you sure that's what you want to do?" my mother asked.

"You'd think I was visiting Hitler in his bunker," I said. "At least somebody in this family is finally getting out into the real world."

Two days later, I flew into Detroit during a snowstorm. "Welcome to sunny Michigan." Rob was unnaturally cheerful when he greeted me at the airport. "The best is yet to come." The closer we got to Muskegon, the quieter Rob became. "Are you nervous about me meeting your parents?" I asked.

"Not really."

"Don't worry, I have very good manners."

After nearly four hours, we pulled into his family's driveway. A glint of sunlight shimmied off the hunting rack on Mr. Casey's Ford truck. As we walked to the front door of the brick Colonial, Rob shouted, "We're home," then turned to me with a smile and mock bow. "Welcome to the house of Casey."

Rob embraced the two people who opened the door. "Mom, Pop, this is Betsy."

"We've heard so much about you," said Pop, mashing my hand in his. "Please, come in."

The Caseys were the tallest parents I'd ever met. Mrs. Casey was beautiful in an ageless way. She had Rob's eyes, wide high cheekbones, and a strong, unsmiling face. Mr. Casey was well over six feet, thick-bodied, with a meager trim of brown hair around his bald head. His hands looked as if they could crush the life out of a rottweiler. Theirs was a house designed for the Jack Beanstalk family. Everything was oversized. There were cathedral ceilings everywhere, beams that went on forever, and miles of built-in shelves containing Mr. and Mrs. Casey's ("Please, call us Audrey and Carl") depression glass collection.

That night, I slept alone in a giant bed. Cramps woke me up on Christmas morning. Excruciating cramps. Had I been anywhere else, I would have taken a Midol, doubled up on the couch and waited for them to pass, but not here.

Audrey served griddle cakes and sausages for breakfast. Everything on my plate seemed to be oozing. God, was I nauseous. I couldn't concentrate on what anyone was saying. I thought I should help Audrey clear the table, but *whoo*, was I dizzy. I took a deep breath and realized that my knees were shaking. If I were home, Mommy would say, "The only thing that'll help these cramps is a shot of brandy.'" Nah, wouldn't make a good impression asking Audrey for a drink. It was nine in the morning.

Rob's sister, Liz, and her husband, Todd, pulled up in a station wagon. For what seemed like hours we carried in pies and armfuls of presents. Then we all stood around the kitchen as Audrey put the finishing touches on a twenty-two-pound Butterball and Liz, the only short skinny person in that family, unpacked a shopping bag full of marshmallows. "A post-Christmas cook-out?" I asked.

I could tell I was going to be sick, really sick, and worried about throwing up in front of all of them.

"No," said Liz, with a stiff smile, "these are for the dinner. Haven't you ever had sweet potatoes with marshmallows?"

Hadn't.

The vision of gummy marshmallows and orange potatoes blobbed around in my head. My knees buckled and the bottom fell out of my stomach. I thought about saying, "A Merry Christmas to all, and to all a good night," before I lost consciousness, but the words never came out. The next thing I remember was lying on the Caseys' brick-patterned linoleum with five pairs of eyes staring down at me.

"Are you okay?" asked Rob, looking anxious.

"Been better."

"She's fine," declared Carl. "Needs a little rest, that's all." He scooped me into his arms and held me against his chest. "Holy Moly," he reported to the assembled Caseys, "the girl's light as a feather. No wonder she's sickly." Carl delivered me to my bed in the Beanstalk. "Now, you get some rest," he said, dropping me onto the mattress. "You sure as hell don't want to miss Christmas dinner."

I tried a smile. "Don't you worry. I'll be in tip-top shape by then."

All I could think about was poor Rob. He brings a girl home from college and she nearly dies on the kitchen floor. I owed him more than that. Whatever it took, I was going to make the rest of the day as perfect for him as I could. By afternoon I rallied in time to join the family for the opening of presents. We gathered around the tree as Audrey handed out the packages. There was a red one wrapped in a silver bow with my name attached to it. "Aren't you lucky?" she said, shoving the thing into my hand.

"Thanks," I said, noting that it was heavy and round and that Rob seemed pleased that they remembered me. Everyone watched in silence as I pulled off the wrapping. It was a jar of something. I recognized the orange on the label and the glug-ging sound it made when I turned it upside down. Spiders raced down my back. There was no pretending that what I thought was happening wasn't. It is a thirty-two-ounce jar of Mani-schewitz gefilte fish. Glatt Kosher.

"Please excuse me," I said. "I need to go outside for a mo-ment." I tucked the gefilte fish under my arm and walked out of the room.

"Don't be upset," Rob said, following me into the hall. "They meant to be funny. Nothing more."

"I've got to get out of here."

"Where you gonna go?"

"Somewhere."

But, of course, there was no place to go. So I walked back into the living room, where Carl, Audrey, Liz, and Todd were talking as though nothing unusual had happened. I sat down on the couch and pretended right along with them.

Later, when we both moved to New York, Rob came with me to meet my grandmother at a little bakery café called Éclair's. It was a place that used seventy-watt lightbulbs and had brown overstuffed banquettes. The refrigerator display cases were crammed with strudels, apple crumb coffee cakes, Napoleons, and fruit tarts. Éclair's was where my grandmother had her coffee and pastry late on Sunday afternoons and where she and her friends stirred sugar cubes into their coffee with tiny sterling silver spoons and gossiped about the week. It was as close as they could come to the Sunday afternoon prome-nades and outdoor cafés they'd left behind.

These were the people I'd known all my life, and Rob was

as out of context here as I was in Muskegon. He was over six feet tall and towered over them all. But it was his manner—easygoing, unreserved, the very things that drew me to him in the first place—that was odd here. These people were formal and rooted in their snobbishness and pretensions. Their thick-heeled shoes and crepe blouses under dark wool suits were a far cry from the casual Wallabies and cotton khakis his parents wore.

Among this group, my grandmother stood out like Eva Peron. Now late into her seventies, she dyed her hair a brassy red and wore handmade silk dresses with large sunflower patterns. If the dresses pulled too tight around her bosom or bunched around her high, thick waist, she didn't notice. In her mind's eye she was still the party girl of Kaiserslautern. Her gold bracelets jangled with every move and she gave off an air of Chanel No. 5 and peppermint Chiclets. The latter, she claimed, were the only things that soothed her stomach after eating too much whipped cream at Éclair's. The one concession to her age were the cloddish "space shoes" she had to wear, the result of too many years of stuffing her wide feet into stiletto heels.

My grandmother was charmed by Rob, although when he was out of sight, she'd ask, "You have other boyfriends, don't you?" She liked him well enough to give him the expensive Viennese butter cookies when we visited instead of the cheap American knockoffs she kept for most company. When the three of us played Scrabble, she cheated by keeping extra letters hidden in her lap. I knew he thought that she and her friends were peculiar and that I was only one generation removed from them.

A couple of months after we came to New York, Audrey sent me a package of homemade oatmeal raisin cookies. In my thank-you note to her, I wrote: "What a perfect way to top off a hearty gefilte fish dinner." Rob told me it made her laugh out loud. I didn't mean for it to be funny.

Fourteen

By 1984 Phillip Moffitt and Chris Whittle were the darlings of the media world. *Esquire* had become a hot magazine. Agents returned our calls and movie stars actually wanted to be on our covers. Young writers hoped that we would discover them and name writers wanted their bylines in our pages. We had so much advertising that we actually had to turn people away, something that now seems astonishing. We were the first magazine to define yuppies and give voice to the "human potential movement." People talked about our stories at cocktail parties and in bed at night.

Soon after I arrived at the magazine, Phillip announced at a story meeting that he wanted to celebrate *Esquire*'s fiftieth anniversary by renting out Lincoln Center and inviting every famous person from the past fifty years. At the time, there were just a handful of us working at the magazine, and we could have no more pictured us filling up Lincoln Center than performing there ourselves. I watched Byron roll his eyes, and I could imagine him bellowing, "What a lunatic."

Yet there we all were, three years later, sitting in Lincoln

Center while Sarah Vaughan sang to a packed house. Purim's idea was a smashing success. Most of "The Fifty Who Made a Difference" showed up that night and the audience was filled with people like Tom Wolfe, Ralph Nader, Norman Mailer, William Styron. Even Muhammad Ali was there. All night, Ali snuck up behind people and made grasshopper sounds in their ears by rubbing his thumb and forefinger together. Pete Dexter later wrote a column about sitting in a too-tight tuxedo waiting for Sarah Vaughan to quit singing so he could go to the bathroom. "And then, just as God made little green apples," he wrote, "he made Sarah Vaughan stop singing." It was quite a night.

On New Year's Eve of that year, the first since my taxi accident, Malcolm and I were getting ready to go to a party. In the corner of our bedroom we had an antique oak full-length mirror, which we could tilt up or down. Standing naked before the mirror, I flipped it so that I had an aerial view of my whole body. I studied the happy-face scar that ran across my abdomen, a reminder of my hysterectomy. My face was beginning to fill out, and lately I'd even stopped covering my mouth with my hand whenever I laughed. I was starting to look familiar again, and it occurred to me that the hunted animal look had disappeared from my eyes. I whispered to the image before me, "Here's the deal. I'll take care of you. I'll feed you well, exercise, get enough sleep, not drink too much. But if you turn on me one more time, don't count on anything." I wasn't sure exactly who or what I was threatening, but I went to the party that night, satisfied that a deal had been struck.

Around the time that Phillip promoted me to editorial director—"A woman will never be editor of *Esquire*," he had said emphatically when he hired me—I got a phone call. The voice at the other end was formal, though slightly hesitant. It sounded familiar. It was Michael, the man from The *Atlantic Monthly* who had set me up with the chief of *Newsweek* correspondents fifteen years earlier. Although we hadn't spoken in all that time, I'd always felt sentimental about Michael: He gave me my first break. Now he was the editor of a major newspaper and was searching for someone to be the editor of its Sunday magazine. "Would you be interested in talking about the position?" he asked.

"Michael! It's so great to hear from you. All these years I've wanted to thank you for what you did for me. I owe so much to you, you were the first person . . ."

There was a congealed silence on the other end of the phone. I thought I heard the sound of an eraser tapping on teeth. "I'm sorry," he finally answered, "I really don't remember you. I have no idea what you're talking about." I didn't take the job.

At the same time as I got my promotion, Purim became editor. The two of us became Phillip's lieutenants, and great allies. Both of us vied for Phillip's approval, then made fun of each other for the obvious ways we tried to get it. Purim's advantage was that he was male. Mine was that I was used to trying to get the attention of paternal figures who never quite gave it to me. Phillip often took Purim and me away on weekend retreats where we discussed his sometimes bizarre but always strangely prescient ideas for the magazine. I can still see Purim and me knee-deep in the mud of an early Vermont spring, begging Phillip not to make us execute one of his most complicated schemes yet. That one was the *"Esquire* Register," a celebration of the most prominent people in the country under forty. We would have national bureaus scouting for these people and a bureau chief in New York who would coordinate the research—a daunting task for a small staff.

Somehow—despite Byron occasionally getting so angry at April that he jumped up and down on her layouts, and Andre bursting into tears because Phillip rejected his selection of belts for a fashion shoot, and Marilyn, one of our junior editors, spontaneously belting out her rendition of Minnie Ripperton singing "Loving You," causing everyone in the office to nearly jump out of their skin—we managed to get it all done. The *"Esquire* Register" became a huge hit, exactly as Phillip predicted, and special issues like that became the trademark of the magazine.

Our offices faced west on lower Park Avenue, which meant that we looked right into the sunset. Some nights, when the sun was a great ball of orange and the sky was streaked with purple and tangerine swirls, a group of editors gathered in Phillip's office just to watch the spectacle. One night, when the sky was spilling over New York City, we all sat there struck dumb by the fact that we were witnessing it from the offices of the greatest magazine in America. Phillip seemed as caught up in the romance of that moment as the rest of us. But as the sun fell beneath the horizon and the sky turned dark, he was the first to break the silence. "I was just thinking," he said. "There must be a way to get more food editorial into the magazine." The man didn't let up for a minute.

One day I was bogged down in writing a knock-out—a bold-faced block of type designed to draw you into the page. According to the art department's design, the first line had to be nineteen characters; the second line, eleven characters; the third, seventeen, and the fourth, ten. That's when the thought hit me: What if *Esquire* was really an expensive mental institution? What if the people who ran the institution filled our days with lots of paperwork and other menial tasks? Suppose they motivated us by praising our efforts and reassuring us that the public was clamoring for the fruits of our labor? It all started to come together. The amount of work we got was commensurate with how much money our parents spent for us to be there. So Phillip's parents had paid the most, and the rest had paid according to where our names fell on the masthead. After we went home at night, the doctors came in and shredded everything we'd done that day, so in the morning we could start all over again.

It made a whole lot of sense to me. Even Purim agreed that it explained everything.

If work was like a funny farm, there was nothing funny about what was going on at home. Malcolm had taken a job as a public relations man for a large investment bank. He stuck it out for about a year and a half, even though it was the worst fit imaginable. He had no head for business and no stomach for the politics of the organization. He longed to be back in the world of journalism. When he got fired in the spring of 1985, we were both relieved. But by summer's end, he was still unemployed, and by fall, he had become detached and frighteningly lethargic. He stopped cooking, stopped caring about his clothes; he withdrew completely from me. Most distressing was his weight gain—six, eight, twelve, fifteen pounds. After all the care that had gone into maintaining his taut body, the weight gain scared me the most.

When I came home from work at night, he'd greet me with a chaste kiss on the cheek. I'd be buoyed by the smile on his face until I'd walk into the bedroom and notice the indentation of his body still fresh on the comforter. "Did you get out much today?" I'd ask.

"God, you sound so icy and accusatory," he would snap. "How am I supposed to answer that?" Lately, he always seemed to be angry with me.

Conversation between us had pretty much dried up. We spent most nights reading or watching television. I couldn't remember the last time we'd made love. Once I even woke him up in the middle of the night and said, "I hate this. I feel like I'm starving to death."

His face got stony. "I don't know what to say," he answered.

I started having daydreams that one of us would die. Divorce seemed out of the question. No one in my family had ever gotten divorced. "Secondhand goods," I remembered my mother saying about a neighbor who had remarried. Besides, I couldn't imagine being alone. I couldn't imagine life without Malcolm.

As he became more aloof, the idea of having something of my own became more imperative. We'd already mailed in our pictures and biographies to the adoption agency. We'd taken each other's photos on the deck of our house, choosing the spot carefully, hoping they'd notice how safely the deck was fenced in and how cozy and unostentatious the house looked. Everything about those photos radiated determination. But what else would they see? Would *you* give these people a child? I wondered when I mailed in our application. I knew we both hoped that putting the adoption plans in motion would change every-

thing. But as I dropped the envelope in the box, I felt my heart
sink.

On the surface, I'd found my place: I was a top editor at a
hot magazine with a stable of my own writers, and I loved coming to work every day. But I was mired in the world of men.
When I wasn't editing a magazine story for them, I was on the
phone with Ron or Pete or some other male writer. I still felt
out of place in this insular world, especially since it left me
remarkably bereft of any female friendships. Between the accident and my daily overdose of testosterone at work, it was hard
for me to retain a sense of myself as a woman.

I first started thinking about starting a new magazine when
I learned that forty percent of *Esquire*'s readers were women.
That was an astonishingly high number for a men's magazine,
and it seemed obvious that women were coming to the magazine
for its great writing. There were a few other women editors at
Esquire, all of us thrown into this bizarre fantasy of what a
man's life was really like. I began noticing that whenever I went
to lunch with one of them, or any other woman, even if I'd never
met her before, the conversation quickly became intimate—
funny in the "can you believe I survived that?" sense—and
forked off in all sorts of surprising directions. No magazine, it
seemed to me, was capturing that kind of whimsy and intimacy.

Most of the women's magazines defined women by their
clothes, the exercises they did, the way they cooked, or how they
decorated their homes. The magazine I envisioned would take
its personality from the voices of urban women. It would assume
these women were resourceful, witty, sensual, energetic, playful,

and smart. It would show how powerful they were and how their work and energy fueled the urban world they lived in. It would talk to women the way women talked to one another—in a voice that was wry and intimate. We'd share gossip, and commiserate about the price of real estate and when to find time to pick up the dry cleaning. We wouldn't pretend to have all the answers, but we would know all the questions. It would be a magazine that was passionate, sometimes neurotic, and often hilarious. I thought I'd hit on the perfect idea.

When I pitched it to Phillip that spring, I could tell he was interested. "I don't hate it," he said, and told me to put together an editorial plan, come up with a name, and get back to him. That night, I taped together two sheets from a yellow legal pad and outlined eighty or so make-believe pages of the magazine. I filled in each page with a would-be article, column or section written by a fantasy list of my favorite authors. The exercise was exciting and looked good on paper; I knew I was onto something. I called it *New York Woman*, to suggest the kind of edgy state of mind I was after.

Phillip liked what I did and by summer relieved me of most of my duties in order to let me work full time on the project. The goal was for me to finish a mock issue and our COO, Wilma Jordan, to finish a business plan by January, and present the whole thing to the *Esquire* Board of Directors by January 24. Then they—*we*, as I was one of them—would vote on whether or not to finance and launch *New York Woman*. All of a sudden, the idea of having something of my own was miraculously within my reach.

.   .   .

In mid-January, Malcolm and I went to an open house in Westchester sponsored by the adoption agency. It was held in a faux English Tudor house with green shutters. Sixteen of us sat around in someone's living room eating fried chicken and coleslaw, all of us pretending that this was just another cocktail party. Our hosts, Jenifer and Len Slotsky, greeted each of us by our first names and asked us individually if we'd like a tour of the house. When we settled in the living room, Len tapped a spoon against his gin-and-tonic glass and announced that Jenifer had some thoughts she wanted to share. Jenifer squeezed Len's hand, stood up, and smiled down at the rest of us.

"Four years ago, Len and I sat in a stranger's living room as you are doing today. Although we all talked about our jobs and the real estate market, in the pit of our stomachs we knew that we were here for one reason—the pain and longing of wanting a child." She talked about the paperwork and how hard the waiting was, but in the end, she said, it was worth it and that we should hang in there.

By this point, all the blood had drained out of the room. No one looked anyone else in the eye.

At that moment, two little brunette girls with giant bows and Mary Janes on their feet ran into the living room and jumped into Jenifer and Len's open arms. The four of them—a family—snuggled on the couch like a brood of puppies. Thirty-two hungry eyes stared at them, the feast at the other side of the glass window. "We'd like to introduce Tricia and Lydia." Jenifer beamed. "Our little angels, our answered prayers. The lights at the end of the tunnel."

Sitting in a metal folding chair, with a long waiting list and interminable interviews ahead of me, all I could think of was how heartfelt Jenifer Slotsky's words had been. I wondered if she'd ever written for a woman's magazine. Everything about that day—Len, Jenifer, those girls, their bows—seemed unreal and beyond my grasp. There was no way I could picture us like the Slotskys—one big happy family.

"You were so quiet this afternoon," Malcolm said on the way home. "Are you sure you want to do this?"

"For some reason, I can't imagine it happening, that's all."

"Don't be so negative. You heard what that woman said, you have to hang in there."

I said I would try, but in my heart—I didn't know how or why exactly—I knew the adoption would never happen.

We were barely hanging in there.

Because Phillip was afraid someone would steal the idea for the magazine before we could get it out, I was not allowed to tell anyone what I was doing. Every day, I came into my office, closed the door, turned on a Patsy Cline tape, and stared out at the assembled parliament of gargoyles that sat atop the building next door. Their immutable faces were friendly accomplices during a time I felt increasingly isolated. One looked like Ernie Kovaks, another like John Travolta. First thing each day, I said good morning to them. And as I sat at my typewriter writing fake headlines and copy, I turned to Kovaks or Travolta and tried to detect some reaction in their stony countenances. Just the way the sun glinted off their heads at a particular moment could set my mood for an entire afternoon. Ernie, Patsy, John, and me. As I said, it was a lonely time.

That New Year's Eve, 1985, took on special significance. By

next year at this time, I hoped to be running *New York Woman*. If not, I couldn't see how I could go back to *Esquire*. Other people had already taken over my work and I had become irrelevant to the running of the magazine. Once that happened, it was hard to put yourself back into play. Either way, 1986 was going to be a big year. So when our friends Bob Randall and Gary Pratt, a couple who had been together for years, invited us to go to New Orleans over New Year's, it seemed an auspicious way to begin the year.

Bob was the creator and main scriptwriter for the sitcom *Kate and Allie*. He was a querulous man whose humor fed off of his own neuroses. Gary was his straight man, kind and attentive to Bob's every whim. As a foursome, we toured some of the magnificent old plantations, walked the streets of the city, and went shopping. They helped me pick out a long chartreuse dress; we chose a white formal shirt for Malcolm. At night, we ate oysters and seafood gumbo and listened to music.

Earlier that year, *Sweet Dreams*, the Patsy Cline story, starring Jessica Lange, had come out. I had become as infatuated with Jessica as I always have been with Patsy. On New Year's Eve morning, Bob and Gary went off searching for a black-widow mask. Hours later they returned breathless. "You'll never guess who we just met," said Bob, his face flushed. "Oh, Betsy, you're going to die. We met Jessica Lange!"

"Oh, come on, you did not meet Jessica Lange."

"Oh, yes, we did, and it turns out she loves my show! Honey, tell Betsy what Jessica said about my show."

Gary didn't miss a beat. "She thinks Bob is the funniest man in television. *Kate and Allie* is the only show she and her kids—"

Bob interrupted: "I told her about you, and what a huge fan

of hers you were. And Ms. Betsoi," he said in a bad French accent, "she wants to meet you for a drink before dinner, *ta dum, ta dum.*"

"She's *sooo* great, *reeeally* sweet . . ." Gary continued, shaking his head, "unaffected, down to earth."

"I told her you'd be at the bar at Brennan's at seven-thirty. This is one night you'll never forget, thanks to *moi,*" Bob gloated, taking a little bow.

"She wants to meet me?"

"Well, of course. Betsoi Cartier ze famous magazine editor? Why would she not want to meet you?"

I went through the rest of the day humming songs from *Sweet Dreams.* I worried what I would say to Jessica Lange. I didn't want to be too fawning, yet I wanted her to know how much I loved her work. Should I bring up Baryshnikov? What about Sam Shepherd, and the farm, and the kids? Certainly I'd tell her about my plans for the new magazine, which, as a woman, I was sure she'd appreciate. We'd talk about Bob and how hilarious he was, and I'd find out how she lip-synched all those Patsy Cline songs so perfectly. I got even more excited thinking how well we would get along.

By 7:20, I was seated at the bar, trying not to stare at every person who walked through the door.

By 7:40, Jessica Lange still hadn't shown. I tried not to look anxious.

By 8:00 I began to feel ridiculous. Maybe she'd gotten waylaid by a fellow celebrity and had forgotten about our drink.

At 8:15, Bob and Gary and Malcolm walked into the bar.

They came over to where I was sitting and with a look of mock horror on his face, Bob said, "What, no Jessica Lange? That pig. She must have stood you up." Malcolm and Gary started giggling. Even when I got that it was a prank, I didn't understand why they went to the trouble.

"Is this what passes for gay humor?" I asked. The three of them laughed even harder. I waited for Malcolm to take my side, to console me even, but who was I kidding? Clearly the three of them had been wallowing in this joke all day.

Just before midnight on New Year's Eve, we walked to Broussard's, where we stood on the veranda overlooking the wisteria-covered courtyard. Lanterns swayed in a drowsy breeze as the band played, "The Way You Look Tonight." I'd already forgotten about the Jessica Lange episode and was feeling all mooey about being in this beautiful place with my close friends and my husband: My own little world. This will be a better year, I thought, as the countdown to midnight began.

Five, four—Malcolm stretched out his arms—three, two— and for one second, I could swear he was going to grab Gary and kiss him—one! The thought came and went as Malcolm swept me up and kissed me on the mouth.

Happy New Year!

Fifteen

Home in New York, the "Vacant" sign went back up in front of our marriage. Malcolm retreated; I returned to my make-believe magazine.

My marriage was slipping away; my professional life was up in the air. In one of those melodramatic swaps with fate, I promised myself that if the board voted to go ahead with the magazine, I would take it as a sign that I needed to repair my marriage—pay more attention to Malcolm, learn how to cook, help him in the garden. And if they voted not to go ahead with it? Well then, it would be clean slate time. I'd move to California by myself, live near the beach, become a tennis instructor. Obviously, this was not a well thought-out plan.

For weeks, April and I put together potential covers of the magazine. We decided that the covers should be candid shots of women doing real city activities. We photographed one woman hailing a cab, another eating a hot dog. One afternoon we photographed an actress friend of April's playing chess with some men in a Greenwich Village park. I made up enough tables of contents to fill up four issues. Meanwhile, Wilma devised a business plan and budget and my project kept moving forward.

Finally, the January 24 board meeting rolled around. At 6:00 P.M. on a starless night, the eight board members went into Phillip's office. No one looked directly at anyone else and we were unusually quiet. Phillip began the meeting by saying, "Well, you all know what we're here to talk about," then all heads turned toward me. I tried not to think about how much I had riding on what happened here. These people were my friends, I told myself, knowing full well that friendship was one thing, business was another. Earlier in the day, Phillip reminded me how fast I talked when I got nervous.

Slow down, I thought, before I even opened my mouth. For the next hour, I presented the mock-up issue of *New York Woman*. I said that the economy was thriving, and this was the perfect time to start a new magazine. Besides, I added, there was nothing like this for women, and given the success we'd had with *Esquire*, I was sure this would follow.

The publisher asked why the world needed yet another women's magazine. The chief of finance worried whether *Esquire*'s budget could withstand the drain of starting a new magazine, and estimated that it could be at least three years before it would start making any money.

It went on like this for a little over an hour. Finally, it came down to the vote. All in favor raise your hands. So simple, like second grade. Two arms (one of them mine) flew up right away. Then another person pointed a finger heavenwards, and another crocked his arm with a little wave, then another hand and another went up, until seven people voted yes. One person voted no. That was it. We all sat staring at one another. Now what should we do? Phillip got up, walked over to me, and gave me a hug. "Congratulations," he said, smiling, "you've got yourself a magazine." People clapped.

"I was just kidding, you know," I said, then ran out of the room laughing and crying at the same time.

My friend Lisa Grunwald was waiting for me.

I threw my arms around her and sobbed into her shoulder. "Oh my God," she said, "they turned it down."

"No, it's not that. Now I really have to do it."

Four days later, I was walking by the conference room at *Esquire*. The television was on—unusual for the late morning—yet it was the silence of the people watching it that caught my attention. On the screen, a great monster was hurtling into the sky, leaving gusts of white smoke behind it. The spacecraft *Challenger* with its seven gung-ho astronauts aboard had just been launched. It took less than sixty seconds for the giant white blossom on the screen to nearly disappear as the shuttle sped into space. Suddenly the blossom seemed to burst and spill all over into the heavens.

We heard the impersonal words from mission control: "a major malfunction," then watched as what looked like a giant rabbit bored a hole through the sky and tumbled back toward earth. Everything went white and silent. The sequence of images sputtered along in slow motion while our brains struggled to comprehend what was happening.

There were the astronauts' families standing on a roof at Cape Canaveral, squinting into the sun, their faces polished with pride, then filled with confusion, then contorted with disbelief. We watched as they shielded their eyes with their hands and craned forward, scanning the sky as if someone up there might have an explanation.

But nobody seemed to have any explanation. "Obviously . . . a major malfunction," was the best they could come up with, leaving us glued to the awful realization of what was happening. The cameras couldn't keep their eyes off the faces of the families. In a moment of grotesque intimacy, we—and the rest of the world—witnessed that naked instant in a person's life when she realizes she has just lost a person she loves. I wanted to shout, "For God's sake, turn off your cameras, leave them alone!"

Inexplicably, that explosion of chaos set off a panic inside of me. The words "blown to pieces" kept playing in my head. I felt my own eruption brewing.

New York after a snowstorm is as quiet as the desert, and smells like fresh sheets on a bed. On a Saturday, four days after the *Challenger* disaster and a little over a week after I got the go-ahead for *New York Woman*, the city was blanketed with four inches of snow. A perfect day for a walk in Central Park. It was time to start fulfilling the promise I'd made to myself: Malcolm and I would spend the day together. We'd plan our spring garden. I felt determined to help bring this marriage back to life.

We walked up to Belvedere Castle, a medieval structure that sits on the highest point in Central Park and has spectacular views of the city. We stood along one of the parapets and looked across Turtle Pond to the east side of Manhattan. The skyline was punctuated with haze billowing from the Metropolitan Museum of Art's smokestacks. The noon sun made the gray streaks in Malcolm's blond hair glisten. In the light, I could see small lines starting to form on either side of his mouth and noticed how they softened his angular features. So this was how aging would play on his face. It would be comforting to grow old with him, I thought.

We walked through the park and down the east side until sundown, then ended up eating chicken fajitas at our favorite Mexican restaurant. Afterward, we went to see *Down and Out in Beverly Hills*, and got home around 11:00. We sat on our queen-sized bed talking, and suddenly I realized this would be another night in which we would not make love, even though it was a snowy night after a perfect intimate day. I asked myself again what was going on.

I started talking about the wall that seemed to have come between us. The thoughts came fast and breathless, how I felt parched in the relationship, how everything I said or did seemed to irritate him so. I thought of Malcolm in the garden, in the kitchen; I envisioned him at parties warding off the advances of flirtatious women; and remembered how he berated me for things like not wrapping presents properly. Then I said something I had wondered but never allowed myself to believe until the words spilled out unwittingly. "You're either having an affair or you're gay, and my guess is that you're gay."

I waited a heartbeat for him to say, "Oh, don't be ridiculous." But the words didn't come. Instead, I saw his face crumble and turn ashen.

The only time I'd ever seen Malcolm cry was two years earlier, when his father died. Now I watched, terrified, as tears filled his eyes. "I don't know how you know," he sobbed. "I wanted to wait and tell you after you got the magazine launched. I've only known for two weeks, and I've been in crisis counseling since then." For some reason, I believed him.

As I absorbed his words, I felt the way I did just before I fainted that day at Rob's house twenty years before—so miserable, I couldn't wait to pass out. There was no relief in what he said and his words kept coming at me.

Everything inside me felt berserk. Blown to pieces. I was gasping for breath, swimming in air. I had crazy thoughts: I'll call my mother, she'll talk him out of this. The two of us hugged ourselves as we rocked back and forth on the bed sobbing. Then, after who knows how long, I felt myself start to laugh, a deep churning laugh. Tears ran down my cheeks, I choked on my own words. Oh Lord, this was funny. Okay, maybe not so funny, but in some way, it sure was a relief.

I'd always blamed myself for Malcolm's aloofness. He wanted someone more feminine, I'd thought. Perhaps he suspected that I was having an affair all those years ago. Why had I allowed myself to get so wrapped up in the magazine? Maybe I was too impetuous. Just last week, when the lock on our front door broke, I insisted we get a new one right away. He told me I was too impulsive. Of course I thought he was right. Now, I realized, he didn't want to change the lock because he knew he wasn't going to live here anymore.

I laughed because for so long, I'd been carrying around the burden of trying to make this work. I laughed at the implications. Was *everything* about the last seventeen years a lie? Did *everyone* else know that Malcolm was gay but me? If Malcolm was gay, what did that make me? Oblivious?

When my laughter drained away, I told him that this felt

like dying. He was the one who'd made it possible for me to be "plucky," to survive the car accident, to try to start a new magazine. Without him, my world would collapse. Life wouldn't work. How could I live on my own? Dread closed in and sucked everything else out. I wish I could say I did something plucky, but I didn't. Instead, I found a bottle of brandy and drank it.

Alcohol is a depressant, of course. Finding out that your husband is gay after seventeen years of marriage is also a depressant. I heard horrible wailing sounds come out of me, sounds I never knew I was capable of making. Malcolm wrapped a blanket around me. "Please don't," he said before I fell sleep exhausted and half drunk. When I woke up the next morning, it was all still there—that plus a blinding hangover. I lay bundled in my bed, getting up only to go to the bathroom and be sick. At two in the afternoon, wrapped in my robe, I hobbled to the couch. Malcolm brought me a glass of ginger ale. He'd thought about what he would do next, he said. He would stay with me for a couple of months, though he'd sleep in a separate room. We could still snuggle in bed—that would be comforting. The only people he told were Bob and Gary, who, it developed, would be coming to visit in an hour.

I thought about New Year's Eve and how much he enjoyed being in on their joke. I wondered if they were all in on this joke as well.

"Are they bringing Jessica Lange?" I asked.

When Bob and Gary showed up, they sat with me on the couch. They told me how wonderful my life was about to become. "You are going to have more men than you ever dreamed of," Bob said. "And the sex? The sex will be so exquisite, it'll make you scream."

Bob could be melodramatic.

He cupped my chin in his hand. "Jesus Christ, you are taking this so well," he said, his voice rising. "You have the dignity of—of Eleanor Roosevelt."

"Gary," he said to Gary, who was seated next to him. "Gary, doesn't she remind you of Eleanor Roosevelt?"

Gary nodded. "Yup, Eleanor Roosevelt. Same kind of strength, grace . . ." His voice trailed off.

I was lying in a fetal position. My eyes looked like bee stings, my hair was uncombed.

"Eleanor Roosevelt? Are you nuts? Janis Joplin, maybe," I said, wiping my nose on my sleeve.

Bob stared at me. Gary stared at Bob. Malcolm handed me a tissue. The room got awfully quiet.

"Okay, Lee Remick in *Days of Wine and Roses*," said Bob.

"Sissy Spacek in *Carrie*," said Gary.

"How did we get onto the subject of Eleanor Roosevelt anyway?" I asked.

Bob shrugged. "How the fuck should I know?"

Some people keep personal disasters a secret, particularly when they involve the sexual orientation of their spouse. But sharing misfortune calms me. The bigger the disaster, the more people I tell. It normalizes things and makes me feel less alone.

First I called my parents. When I told my father, his voice got soft. "Oh Bets, I don't know what to say. This is horrible, I'm so sorry. I'll get your mother." He hadn't called me Bets since I was a little girl.

My mother got on the phone. "Oh brother," she sighed when I told her the news. "I'll come to New York as soon as I can."

Next, I called Miriam.

"Malcolm and I are splitting up," I said.

She started to cry.

"He's gay," I added.

She stopped crying. "I always thought he was gay," she said. "The first day I met him, I looked at him and knew."

I thought back to that first meeting. Malcolm was wearing a white T-shirt. Later on the phone, Miriam said how handsome he was and asked, "Has he ever done any television commercials?" I realized now that was her cryptic way of signaling to me what she really thought.

"And you're telling me now, seventeen years later?"

"Well you wouldn't have taken it very well then."

Next, Malcolm asked me to call his mother and stepfather. In my panic I didn't try to prepare them for my words. I just said, "Malcolm and I are splitting up. He's gay."

I heard his mother take in a breath. "Oh, my God," she said. "Oh, my God," she said again and again. It struck me then that I was not the only person who would be shaken by the news. Later, I realized I'd gone and outed him to his parents. I will always regret my clumsiness.

Malcolm stood by as I called close friends. If I said the words often enough, maybe they would start making sense. I wanted Malcolm to watch me as one by one I told people that our marriage was over. Was I punishing him or waiting for him to say it was just a bad joke? I counted on my friends' stunned reactions. "What? After all this time? You were such a perfect couple." Even though the logic escaped me, I took it as a vote for my side.

I called Purim, who lived a few blocks away. "I need to see a straight guy," I sniffled into the phone. "Can you come over?"

"What you need is to put on clothes and get out of the house," he answered. "I'll be right there."

In an act of kindness that wiped away every contentious story meeting, Purim showed up, poured himself a scotch, and was the first person all day who asked Malcolm how he was doing. Then he took my arm and led me out into the frosty evening.

We walked for a little over an hour. I cried and he listened. I told him everything that was going on in my head: I was scared that I'd stop functioning, become a bag lady; that I didn't know how to live alone; how I doubted that any man would ever want me again. He told me I'd be fine, there would be plenty of men, though in typical Purim style, he told me that he would not be one of them.

When we got back to the front of my building, I grabbed his arm. "It's too depressing, I can't go back up there, to that house of mirth," I said. We both laughed weakly. Then I walked up the stairs. I opened the door and smelled something familiar.

Pot roast. Pot roast and garlic mashed potatoes. Unbelievable. The table was set and in the kitchen, Malcolm was putting the finishing touches on the green beans. It was a night like every other night in our house, only Malcolm was about to start dating men, and so was I.

As we ate, he talked about moving into the upstairs bedroom. I flashed on us calling good night to each other like sisters in a sorority house. It seemed unbearable. If the past seventeen years were a lie, I couldn't stand another moment of living in it. I don't know if I hated him just then; all I knew was I couldn't bear to look at his face.

"You have to leave," I said.

"I know," he answered. "I figured in a couple of months."

"No, right now."

"Now? Can't I even finish dinner?"

"No, you have to leave now."

Malcolm got up. He packed a few things in his suitcase.

"I'm not sure where I'm going to go," he said.

"I don't care."

He left the house. I cleared the table and did the dishes, wondering if there would be enough leftovers for me to eat the following night. It's amazing how the mundane stuff fills your head even while your heart is breaking.

The next morning I went back to work. As I stood in the elevator heading up to *Esquire*, I held on to the metal bar wondering how I was going to make it through the day. Leslie, our public relations person, walked into the elevator after me. She had a weary, been round the block kind of humor, and a sandpaper voice from a lifetime of smoking. "Jesus Christ, you look like shit," she said.

"Thanks," I said, "and how was your weekend?"

"Seriously, you look awful. Are you all right?"

"Well, not really," I said. "Malcolm told me he was gay this weekend."

Leslie shot me a look as if to say, "You've got to be kidding," then started to laugh her raspy smoker's laugh.

There's a famous episode of *The Mary Tyler Moore Show*, when Chuckles the Clown dies. As the priest delivers his eulogy, Mary bites her lip. She fakes a cough. She makes strange guttural noises. And then finally, she nearly falls down laughing. That's what happened to Leslie. Every time she tried to say something comforting, she laughed even harder. This went on for fourteen floors. When the doors opened, Leslie threw her arms around me. "Oh, Betsy," she said, "I don't know what to say. This is so awful, I thought you were kidding." She looked distracted.

I knew Leslie wished me well. I also knew she couldn't wait to get away from me and call everyone she knew. I didn't blame her. I'd have probably done the same thing.

Obviously, the news had already hit *Esquire*. A hush came over the office when I walked in. People folded their hands and looked at the floor. No one came over to talk to me although someone had placed a sad bouquet of irises on my desk.

Then our production manager, an empathetic woman from Texas named Kit Taylor, walked over. "This sucks," she said. "But you're going to be great. Everyone's going to fix you up." She told me how she and her husband, Jack, had a man in mind for me. "We've always thought the two of you would be perfect together. He's in a bad marriage now, but when he gets out of it we're going to bring the two of you together."

Phillip called me into his office. I sat on his couch and started to cry. He handed me a box of tissues, then told me how we all get used to our prisons and that I had gotten comfortable in mine. "You know, this will turn out well for you, your life will open up in exciting ways," he said, then added: "Now, I don't want you to think I'm going to be available to date you. I could never do anything like that."

Here I was, not even thirty-six hours out of my marriage and two men had already told me they would never go out with me and the one mythical man who was perfect for me was tied up in another marriage. So this was what getting divorced was going to be like.

In a way, it was like being pregnant. Everybody had an opinion. "What a scumbag," came up frequently. One woman, who'd been friends with both of us for ten years, said, "Do you suppose it was your success and ambition that drove him to it?" (She was married to a shrink, no less.) Telling me that was like telling someone who'd just been diagnosed with a dreadful disease that they must have brought it on themselves. Others were kinder, they told me what fun dating would be, and would I like to meet a cute dermatologist that they knew. And then there was the inevitable, "I always *thought* he was gay. Come on, you must have had some clue."

Of course, in hindsight, the evidence was there: great-looking guy, women came on to him all the time but he never seemed to notice. He cooked a mean *kalubiac*, and he was adamant that he help me pluck my eyebrows. He was the only man I ever knew who had never been to a sports event; we used to joke that he thought Thurman Munson was a type of bundt cake. But there was also evidence to the contrary. He was affectionate, always holding my hand, kissing my face, wrapping his arms around me. Our sex life, until the last few years, had been amazingly all right. In bed, he was tender and thoughtful. If sometimes our lovemaking felt rote and routine, I figured that's what happened. We were doing the best two people who had known each other for seventeen years could do. When you get married at twenty-two, there are dreams and then there is real life and somewhere down that path, there are shattered illusions. They could be about money or secret affairs or stupid things like being a bad dancer. I assumed that unless you're one of the lucky few, everyone had times when they straightened their spine and admitted to theirselves, "This is not what I had in mind. Not at all what I had in mind." But I also assumed that they then went on.

I loved Malcolm and never seriously thought we'd ever split up. Like most couples, we had intimate conversations about everything having to do with sex: "Did you ever think you might be a lesbian?" No. "Did you ever think you were gay?" "No."

When it came, the truth tore through me, uprooting everything that held me together.

The weeks after were excruciating. Scared that I would start drinking and never stop again, I threw away every bottle of wine and liquor in the house. Friends stepped in and walked me through my life. Jeanie took me out for pizza; my oldest friend from childhood came over and made soup. Lisa, in her tiny fine handwriting, made lists of surprises that lay in store for me; Purim picked me up in the morning and walked with me to work. Pete came to New York to see me and looked stricken when I cried in front of him. Miriam crawled into bed with me when I couldn't get up, and took long walks with me when I could. I was rarely alone.

The first Friday night after Malcolm moved out, I stayed at the office late, not because I had work but because I couldn't face the empty house, couldn't imagine getting through the weekend. Numbly, I reached for the phone and without thinking why, dialed Ron Rosenbaum's number. Though we had a comfortable, respectful, professional relationship, we were not that close, certainly not close enough for me to call and ask him to rescue me. But something about Ron—his kindness, his intensity, how smart he was—instinctively made me feel I would be safe with him. I asked if he'd have dinner with me that night. Like a Red Cross worker summoned to an emergency site, Ron snapped into action. Over the next couple of weeks, we went out to dinner, we went to the movies. We hung out in coffeehouses, rummaged through bookstores, went running in the park.

I still believe that Ron saved my life. Whatever rage or anger I didn't feel, he did. If someone made an uncomfortable comment, I didn't have to get indignant. Ron did it for me. Whenever Malcolm came to visit—which was often in the beginning—he had to pass the sentinel that was Ron. "How come you're here?" he would ask in a flat, angry tone. "I've come to do my wash," Malcolm would answer.

"What's the matter, you can't find a Laundromat anywhere in the Village?"

While I was barely able to digest consommé, Malcolm was making a miraculous comeback. It's hard to see, when you're the one feeling damaged, that the other person is feeling many of the same things. I thought Malcolm had moved on to a grand new life, while I was left in the wreckage of what once was ours. But later, when we were far enough away from it to talk about it, I learned how much it had hurt him to lose a life that he believed in and had struggled so hard to hold on to. Still, after more than thirty years, he felt euphoric about finally coming out. He discovered hair mousse. He moved to 1 Christopher Street (the center of gay New York). He did the wrist thing and it seemed to me he went dancing every night. He would call me up wanting to chat. "You should see my new leather jacket,"

he'd say. "I'm going to have to lose another five pounds so it fits
perfectly."

He wanted to discuss his dates. "Zeus and I had the best
time at the Monster last night. We danced until two-thirty.
Then we went back to his place. Oh, my God, you wouldn't
believe his body, I mean, we didn't sleep all night—"

"Nnnnnnn. Time out! Don't tell me more."

Ron insisted that I not let him talk to me about his dates,
but part of me was curious about this new Malcolm. It was like
finding someone's diary after they've died. Of course you
shouldn't read it—who knows what you'll discover—but how
can you resist? It was also important to me that Malcolm and I
stayed friends. If I wrote off my marriage entirely, it would un-
dermine everything else that had happened during that time.

As the anxiety loosened its grip, and the shock of what happened abated, I started to feel excited about what could lie
ahead. There would be men, I hoped, the kind of men I'd
flirted with and fantasized about while I was married. I could
be more myself, not someone who was trying to please another
person or get his attention. Maybe I'd meet someone who was
more of a friend, less of a teacher. Friends kept asking me if I
felt angry or betrayed. I told them the truth, that in many ways
I was relieved the marriage had ended. I was just eager to get
on with this new part of my life, as scary and impossible as that
seemed.

Besides, if Malcolm had betrayed me, he also betrayed himself in the process. Trying to pass as someone you're not was

the hardest thing to do; I knew that from firsthand experience. I was glad that he could finally be himself. We'd become what we should have been all along, the best of friends. So when Malcolm took up with his first serious boyfriend, I was curious to meet him.

Luis appeared on the scene only weeks after our breakup. "He's beautiful," Malcolm reassured me before he introduced us.

Luis was wearing a silk mango-colored shirt that draped slightly off his shoulder. "Isn't this a great color for him?" asked Malcolm, his eyes shining. Luis's sensuous full lips parted in a soft smile as he turned slightly so I could study his profile. Clearly, Luis liked compliments.

Everything about Luis was dramatic. When he talked, bracelets clattered, he tossed his shiny black hair, and traces of last night's makeup accentuated his dark gypsy eyes.

Malcolm was in love.

Luis was sixteen years Malcolm's junior. He had recently moved to New York from Venezuela and was quite dazzling to look at. I got the feeling that Luis played better in Greenwich Village than he did in Caracas and like Malcolm, he was basking in the freedom of being openly gay. Underneath all that posing, he seemed vulnerable, and a little scared. In Malcolm, he had found a kind father figure. In Luis, Malcolm found a companion who was as jubilant about his new life as he was. Lucky for both of them.

After I complimented Luis on his shirt, I didn't know what else to say. Then I noticed the large hunk of glass hanging on a leather band around his neck.

"Ahh," I said, cupping the pendant in my hand. "This is beautiful, I've never seen anything like it."

Malcolm's voice tightened. "You shouldn't have touched that," he said. "It's Luis's crystal. No one should touch Luis's crystal but Luis."

"Whoops," I said, letting the crystal fall to Luis's chest. "I didn't know."

Luis did one of those whfff, motions with his hand. "Don't even think of it," he said graciously, "I will wash it."

Luis took off the crystal, carried it to the sink, pulled out a sponge and some Comet, scrubbed it, then placed it back around his neck.

"Think you got it all?" I asked.

"Oh, yes. Is fine now."

Malcolm breathed a sigh of relief.

Three weeks later, Luis and Malcolm called to tell me that they were the equivalent of engaged and were throwing a big party to celebrate.

I wondered what would have happened had I dropped Luis's crystal on the floor.

"Will you come to our party? It would mean a lot to us," asked Malcolm.

"Oh yes," said Luis on the extension, "My mather ees coming from Venezuela. She looks forward to meet you."

"She sounds great," I said. "What's everyone going to wear?"

Still, I couldn't help wondering if Malcolm rubbed Luis's head when he couldn't fall asleep at night, or if he ran a hot bath for him after he'd had a bad day. In time it got easier and

I stopped having thoughts like these, but Luis was the first. Ten years later, during my tenure as editor of *New Woman* magazine, Malcolm brought his latest friend, Simon, to meet me. We sat on the striped sofa in my office as the sun shone on Simon's flawless face. Before they left, Simon reached over and took my hand. "Malcolm loves you very much," he said.

"And I know he feels the same way about you," I said, squeezing his hand back. I was genuinely glad to see Malcolm happy.

Immediately after Malcolm's departure, launching *New York Woman* kept my mind off my problems, at least during the day. This thing that had, for so long, been between me and the gargoyles on the building across the street, was starting to breathe its own life. Other people needed to be hired, and quickly. Ron told me to call Helen Rogan, an English editor he'd worked with at *Harper's*. "You'd be a perfect team," he said. "You should hire her as your number two editor." That was during the time when Ron seemed to hold the key to my survival, so naturally I called her.

"Can you come in for an interview on Tuesday?" I asked.

"I'd love to," she answered. "But I can't. Tuesday's my birthday. However, Thursday is not my birthday." I liked her already.

From what Ron had said about the way her mind worked, and from the crisp way she spoke on the phone, I expected Virginia Woolf to walk through the door. Instead, a vibrant blond wearing a sweet dress with tiny blue cornflowers that matched her eyes exactly showed up. When I asked about her past jobs, she answered by telling me about the bizarre sexual habits of one old boss. Her laugh lit the room like fireflies. She'd worked at *Time* for a short while, she said: *"Grrrueling* experience, but great benefits. And all those hideous men in gray suits: You could hear them in the elevator, muttering under their breath, 'Thank God I'm covered, thank God I'm covered.'"

When we met again the following week, she told me how she had recently married a humor writer: "They are the most depressed people in the world."

I told her about my separation, and about bad blind dates. "No one should have to date and do job interviews at the same time," I said. "Good God, your life is absurd," she answered. That afternoon, I offered Helen the job.

Exactly one month after Malcolm and I split up, I left Kovaks and Travolta and moved to a tiny office in what had formerly been a shoe showroom. All of the shelves in that room sloped downward in order to display the goods. By now there were six of us, and we were forever picking up files that had fallen to the floor.

Our first issue was to be on newsstands by September, which meant that by June everything had to be finished. It was March—not a lot of time at all, considering we were starting with nothing. During the day we sat together at the round oak table in the shoe room and talked about story ideas and the way the magazine should sound and look. We ate constantly— bananas, popcorn, grapes, apples, watermelon slices—so much food that by mid-summer, a scourge of fruit flies had invaded our windowless office. When I would say something that struck Helen as ridiculous, she rolled her eyes and gave an exasperated sigh. "Oh, you are such a foolish woman," she'd say, breaking up the high-wire intensity.

At night, we staggered out of the world we were creating, purple in the face from airlessness and exhilaration. It was a magical time. That we thought what we are doing might change the face of journalism made us feverish with energy and ambition. There were no angry readers or bad newsstand numbers to cloud our dream yet. "Perfect idea," Helen cheered when someone suggested we do a story about women and their hairdressers. "How brilliant is that?" I exclaimed when she came up with the headline: "Getting Done."

If this was to be a magazine for urban women, the design would have to be sophisticated, clean, and sexy. Finding the right art director was the key to designing our words in just the right way. The blending of colors and words and the choice of photographs all rested with that person. Editors feed a magazine; art directors dress it. They're the ones who make it look cocky or seductive or like it's spoiling for a fight. Several people had told me to check out Fabien Baron, a French designer at GQ. Very young, they said. Slightly immature, needed to get his own way, but absolutely brilliant.

"Does the thought of starting a magazine seem daunting to you?" I asked Fabien when we met.

"Pssh," he said, shrugging the way they teach them to do in France. "Piece of cake."

"How do you feel about doing a magazine for women?"

His ears pricked. He licked his lips. "Women? I love women."

"So how would you feel about working here?"

"Sure," he raised his eyebrows. "Why not?'

Fabien *was* brilliant, a total original. He used type and photography like a weapon. As far as he was concerned *they* were the story. A single letter could take up half a page. In our second issue, we did a fashion story on hats and bathing suits. He created a block of text as delicate as an ice sculpture that floated in the middle of an all-white page. On the facing page was the silhouette of a woman in a black hat, yellow bathing suit, and a black satin bow wrapped around her arm. We worked hard to make our words live up to his design.

Fabien later redesigned *Harper's Bazaar* and turned the world of magazine design on its ear. His debut issue featured supermodel Linda Evangelista photographed from the neck up. Her cocked arm hid the left side of her face. The second A in *Bazaar* appeared to be slipping from the logo onto her hand. She held it as if she had just caught a Fabergé egg. The only words on the cover were: "Enter the Era of Elegance." Magazines and advertisers are still copying him.

For a long time it looked as if *New York Woman* would not have a first cover. Fabien came to work and played darts with his photographer friends. Or they played the stopwatch game. One person tried to count to ten in perfect one-second beats, tapping his foot to keep the rhythm while the person with the stopwatch tried to throw him off by counting out of sequence or shouting animal sounds to distract him. From where I sat, all I could hear was "Hooot," "Baaaah," "one, four, seven, three." "Honnk." It was hard not to feel panicked.

One morning, after a couple of rounds of the watch game, Fabien came into my office. He gave me one of his bulldog grins. "So you want a logo, eh? Okay, is time." In a matter of hours he came back with a white piece of paper the size of our cover. *New York Woman* was spelled out in large serif capital letters. All the letters were black except for the W, which was larger than all the others and in lipstick-red. There was an impudence about those letters, something daring and graceful at the same time.

"Is perfect. No?" he said (asked? demanded? Who knew?).

"Yes, it's perfect." It really was. Later he added the price of the magazine to the cover in American dollars, English pounds, and French francs, even though it was only for sale in New York and Los Angeles. He kept the background white—which would become our trademark. The cover model for the first issue was a woman named Lara Harris, who looked like a young Isabella Rossellini. Her beautiful unsmiling face stared directly at you, daring you not to stare back. She was wearing a pink sweater with the collar half up and half down, and the buttons askew. Wisps of hair escaped here and there, suggesting that like all New York women, she was too much in a hurry to care about things like hair and buttons . . . or was she? The words, "Our Marvelous Maddening Lives," appeared next to her head.

It's before the launch of a magazine that you learn about the things you wish people had put in their résumés. Under "Hobbies," for instance, why don't they just write, "Controlling everything and everyone around me," or "Pathological lying." We were going to find out anyway. One editor stayed late after everyone went home and rewrote the headlines or captions we'd worked on that day. The editor in charge of keeping us on schedule and getting everything out on time came to me after work late in June. "I have a confession to make," she said, large tears falling down her face. "We were supposed to have everything done today and I forgot." I was sitting on the window ledge when the word *forgot* landed on my lap. I considered falling backward. Another of our editors kept all the stories she was supposed to edit locked in her drawer. The day they were due, she took them out of her drawer and revealed she hadn't edited them. There was not a pencil mark anywhere. Thank God for Helen, who in a matter of days was able to transform even the most convoluted writing into stories that were funny and alive.

Fabien turned out, as they say in America, not to be a team player. If he didn't like a story or a photograph, he flicked his hand and announced to everyone present, *"Ees sheet."* If he really hated it, he added, "What is this? A magazine for menopausal women?" Many of the photographers Fabien brought in spoke only French. Our fashion editor, a high-strung woman with impeccable taste, only spoke English. Before each fashion shoot, Fabien, the fashion editor, and I discussed what the mood of the photographs should be, and where we should take them. Fabien always said, "No problem," the photographer agreed, and off they'd go to shoot exactly what they wanted. Fabien would come back the next day and tell me, "Iss beautiful. You'll love it."

Then the fashion editor would come into my office, slam the door, and start to cry. "It was a nightmare," she'd sob. "They talked French the whole time and totally ignored me. They laughed—how do I know they weren't laughing at me?"

It was a wearing process, though the results were often beautiful—sometimes stark and bloodless but always controversial. In our first issue, we ran a story called "Matters of Taste," which showed six different women modeling fashion classics. The women, while elegant, looked so melodramatic and depressed that Helen said we ought to call it our "Graveside Fashion." Still, this was years before heroin chic became the staple of fashion magazines, and no one in this country had seen anything like it.

Nobody on staff had ever created a magazine before. We knew no rules, and had no idea who we'd offend and who would love it. The first item in our first issue was about High Rise Syndrome: *"Every year, various organizations send out press releases warning of the danger, but still, the first time most people hear about it is when their own cat lands belly-up on the sidewalk, or the awning."* For years after that piece ran, every time I heard a whooshing sound outside my window, I assumed it was a cat going by. In that same issue, Elmore Leonard wrote an erotic little piece about women's mouths. We featured Little Debbie's Nutty Bars, prominently, recommended that our readers check out The Dog Museum of America, and ran the first of many entries of "The Filofax File," updates on new things to buy for your pocket calendar.

It was all a bit overwrought, but it had energy and spoke to women in what we thought was a totally unique voice. The magazine got a terrific reception. Marvin Traub, the president of Bloomingdale's, liked it so much that he put copies of it in all of his windows. He also gave us a big party in the china department. The guests included everyone that was in our first issue, from Velma Newton, a subway superintendent, to the glamorous Mandelbaum sisters, jewelry designers from SoHo. As Traub presented me with a silver frame, I looked around and saw the faces of our little troupe. Beneath our frozen smiles, I think we were all thinking the same thing. How the hell did we get from the shoe display room to Bloomingdale's?

. . .

Phillip called one morning just after the first issue came out. "Have lunch with me today," he said. It wasn't a question. We went to the Swan coffee shop, an old-fashioned New York lunch place with liver-colored walls and the best egg salad in town. Eating egg salad's a little like walking into a spider's web: Once it gets on you, it sticks to every part of you. That afternoon I was up to my elbows in it when Phillip told me that he'd made a decision. "Mmm," I said, wiping my chin with a napkin.

"I'm selling *Esquire* and *New York Woman*," he continued. "Hearst is buying *Esquire* and American Express is going to buy *New York Woman*." Was there egg salad between my teeth? Phillip kept talking. "In forty-five-minutes you'll get to meet the new owners. There's a meeting uptown in the First Boston offices. You should be prepared to speak about the future goals of the magazine."

It was the '80s and magazine editors were like baseball players: bought, sold, in, out. But that afternoon at the Swan, I had no time to understand what any of it meant, just that I had to give a speech to strangers in forty-five minutes and that Phillip was abandoning me. "What will you do?" I asked him. "I don't know yet. You need to go now."

I ran back to the office to brush my teeth, then grabbed a cab. On the way up to First Boston, I wondered what had brought Phillip to this decision. I couldn't imagine not having access to his braininess every day. I wondered if this sale would change everything. Coming to work had been like going to camp: I loved how we sat on the floor in jeans and looked at layouts; how we knew everything about one another's lives, then used what we knew to poke fun at one another like old friends.

We were anachronisms, really, in this heyday of Dressing for Success, Going Corporate, Growing the Company. Of course things couldn't stay the way they were.

Walking through the doors of First Boston was like entering the New World: granite, marble, atriums. A receptionist was waiting for me outside the designated conference room. "Yes, they're expecting you," she said, pulling open a brushed metal door. Inside, there were fourteen of them, all men. They sat around a U-shaped conference table with fourteen metal briefcases at their feet. I wondered if they were bulletproof, the cases anyway. They thanked me for coming at such short notice, then asked me to talk about how I saw the future of *New York Woman*.

In truth, I hadn't thought beyond getting out the second issue, but I heard myself give voice to things I'd never said aloud. I said that I saw *New York Woman* becoming an international magazine. That we were talking to a community of urban women who basically had the same concerns and similar tastes. They were smart, sophisticated, funny, and wanted to read a magazine that spoke to them the way they spoke to each other. "This will be a groundbreaking magazine," I said. "It will forge a new type of sisterhood. As its editor-in-chief, I believe I have the best job in American journalism." Over the top, maybe, but every word was heartfelt.

The men wrote furiously as I spoke, and when I finished, they put down their pens and smiled wanly. "We appreciate your time," said one of them. "It's nice to meet someone who loves what she does."

I didn't know who they were or what I was supposed to have said, but as I left First Boston, I knew one thing for certain. It was time to buy some business suits. A few weeks later, I received an expensive piece of crystal with American Express's name on it and the *New York Woman* logo. The deal was done. Phillip announced that he was moving to San Francisco.

On the first day of work at American Express, I went in to see my new boss, Tom. He had a hearty laugh and confident president-of-the-class handshake. We faced each other across his mahogany desk, which was empty but for a yellow legal pad. Reading upside down, I saw my name on top of the mostly blank page. Underneath it was printed in tiny square letters: "Ask her how she feels about the move." Before he could say a word, I leaned forward in my chair and said, "You know, I am so excited about coming to American Express. I feel great about the move."

His face got pink. "That's exactly how I feel," he said with a large grin. "We're going to have a *fabulous* time together." I believed him.

At the celebratory dinner that First Boston gave for American Express, I sat next to Tom. Everybody was feeling self-congratulatory that night: the American Express executives, because this was the first in what they hoped would become their empire of city magazines; the First Boston bankers, because doing media deals was considered cool, and me, because I was in Côte Basque, one of the fanciest restaurants in New York City. Tom and I were talking about my next issue, the first to have his company's name on the masthead. "The word *pussy* is going to show up in a piece about bimbos," I said earnestly.

"Oh, really?" he said, his cheeks flushing.

"Well, yes. I thought you ought to know that."

.   .   .

By now, we had assembled a young staff—women mainly—all with an urgent need to express their opinions. Our story meetings took place first thing in the morning, every other Tuesday. All of us, our hair still wet from the shower, sat in my office talking about everything. If you didn't know who we were, a coffee klatch at a hair salon would be an obvious guess. During one meeting, Lori Nash, one of our younger staffers, brought in a tape that she'd asked us to watch with her. It was the video of her father's marriage to his new wife. Dad was a lean athletic man in his mid fifties. He wore a dark suit and hiking boots. Starburst, the new wife, was barefoot and wore a slinky slip dress and a garland of mountain laurel on her head. She was in her early thirties, about the same age as Lori. They stood on a windblown mountaintop in Colorado and exchanged vows, that, of course they had written. For most of the two tedious hours that we watched the tape, all we could hear was the wind whipping through the microphone. The sight of his new wife, Starburst, with her father was obviously a painful one for Lori, which made it even more excruciating and was why we were watching it in the first place. We were determined to keep ourselves intact, in spite of the men in suits with bulletproof briefcases.

The new offices were in midtown. They were real offices with doors and bookshelves that didn't slant. Outside our window was a concrete rooftop, a kind of a terrace where pigeons roosted. We weren't allowed to use it, but every couple of weeks, a man in a white jacket walked along that terrace throwing pellets like chicken feed. One morning during a story meeting, my assistant Stacy Title burst into the room. "I'm sorry to interrupt, but that man out there, I know he's killing the pigeons." She swirled her black curly hair around her fingers. "Come on, you guys, we have to do something. We can't let that Nazi bird-killer get away with it. I'm going to get to the bottom of this," she said.

We forgot the whole thing until several weeks later when, during one of our many birthday parties, Stacy stood up and said she had an announcement to make.

"I've done some research, and of course I was right," she said, arching her neck to crack her back in just the right way. "That evil man out there is feeding birth control to those pigeons. I think we should leak this to *The Village Voice*."

No one said anything, we just kept eating cake. Stacy shook her arms up and down like a child about to have a tantrum. "Oh God, Stacy," Helen said with exasperation. "You are a parody of a person."

Every couple of months after that when a man in a white coat appeared outside our window, one of us would say, "The pigeon killer is back."

"Oh yeah," someone else would say, then we'd go back to whatever it was we were doing.

Stacy has since become a Hollywood director whose first film was nominated for an Academy Award. To this day she worries whether or not Helen really meant it when she called her a parody of a person.

Our personal lives and quirks spilled over into the magazine. Fabien continued to do exquisite covers that made people nervous. The women on them were pale and dramatic, often striking arch poses that were a chiropractor's nightmare. He hectored us into using more celebrities and sent out secret ballots to the staff that everyone knew were from him asking whether or not we should put Madonna or Meryl Streep on the cover instead of some unknown model as we were inclined to do. Then, he reported to me that the majority of those polled were in favor of Meryl Streep.

In an early issue, we did a photo essay chronicling twenty-four hours in New York's meat-packing district. At night, this area was most famous for its transvestite clubs. The photos were raw and powerful, and I heard from Tom that they got the attention of my new colleagues, who were just beginning to understand that the classy women's magazine they thought they had bought wasn't turning out to be exactly that.

Several months later, we ran a story about the Jewish American Prince. *"No one worries about precipitating the next Holocaust every time they make a JAP joke. And I ask you, why are there so many Jewish American Princess jokes and no Prince jokes?"* Marcelle Clements said in her story. We accompanied the piece with photographs of Jewish boys with their mothers—Sigmund and Frau Freud, Sammy Davis and his mom. One of the pictures showed Henry Kissinger with his mother, Paula. Only later did I discover that Kissinger was on the board of American Express.

No one from American Express ever said to me directly, "What are you trying to do, kill us?" Instead, they would let it drop that someone's wife was upset with some dirty word we'd used. "The magazine needs to be more friendly, approachable, warm," Tom told me. "Less—you know—neurotic."

Shortly after the Jewish American Prince piece appeared my mother called me at the office. "Your father hit the roof when he read that story," she whispered. "He . . . oh, my." It was the oh my that made the hairs stand up on the back of my neck. Two days later I received a letter from the B'nai Brith Anti-defamation League, saying that a complaint had been registered. The next day, a man from the league called me. "That piece has people upset," he said. "I have an outraged letter here," he said, reading bits from it.

"Who wrote that letter?" I asked.

He must have heard me gasp when he said the name.

"Anyone you know?" he asked.

"My father."

He paused, "This is a new one."

"Not really," I said.

When starting a magazine was just something that lived in my daydreams, I had visions of myself as the editor-in-chief, feet propped up on my desk, thinking, Ahh, this is all mine. I've done it. But the truth is, when you're a magazine editor, you've never really "done it." There's always a next issue to put out. As it happened, the only time I ever put my feet up on the desk is when a family of mice that had been living in my rubber tree plant came rushing across the carpet heading my way. Besides, most of the time, the melodrama of my personal life cut such a gaping swath through everything else, I barely had time to enjoy what heady days those turned out to be.

Sixteen

Spring came, I felt hopeful. With hope came a shopping trip to Saks Fifth Avenue. Nothing speaks of possibility like a well-stocked shoe department. Gold hooker spikes, soft-toed ballerina slippers, Hike-the-Adirondacks boots, run-your-own-firm suede pumps. It was the Katharine Hepburn *Pat and Mike*, spectator shoes with their blue tips and white leather that spoke to me. This was fate at its most obvious; if I bought those shoes, my life would right itself again. The sticker on their soles said $117, a small price for happiness but a bit too large if you don't have any money in the bank. With a car, a house, and poor investments, Malcolm and I had run up a pricey life. "I'll try them please, size seven," I said to the salesman. He never said a word, just got the box of shoes and dumped them at my feet. I had a feeling we both knew I couldn't afford them but I slipped them on anyway.

"Perfect, I'll take them."

He rang them up in silence.

"Thanks so much," I said, signing my charge.

There was not even a "You're welcome." One month later,

the bill came. The shoe maven had left a digit off my bill, so it came to $17—a sure sign that my life was about to improve.

H ello, Betsy Carter, this is Julius Singer. Bruce said I should—uh—said we should meet. How about dinner Saturday night?" That was it. No small talk, no "What would you like to do?" The voice was high-pitched and nervous with a Brooklyn accent thick as an egg cream. He sounded in a hurry to get the deed done.

Another one of Bruce's lawyers.

Bruce Wasserstein was the kid genius on *The Michigan Daily*. He was several years younger than the rest of us and rumpled in the way that people who live in their heads can be. We all knew he'd be wildly successful when he got older, we just weren't sure at what. He was probably one of the people at the *Daily* who found me irrelevant, but when we met up again after college, he became one of my closest friends. He brought me into his family, which, given how small mine turned out to be, was a great gift. Bruce was a big-picture guy who saw all the angles, and he did become wildly successful as an investment banker. He had always been an invaluable adviser in my professional life—he was one of the key players behind the *New York Woman*/American Express deal. Now he turned his strategizing toward my personal life.

He was one of the first people I called after my marriage broke up. Typically, he zeroed in on the one thing I needed more than anything: dates. Bruce knew everyone, and I can only imagine how he worked his Rolodex. All I can say is that within a week after Malcolm left, I started to get phone calls from every unattached investment banker and corporate lawyer in New York City. Dutifully, they took me out. Some were interesting and fun to talk to. Others, I could tell, were perfunctorily crossing me off their "to do" list, paying their respects to Bruce. One never spoke, except to answer my questions. Finally, when there was nothing left to ask, I pleaded illness and went home. Another gave me exquisite details of his premature ejaculation problem—including the interval, in exact seconds, between arousal and the aforementioned ejaculation. After that, I vowed never again. Yet there was Julius Singer on the other end of the phone and here was I saying yes to another blind date. Julius Singer couldn't be as bad as the last one. Could he?

That Saturday night I put on a black leather skirt, black stockings, and a red off-the-shoulder sweater. My friend Greg dropped by just before I went out. "You look like a juvenile delinquent," he said.

"That's exactly how I feel," I said. The bell rang at precisely 7:30. I opened the door expecting to see a plump, balding guy in Gucci loafers. Instead, there was a wiry man about my height wearing a black-velvet Isaac Mizrahi jacket. His dark brown eyes and nimbus of black hair were shot through with an intensity that went to the pit of my stomach. Later, I found out his nickname was Einstein.

Dinner was at a quiet, romantic SoHo restaurant. When Julius spoke, his voice burst through the air like the rat-tat-tat-tat of old wire machines. He told me that his wife had packed up the house and kid and moved out while he was in London, leaving a matchbook with her phone number in the kitchen and

a futon on the bedroom floor. I told him about Malcolm and
Luis and rat-tat-tat-tat.

After dinner, we walked by a Korean grocer. It was late
March, tulip season, and there were buckets of them in every
color. Julius told me to pick some I liked. I chose the apricot
tulips. "What else?" he said. I giggled and point to a pomegranate bunch. Julius handed the clerk some money, then made a
bowing gesture to me, placing the bouquet in my arms. Six
weeks earlier, my marriage had blown up. Now a man whom I'd
met only hours earlier had just bought me two dozen tulips. I
was clearly right about the shoes.

Back at my apartment, I took a long time arranging the
flowers, worried about what to do after I'd finished. "You like
them?" I asked, holding up the vase for him to see. Julius stared
at the tulips. He pulled a pomegranate petal off the stem and
put it in his mouth. Then an apricot one, then another pomegranate, then an apricot. He didn't say a word or even crack a
smile, determination was all I saw in his face. This was the first
of what he would later call "The Grand Gestures."

"Want to wash that down with E-Z Grow?" I asked, trying
to become part of the joke.

"No," he answered, downing another petal.

"You have pollen on your lip."

He took my face in his hands and kissed me. "So do you."
We came together like two drunk drivers, hands everywhere,
clothes strewn all over the floor. We fell off the bed making
love. Days later I realized I'd cracked a rib.

Back at work on Monday, I gave a no-big-deal shrug when
someone asked about my date Saturday night. Late Tuesday afternoon, a large Federal Express package from New Orleans

landed on my desk. I vaguely remembered that Julius had gone there for business on Sunday afternoon.

I shut my office door and tore into the box. Inside was an enormous black mask made from what looked to be vulture and crow feathers. It was grotesquely gorgeous. Dark and dangerous, I thought. A far cry from New Orleans three months ago. The note was penned in a graceful wide-looped script. "Sometimes even New York Women need to hide. I loved our date. Julius." Another grand gesture.

"Can I come in?" Helen knocked.

"Sure," I answered, hoarsely. "Door's open."

"We should . . ." She dropped the end of her sentence.

"What is *that*?" she shrieked, pointing to the thing.

"Oh, you noticed," I said, patting a feather.

"Noticed? Christ, it looks like the remains of a human sacrifice."

"It's from the guy I went out with Saturday night," I whispered. "It's a bit unnerving."

"Well, I'll say it is."

"He's sexy."

"Be careful."

"I think I like him," I said knowing how dumb it sounded.

Helen extended her arms announced dramatically, "*And so it begins.*"

And so it did.

One night Julius brought his calendar over and filled in every weekend on mine until the summer. There were formal dances, dinner parties, parties on yachts. I rode around in limousines and wore drop-dead dresses that I borrowed from the fashion closet. That Julius was a little autocratic and not too communicative didn't bother me much. At this point, I was much more hell-bent on having fun than talking anyway. During the week, I returned to earth and life at the magazine.

In the evenings, I often represented *New York Woman* at functions around the city. One night I went to a benefit at Rockefeller Center for Meals on Wheels. The room was filled and the chairs were crowded around the tiny tables where we ate. Robin Leach, host of the TV show, *Lifestyles of the Rich and Famous,* and his bosomy date were at my table. Leach chatted amiably with everyone in our little group, all the while picking petals off the white roses in the centerpiece and dropping them down the front of his date's low-cut yellow gown. Julius and the tulips, Robin Leach and the roses. Was this a trend? I made a mental note to bring up flowers-as-sexual-aids at the next story meeting.

Long before black became a fashion statement, Julius wore it and little else. He had no patience for visual excess. Even white was too garish for him. His penthouse apartment had black floors, gray walls, and no furniture. There was a mattress on the floor in his bedroom, and an overstuffed chair in the television room. That was it. He claimed that my clothes gave him a headache.

"Let's see what's going on in here," he said one Saturday afternoon, rummaging through my closet. "I have an idea. I'm going to edit your closet."

He got an oversized Hefty bag from the kitchen and started yanking things off their hangers, dumping them into the sack. I sat motionless on my bed as he narrated my wardrobe.

"I can't believe you'd be seen in these" (green cords). "Looks like a *shtetl* remainder" (floral rayon dress). "A Miami leftover" (peach blouse). "Must've been part of a Halloween costume." (Royal blue bell-bottoms).

By the time he got to "Sears close-out sale" (lime-and-white striped sundress) my closet was nearly empty.

"Better," he said. "Now you can start to dress like a real person." (Have I mentioned that he could be autocratic?)

When I told Helen how Julius had thrown all my clothes into the garbage, she wrinkled her nose and said, "He sounds awful."

But Julius was only half the story. One Saturday night we went to see, 9½ *Weeks*, which happened to be playing right around the corner from his office. After the movie, he said he wanted to go upstairs and get some papers he'd forgotten. Papers, my ass, I thought, still vibrating from what I had just seen on the screen. I had fantasies of Julius making love to me on his desk, tying my hands together with the cords from the venetian blinds.

His large corner office was bare, except for his desk and a credenza topped with hunks of Baccarat crystal—mementos of deals done and companies acquired. When it was clear that there was to be no desktop bondage and seduction, I began reading the stuff on his walls: laminated newspaper articles about him; formal group photographs from firm functions. In the middle of all this professional hoopla was a snapshot of a little boy with green eyes. He was wearing a yellow slicker, and a wisp of blond hair, damp from a recent rain, fell onto his forehead. The boy's head was turned slightly, as if to get away from the camera, yet he was smiling the half smile of a kid trying to do the right thing.

"Who's this?" I asked.

"That's Nicky."

I knew Julius had a son, but I was not prepared for how fragile and angelic he looked. "What an adorable child," I said, still staring at the picture. Julius seemed uncomfortable.

"Yup, you'll meet him soon."

A few weeks later, on a weekend in early May, Julius, Nicky, and I drove up to my house in upstate New York. "We'll see horses," I promised. Nicky sat silently. "Maybe we can find an arcade with Asteroids and Space Invaders." Being away from his mom was scary for Nicky, so spending the weekend at my house was a courageous ordeal. But he was also eager to please his dad. He sat upright in the backseat hugging his Snoopy doll. This kid clearly felt frightened and abandoned and probably sensed the same about me. When Malcolm left, I also lost a family. I used to tease him and say, "If we ever get divorced, I get your parents." It didn't work out that way. Suddenly, I wasn't part of any family holidays or get-togethers.

Nicky became the cornerstone of my weekends. The three of us picked out shorts for him at the Gap, or went to bad movies together. Some afternoons we sat on his bedroom floor and played games, or we walked around the neighborhood and poked around in the local hardware store. The best part was when he took my hand or settled into my lap or told me a story in that funny quacky voice of his. So this was what normal families did. I wondered if I was doing it right and marveled at my good fortune.

. . .

When everything changes, you long for your old rituals. Then one day you realize that how you are living now is, in fact, the routine you will yearn for some day.

That spring, Julius and I rode the crest of a giddy romance. We were the first onto the dance floor at parties, and we made out shamelessly in restaurants and on street corners. And of course, there was Nicky. I was forty-one and life seemed to be falling into place in ways I could have never imagined. Sometimes I worried that it would all career out of control; other times I just held on for the ride.

If there is a more optimistic holiday than July Fourth, I don't know what it is: the food, the spectacle, the picnics, the reminder that there are still a delicious nine weeks left until the end of summer. That weekend we rode around in Julius's convertible, top down, an American flag jammed into the spot where the antenna used to be. We grilled steak and blasted Bonnie Tyler and The Petshop Boys across the Hudson Valley. It was one of the best weekends we'd had together; it was also the first time Julius had ever said "I'm sorry"—after we fought about how to start up the barbecue. The pictures I took at my house that July Fourth had a dark grainy quality about them. I don't know if it was the camera or something else, but in each shot of Julius by the barbecue or me backlit by the sunset, there were black streaks raining over us.

Monday afternoon we drove back to the city. Julius never spoke while he drove. When Nicky was there, I had company; when he wasn't, I had time to daydream. That afternoon, I worried about the week ahead: We were just starting to work on the second issue of the magazine. Would we meet our deadlines? What if people hated what we were doing? I thought about Julius and what an odd couple we made. My friend Susan even used the word *scary*, to describe Julius. Was I wasting my time? Did he really make me happy? Then I did what I always did when my thoughts went brackish. I thought about Nicky's green eyes and squeaky voice until everything felt okay again.

On Tuesday I woke up eager to get back to work. "Hi, guys," I said, breezing into the reception area. Julie, our publisher, was there, as was Marney, our marketing director. What were they doing here? Why didn't they smile back at me? I kept on chatting. "How was your weekend. Pretty amazing weather . . ."

Marney cut me off. Splotches of red stood out on her wide pale face. "Betsy," she shouted at me. "Your house burned down! Your neighbor's on the phone, and he wants to talk to you!"

"What do you mean, my house burned down?"

"Your neighbor, he's on the phone. Your house burned down!" She kept shouting.

Julie helped me to a chair. I put my head below my knees and tried to catch my breath. Marney's shrill voice wouldn't stop: "He wants to talk to you. The fire department's still there. Here," she said and pushed the phone into my face.

I fought the urge to slap her and shout, "You stupid cow, shut up." Instead I took the receiver: ". . . been burning since seven this morning . . . nothing left . . . arson . . ." The words jutted in and out of clarity. ". . . anything I can do for you?"

If I said, "Yes, please water the roses," could I make what was happening go away?

I hung up. This was one that was going to get me, I thought. I called Malcolm. "I'll be right over," he said.

I called Julius. "We'll discuss this at dinner," he said.

The *New York Woman* staff had never seen me through a crisis, and I made no effort to hide my despair. I felt so naked. I was so naked. Everything was gone now. Crying in front of everyone didn't make me feel ashamed. It felt like my due. It came from the deepest, most hurting place inside me. And yet, there was a magazine to get out. It didn't occur to me to cancel meetings or go home. I ran the meetings, sniffling and wiping my eyes as I talked about the cover and an upcoming fashion story on evening dresses. Even Fabien was sympathetic. "Is horrible," he said. "But now you can build the house you've always wanted."

When the receptionist called to tell me that Malcolm was outside, I started to laugh. "Well, here we go," I said to Helen. "Welcome to my life."

That night Julius took me to a Japanese restaurant. We sat on the floor barefooted and cross-legged, picking at our sushi. "What about insurance?" he asked, pulling out a fountain pen and notepad. "Can you itemize the things you lost and their approximate value?"

Each question made me more tearful. Julius wrote down the items I would need immediately: tennis racket, bathing suit, shorts, cotton sweaters. I watched how carefully he penned the words, not abbreviating a single one. Pragmatists like Julius are not easily derailed by sentiment. At this moment, I was grateful for that. Seeing the words *shorts* and tennis racket in black ink under my name lifted me out of my despair and into a future where once again, shorts and a tennis racket would be necessary. That weekend, he helped me choose the only black tennis outfit I have ever owned.

Putting one foot in front of the other: I was getting very good at that. Understanding the pattern and meaning of what happened over the past couple of years was harder. I'd lost my teeth, my ability to bear children, my husband, my house, and everything in it. Stripped bare again and again. If this were a movie, I'd skip to the end and pray for a happy ending. But this was my life, and there was no easy fast forward. I was stuck with every miserable moment of it. If it weren't me, I'd be the first to notice the irony of my own life. The editor of a magazine that purported to conduct a smart tête-à-tête with the most sophisticated women in America had a life that was an endless series of melodramas that she would never publish herself. At night, I lay sleepless trying to make sense of what was going on. God hated me and was trying to tell me I must start over, I decided, not realizing that whoever I was becoming was already under way.

Seventeen

From where I stood, everything looked normal. The pines lifted their arms skyward; the air was still and sweet. I followed the gravel road for a quarter of a mile, wondering when I'd see the first signs of the horrible thing that happened here days ago. The path narrowed and bent into a hill. I climbed slowly, my heart pounding. And then, there it was. Or—there it wasn't.

There was a cavity in the ground covered with charred bits of things that used to be something else. There was no evidence of the books, the ten-speed bikes, the rocking chair, the antique cupboard, the Guatemalan blankets, the slides and photographs, the washing machine, the heirloom china, the diaries, the letters from camp friends, the disco records and Broadway musicals, the pine dining room table. Just ten-day-old ash and a scarred piece of earth.

It was the middle of summer, and the trees were scorched and bare. The pool was empty and its walls were warped. All that remained of Malcolm's garden—the snapdragons, dahlias, lilies, and marigolds, all carefully planned so there'd be color from May to October—were incinerated stalks that poked out from the blackened earth. Miraculously, one rose survived. It was pale and pink and barely hanging on.

I walked to the bluff overlooking the Hudson River. From up there, you could hear the sound of the train rumbling back and forth from Albany six times a day. In the winter, the frozen river groaned as barges nosed their way through. Early in the morning the whippoorwills called to each other with a cooing that sounded exactly like their name. This was my house. The most beautiful place on earth.

From that day on, I unwittingly conducted private rites for what was lost. An object came to mind and I visualized it in flames, burning to extinction. A lamp, a *Chorus Line* album, a swimming trophy from camp, the drawing of Snoopy with "Nicky's Room," written beneath it. It took me six months to decide to sell the land and give up on the dream that I would ever rebuild there.

The people who bought my property planned to construct an enormous house on it. There would be a front porch overlooking the river and a gazebo where the garden was. "Think about it," said Phillip, when I told him. "From ashes to a mansion."

Eighteen

After the fire, I never again took luck for granted. Bits of fortune cookies that promised good times ahead and lots of travel lay wadded up in my wallet, I kept a twenty-dollar bill that I found on the sidewalk in my jewelry box, as an omen of good luck. Each crack I stepped on spelled doom, and every time I rode over a railroad crossing, I lifted my feet and shut my eyes. "Peace of mind," I wished. It wasn't the kind of thing that had ever crossed my mind to wish for before. One day I half-kiddingly told someone in our advertising department that the way my life was going, I was thinking of seeing a psychic or a card reader. All of a sudden, people I barely knew were slipping me sheets of paper with names of people who read palms and interpreted auras.

Harriet the tarot card reader came highly recommended by two people in our research department. They ought to know, I thought. Harriet read her cards in a room in Greenwich Village that was heavily decorated with batik. She had henna-colored hair and pants to match. The blue scarf draped around her shoulders was the identical color of her eye shadow, and offset her pale freckled skin perfectly. Clearly Harriet had had her colors done.

"We'll start with your past," she said, snapping her oversized cards on the table. The first card she turned over had a drawing of a man draped in black. His head was turned to the side and with one hand, he shielded his eyes. "Five of Cups," she said. "The card of loss, bereavement. You've had something taken away, you're feeling grief. You've let go of a hope and you're experiencing sorrow."

"I'm unable to have children," I said, thinking that Harriet talked like a law school dropout.

Next she flipped over a card of two men struggling through a snowstorm. One was on a crutch, the other had rags covering his body. "You're going through a period of hardship. You have been rejected. You are standing alone and struggling to make ends meet. You don't have a lot of money."

"Mm-hmm, I've recently gotten divorced. I'm kind of broke."

She sucked in her cheeks as she turned the next card: the Tower. It was a picture of fire, lightning falling on jagged rocks. Before the words *upheaval, explosion* even came out of Harriet's mouth, I shouted: "Yes! Explosion! My house exploded, burned to the ground!" This was starting a game of charades, and I was winning! But the beads of sweat that broke out on Harriet's upper lip made me remember it wasn't so.

Was it my imagination, or did she actually shudder as the next card came up. The Death Card. "This means *ending*. Cutting out what isn't necessary. Going through what can't be avoided. Getting pared down to the bare bones."

Her body tensed as I shook my head. "There was an accident, I lost all my teeth."

"It's obvious you've been on quite a journey," she said, bending down to do something under the table. I assumed she was dialing 911. But when she sat back up, I noticed a booklet in her hand. The cover had a rainbow on it with a crown floating beneath it. Above the rainbow and the crown was the title, *Journey to I Am.*

"Here," she said, pressing the manuscript into my hands. "I wrote this myself. I think it will help you." That's when I noticed tears streaming down her freckled cheeks. I had made my tarot reader cry. It occurred to me that maybe I should try a different avenue of self-exploration.

At night, when I couldn't fall asleep, I did anagrams in my head. Bedroom became boredom; miracle, *reclaim.* Letters tumbled over one another, words disassembled, and I put them back together again. There was comfort in creating a new order. Sometimes my word games delivered poignant messages. *It's all gone* lolled around in my head late one night and slowly came back to me as *angels toil.* Though I didn't know why, I found it strangely comforting. Another night, *start over* turned into *overt star.* A few weeks later, when *strip bare* rearranged itself as *best repair*, I decided it was time to get some help and work on that.

New York City has no shortage of psychiatrists. Everyone you meet has stories of miraculous transformations brought about by some guy who worked upstairs from a Benetton's. From the dozens of recommendations I got, one name stuck out—Dr. Phoebe Slom. It wasn't very scientific, but the moment I realized that *phoebe slom* was an anagram for *o help me sob*, I knew she was the one for me.

Once a week for the next several months, I dragged poor Phoebe through the morass of my life. She never said much. Mostly, she nodded sympathetically, or jotted down notes. But every now and then she'd seize upon a detail and turn it into a theme. Like banana peel.

I had told her about one afternoon when my mother had a group of friends over for coffee and her famous yeast cake. While they were eating, I dashed through the dining room peeling back a banana. "Hi," I said, barely noting that one of the little strings inside the banana had fallen onto her favorite Persian carpet.

"Pick that up," she demanded.

Even at twelve, I didn't like to be given orders. Without saying a word, I ground the peel into the carpet with the ball of my foot. She jumped up from her chair and slapped me across the face.

"Banana peel" became Phoebe's code word for my problems with authority. Whenever I disagreed with her, she'd shake her head and give a *haw haw, gotcha* laugh. "There's that banana peel issue again," she'd say. Other times, she'd get visibly emotional. The first time I told her the details of my car accident, Phoebe's cheeked turn rosy. She started massaging her temples with her thumbs.

"Do you mind if I'm honest with you?" she asked.

"Of course not."

"What you have told me has just made me physically *sick to my stomach*," she said, deliberately enunciating the words *sick to my stomach*.

"I understand how you feel," I said, making a mental note

to talk to a shrink someday about my need to be polite to my shrink.

Over time, Phoebe became convinced that I hadn't allowed myself to feel proper anger toward Malcolm. "We won't get anywhere here until you get in touch with your rage," she insisted.

"Honestly, I don't feel inner rage."

She shook her head so imperatively that her glass-bangled earrings slapped against her cheeks. "Of course you do, dear. You've always turned your anger inward. That's why you have such self-esteem problems."

"But I don't."

"That's something else we need to talk about."

It was pointless to argue.

When I walked into her office a week later, Phoebe was holding a plastic bat between her legs.

"Gee, I forgot my glove," I said.

She didn't even acknowledge my attempt at a joke.

"Listen, I think we can get at this another way. Clearly you're uncomfortable talking about your anger. Maybe you'll be more at ease dealing with it in a physical way."

Phoebe wanted me to beat the couch with the bat as hard as I could. I made a few feeble swats at it.

"Cry. Scream if you like," she coached. "That son of a bitch, he took seventeen years of your life. Robbed you of ever having children." Dots of sweat broke out on her brow. "Go on, say it, that little shit left you broke," she was nearly wailing now. "Not a penny. Took the prime of your life. Can't get that back again, no sirree. The prime of your life!"

I tapped the couch a couple of times, even gave it some

halfhearted smacks, but I became so engrossed in what Phoebe was saying that I lost my concentration.

"You hate him! You hate him!" she shrieked, looking wildly around the room. "How will you ever trust another man?" Then her voice dropped and she fixed me with a glassy stare: "There now, don't you feel better?"

A couple of weeks later, Phoebe decided that the bat and couch exercises hadn't worked all that well, that we hadn't made a dent in all the rage that was still roiling around. "You're a perfect candidate for hypnosis," she told me. "You'll see. We can get at some of the baggage that prevents you from releasing your feelings. This will make you feel so much lighter." So for the next few weeks, I lay on her beanbag couch as she swayed a pocket watch in front of my eyes and waited for me to fall under her spell. Nothing much came up until one afternoon, while I was talking about my childhood in Washington Heights.

"I smell garbage burning!" I said.

Phoebe's voice rose in triumph. "Garbage burning? Tell me more. What does it remind you of?"

"It reminds me of cans filled of incinerated garbage that were lined up under my bedroom window in Washington Heights when I was a kid."

I could hear Phoebe scribbling.

When she finally spoke, her voice was lilting. "Well, I think we've made quite a bit of progress for today. Let's stop here."

During our next session, we did the watch thing again, and she brought me back to Washington Heights. Again I smelled the cans of incinerated garbage. Did the odor scare me? Make me feel comforted? Angry? Phoebe went at me like a dog after squirrels.

"Umm," I said, "it just makes me feel that soon the garbage men will come and dump the incinerated trash into their trucks, and the cans will stand empty outside my window."

Phoebe sounded exasperated. "Betsy, it is so important that you get past this. We are close to a real breakthrough."

I tried, I really tried. I talked about the compactors I had seen at *Air & Water News* and attempted to make a metaphor out of all things eventually being returned to dust. Phoebe didn't bite. "Perhaps at our next session, we can talk about your need not to take our work together seriously," she said, frostily.

I walked out into the street, annoyed at how bad I was at therapy. As I turned the corner, I absentmindedly tried to peer through the window into Phoebe's ground-floor office. But I couldn't. Phoebe's windows were blocked with cans. Garbage cans lined up like bowling pins. Garbage cans filled with freshly incinerated garbage from her building.

Screw therapy, I thought. I was going to quit. I was tired of Phoebe using me as her guinea pig to try out every new shrink trick in the book.

But Pheobe, with her bottomless capacity for empathy, kept me coming back for more. She paid me compliments. She said things like, "I've never noticed how strong your hands are," or "We have a connection that goes beyond therapy, you know." They were things that, though often out of context, boosted my insatiable need for approval. And Phoebe was filled with practical suggestions and common sense: Be kind to yourself, she counseled. Keep warm. Wear sweaters. Cook homemade meals. You are your own family now.

Her advice seemed sound, and I translated it into a simple formula. Every couple of days, on my way home from work, I picked up a package of chicken parts. My intention was to broil the chicken, make some salad and potatoes, light a candle and sit with myself through a cozy meal at home. But it never happened that way. Sometime early in the evening, I'd cram the uncooked parts into the freezer along with my swelling collection of other roasters and fryers, and order a pizza or Chinese food. Years later, when I moved out of that apartment, I found that my freezer had become an arsenal packed with frozen thighs and drumsticks—reminders of so many intimate home-cooked meals I had failed to share with myself.

The last time I went to Phoebe's office was on a rainy Thursday in January. Chilled, I settled onto her couch soothed by the hissing of her radiator and the blinking eye of her ionizer. She dispensed with her usual "How are you today?" She was in a hurry to begin.

"Given all the things that have happened to you in the past few years, it's made me seriously think that you have lived a past life," she said, fidgeting with her worry beads. "I suspect that in your other life, you were an evil person. I think you did a lot of very bad things, and now you're being repaid for them in this lifetime. Betsy, I want you to consider this. I want you to think about having an exorcism. It's the only way you can put a stop to this. I know somebody who can help you."

I stared at Phoebe with disbelief. The longer I stared, the more distorted her dark, ferret-face and pinched brown eyes became. She looked more like an Indonesian mask than a shrink from Jersey City. Normally I'd be curious enough to ask where in New York City you could go for an exorcism. I'd have even jotted it down in my notebook as a possible service piece for *New York Woman*. But the chill of her words and the possibility that she could be right stunned me into an unnatural silence.

Lately I had been anxious that if there was some dark force warring against me, it might accidentally strike Nicky as well. When friends called me nicknames like Bloody Mary, Job, Typhoid Annie, I laughed it off. But deep in my heart I worried that they didn't think it was very funny. Maybe this wasn't just a matter of when it rains, it pours. Maybe I really was a marked woman.

I'd just had my first asthma attack, in a subway station while on my way to a Christmas party. I had developed a nerve-wracking cough, and things I assumed I could always do, like dancing and running, left me breathless. On this evening, as I tried climbing the stairs, I couldn't get past the fourth one. My cough rattled and my breath came out in rickety bursts. What followed was a trip to the hospital, many tests, and later, color-coded canisters of inhalers that are still never far from my body. Since then, each time I cough or have a catch in my throat, I search for signs that I might stop breathing.

But when every other molecule in my body wanted to give up, lie down and declare a state of emergency, there was another part of me that goaded me to keep going. I was learning to breathe again, to feed myself, to get on with my life. There was someone in there who was taking charge and doing okay. I wasn't in the mood for some has-been exorcist on the upper West Side to snuff out whoever that person was.

Phoebe picked at her cable-knit sweater and waited for my

response. As she looped a loose thread around her pinky, I felt indignation and resolve. So many times she had told me to be kind to myself, to nurture and protect myself. Now was the time to show her that I'd learned those lessons well.

"This thing about my past life and being a bad person," I said. "I don't believe that. I think my body betraying me has been a wake-up call to things that needed to change or be improved. It's been horrible, but I don't think there's a bad person in there who needs to be exorcised."

"I know, it's a radical thought," Phoebe said.

Clearly she hadn't heard a word I said.

"Maybe you'd like some time to think about it."

"I have thought about it. I'm going to pretend you never said what you just said. I think I need to leave. Thank you for all your help."

That was the end of my therapy with Phoebe Slom. I was sure I was a big disappointment to her, and after I walked out her door, I imagined her massaging her temples and muttering, "Banana peel" to herself.

It made me laugh when I realized that an anagram of *banana peel* was *enable a nap*.

Nineteen

If you're going to try and figure out the meaning of your life, I discovered, the best time to do it is while you are wearing a short red-beaded Donna Karan cocktail dress.

Julius's friends on Wall Street were making money faster than they could eat it. They gave parties where caviar flowed like onion dip and the favors came from Tiffany's. Gladys Knight and all of the Pips entertained at their sons' bar mitzvahs. They wore T-shirts that said; "He who dies with the most toys wins." Winning is what mattered. Conversations became contests of who could talk faster and louder. The men in his firm exchanged the names of important decorators and jewelers like other guys did ballplayers. Julius guessed that one of his partners was about to become engaged to his girlfriend when he asked another colleague for the name of his furrier. They bought enormous Georgian-style mansions as their summer homes. When they ran out of things to renovate inside, they took on the land outside, building hills where there were none and cascading waterfalls where a detached tool shed used to stand. It was a time of insane excess, and I got to watch the whole thing.

One evening, we went to a dinner party for a famous British corporate raider. The party was in a sprawling Fifth Avenue penthouse overlooking Central Park. Julius always looked great at these events: His lean body filled an Armani tux just so, and with his hair slicked back, he looked like Michael Douglas in *Wall Street*—which, I suppose, wasn't a coincidence. English antiques filled the penthouse. The overstuffed chairs were upholstered in cabbage rose fabrics, and the living room walls were lined with satin. "Kid-friendly place," I whispered to Julius.

"Grow up," he said sharply, afraid I'd embarrass him. Waiters offered us champagne and little crepes filled with crème fraîche and caviar. A chamber music quartet played off to the side.

At dinner, I was seated next to the corporate raider. He had manicured nails, initials on his cuffs, and a blue handkerchief poking out from his suit pocket. I couldn't tell how it would go.

"Are you one of them?" he began by asking me.

"Are you kidding?"

"What do you do then?"

I told him all about *New York Woman*, and how I imagined that Julius and his friends thought I sat on the floor all day, cutting out dolls and coloring.

"It's a small world they're in. Small world, big bucks," he smiled, stretching out the word *bucks*.

During the lulls in our conversation, he shook the hands of those who came to pay their respects, and chatted politely with them. The woman seated to his left was wearing a skin-tight sheath. I had no idea he'd noticed until he turned to me, gesturing toward her. "If that dress were any shorter, she'd swallow it." He spoke the King's English like someone upon whose every word other people hung, which made what he said even funnier.

Just before the servants brought out the racks of lamb, our host clinked his glass with a knife and stood up. He welcomed his colleagues and paid lavish tribute to the guest of honor. Then, with a flourish, he turned to the raider: "And now, I would like you to meet the two most important mergers in my life: Ashley and Parker." He waved his hand and out they came. Seven-year-old Parker wore a tuxedo and a perfect pompadour. Nine-year-old Ashley had on an Alice in Wonderland dress, tiny pumps, and dabs of blush that emphasized her weasel-like features.

On cue, they marched over to the raider's chair. With her dress in one hand, Ashley did a deep curtsy, nearly touching her head to the floor, while Parker bowed himself in half. In unison, they said, "How do you do. We are so pleased to have you in our home." The raider returned their greeting effusively. Ashley and Parker turned on their heels and ran from the living room. Only when they were out of earshot, did he turn to me and whisper: "The children are ruined."

That was around the time when it started going sour for me. I stopped thinking excess was interesting. I loved the dancing and the spectacle of the clothes and beautiful houses, but I was tired of always feeling as though I'd been dropped into another planet. Julius and I had been together for two years and had not talked about anything more intimate than my ugly clothes and our schedules. Whenever I thought about breaking up with him, though, I thought about Nicky. And I thought about sex with Julius. That never got uninteresting. I was not used to my sex life being written all over me. Julius would drop mention of it into the conversation, and say things at dinner like, "Betsy gets hungry after sex," or, "If we stay at this party much longer, it will cut into our sex life."

Even when he said nothing, people saw it. One weekend, we went to Miami Beach and stayed in a plush condo, the type of place where there were steps leading up to the marble bathtub and the walls around it were covered in mirrors. As we gave my parents a tour, my mother stopped to take in the spectacle of the bathroom. "What a tub!" she whispered. "Bet you could have some fun in there." I swear she winked.

Sex was the only thing my mother and I never discussed. Months after I married Malcolm, she asked me if there was anything I needed to know. "About what?" I asked.

"You know, about marriage, or your personal relations," she said.

I told her everything was fine, and that was that. This was a woman who honestly didn't know the difference between a lesbian and a gay man until my husband became one, and now she was talking about bathtubs and smirking at me as if to say, "Who are you kidding?" I smiled back as if to answer, "Certainly not you."

I used to tell Phoebe that Julius was moody and negative. He had a clipped way of saying *No* to anything I wanted to do that felt like a slap. Want to go to the movies? *"No."* Want to take a walk? *"No."* Denying me seemed to give him pleasure. Phoebe agreed as to how this was possible. "It sounds as though he might have a personality disorder," she'd put forward.

"Then why is the sex so great?"

"Dear, as soon as you start feeling healthy, you'll want more out of this relationship than weekend sex. Right now, it works for you since you have nothing to give emotionally anyway."

What a gift for words that woman had. But for a change, she was right.

Not long after the raider dinner party, one of Julius's colleagues threw a party for his wife's fortieth birthday. He chartered a bus to take a bunch of us away for a weekend in the Pocono Mountains. Julius put his arm around me in the bus, something he rarely did in public. We went rafting and swimming and danced by a campfire at the side of a lake. That night we made love in a round queen-sized bed, and again in a bathtub in the shape of a champagne glass.

Sunday afternoon, the bus dropped us at Julius's apartment, where we made love again. Afterward, we lay side by side listening to the buses wheeze up Madison Avenue.

"I don't think I can see you anymore," I said, wondering where the words were coming from. "It just doesn't seem right."

Julius never talked after sex, so his silence wasn't that unusual.

"I probably should go. It wouldn't make sense for me to stay."

He stared at me but said nothing.

The more he didn't speak, the harder I tried to get his attention. Had he said anything, things might have been gone another way, but he didn't.

I talked about the ways in which we were different and how ultimately we weren't right for each other. He didn't argue. The more I talked, the more I convinced myself I was doing the right thing. I got out of bed and put on my clothes.

"I've loved being with you. But I guess we both knew this

was inevitable," I said, tucking my shirt into my jeans. "I mean, in the end, we're such different people. I'll miss you." I bent down to kiss him good-bye.

"I hope we can stay friends. You, me, and Nicky."

A sob caught in my throat. Part of me just wanted to crawl back into bed and snuggle in next to him.

Get out now, I thought, or you will never leave. "Good night," I said, then closed the door quickly.

I stepped inside the elevator, with its familiar wet wool smell. On Friday nights, when I'd come to Julius's house, that smell was my welcome. It promised Nicky, and making love with Julius, and the three of us being tucked in for the weekend. Now I stood engulfed by the musty odor, knowing I'd never be back. I wondered if I would ever see Nicky again. I already missed the intensity of Julius's eyes. Why did he lie there without saying a word? Had I just broken up with myself?

Once, just as we were getting ready to leave on a trip, I looked at his nervous face and said, "You're dreading this, aren't you?"

"Yes, I am," he answered.

I didn't think he'd take the break-up all that hard. Shows you how wrong a person can be. There were letters, pages and pages of them. He talked of marriage and even mentioned the possibility of us adopting a child together. Exotic flowers that looked like predatory birds started showing up at the office. One day, a messenger arrived at *New York Woman* with a tiny package that could only mean one thing: important jewelry. Helen sat next to me as I opened the navy blue box. In a nest of maroon velvet sat a ring with diamonds and blue sapphires that sparkled like a summer night.

"It's beautiful," I said, holding it up to the light.

"It's very expensive," said Helen.

"I could get a car for what this cost," I said, only half joking.

"Send it back," she ordered.

"I could put a down payment on a co-op"

"I'm not leaving until you put it back in the box and return it."

It was tempting to keep the ring and pick up where I'd left off with Julius. With Nicky. I thought about how Julius's fingers felt on my face, caressing my neck. I remembered teaching Nicky to ride a bike and the time he sat on my lap while I wrote my column for the magazine. I could see the three of us in Disney World and how we laughed when Nicky, then about six, whispered to us that he didn't think Cinderella was American. Maybe I should try again. Julius and I weren't a perfect match, but maybe I'd reached the age where you couldn't be too fussy about such things.

Then I caught myself and got scared. Being alone frightened me, but feeling alone while I was with someone else was even more frightening. Still . . .

"What if Julius is the only man who will ever ask me out?" I asked Helen one day.

"That's nonsense," she said, looking concerned. "You're already housebroken, you know how to live with someone else. Men like that. Anyway, imagine what it could be like to be with someone who isn't always trying to make you over? It could be incredible."

Oh God, let that be true, I wished silently. Just let me be strong enough to stick this one out.

A message appeared on my desk one morning, several weeks after I'd returned the jewelry. Bruce and one of Julius's other friends, Stan the cosmetics mogul, summoned me to lunch at a fancy Italian restaurant. "Don't go," said Ron on the phone. "They're just going to browbeat you about Julius."

"What if they want to see how I'm doing?"

"Fat chance."

Of course I went.

They had already ordered my food by the time I got there. "Gentlemen, your guest has arrived," the waiter said as he held my chair. It was that kind of place.

"Are you sure you know what you are doing breaking up with Julius?" said Bruce.

"We didn't really have that much in common."

"You're giving up an awful lot. Julius is a great guy," said Stan. "And then there's the lifestyle. He offers you things you could never get yourself."

"I know that. But I need someone who will take my calls and see me more than once a week."

"You know, Julius is one of the top lawyers in his field," said Bruce. "I'm sure you've seen him quoted in *The New York Times.*"

"Yes, but that's beside the point. I need to be with someone who has more of the same interests as I do." I was beginning to hate this. "You both have wives who are kind to you, a comfort to you when you come home . . ."

"That's silly," said Stan, cutting me off. He made his living by getting his way; he wasn't interested in being contradicted.

The salads came. The waiter's face was expressionless, but his arm brushed mine as he placed the plate in front of me. I took this as a sign that he was encouraging me to hold firm.

True or not, it bolstered my nerve. "They like you and make you feel good about yourselves," I continued. "Why shouldn't I be with someone who makes me feel the same way?"

The answer came back at me in an instant: "If you want to be with someone like us, well then, the other stuff is just part of the deal."

Someone like them? The deal? So that was it? This was about the deal—the thing I'd screwed up by leaving. By the time the waiter came back to clear the tuna, my voice was harsh.

"Did it ever occur to you that maybe I don't want to be with one of you, that maybe I'd prefer to be with one of, one of—me?"

The waiter averted his eyes.

"Check please," Bruce ordered.

As they paid the bill, Stan turned to me. "It's your loss," he says. Not really, I thought, tallying up how much they billed for their time. We'd been here an hour and twenty minutes and they hadn't closed the deal.

What a relief it was to go back to the magazine. I walked by Stacy's office. She was lying face down on the floor while Ann Kwong was walking on her back. Ann had taken over from Fabien when he left to be the art director of a hip downtown magazine. Even though Ann was under five feet tall, her-take-no prisoners style had earned her the nickname "Queen Kwong."

Two weeks after my fancy Italian lunch, I received an invitation printed on sunshine yellow paper. It was from Miami High School, inviting me back to my twenty-fifth reunion. "Stingarees from all over the world will gather," it read. "You don't want to miss this once in a lifetime opportunity to greet old classmates and catch up with your favorite teachers." The dancing Stingaree with a happy face was drawn in blue: yellow and blue, the school colors. I studied the notice thinking about how I'd feel, Princess Poo-bah, showing up alone: no husband, no boyfriend, no children. Why was I even considering it? There was no way I was going to go.

Soon after, I got a phone call from my old friend Sherry Lee.

"So, Miss Betsy, are we going to the reunion?" she asked in her usual mocking tone. Sherry Lee still lived in Miami and was an on-air personality for the local public television station.

"No, we are not," I answered firmly. "I can't show up without a date."

"What if I told you I'd take care of it? Would you come then?"

"Oh, that's all I need is for you to take care of it. Is Charlie Manson out on parole? Claus von Bulow?"

"Trust me," was all she said, laughing.

And against my better judgment, I did.

Two months later, on the night of the big Miami High dinner dance, I was primping with Sherry Lee in a hotel room at the Americana hotel. At 7:00 P.M. the phone rang. "Ms. Carter?" said the operator. "Your date is here. He'll meet you by the check-in desk."

"How did this happen to me?" I groaned, crunching my damp hair. "I'm having a blind date *and* in front of my whole high school class! I've hit rock bottom."

The first person I saw as I walked out of the elevator was Ralph Renick. If you grew up in Miami in the fifties and sixties, there was only one anchorman on television: tall, handsome Ralph Renick, with his black-framed glasses and frat-boy congeniality. In my twelfth-grade career book on journalism, Ralph Renick was the first person listed under celebrities in my field. When Fidel Castro overthrew Cuban dictator Fulgencio Batista in 1959 and instantly became the darling of the left, our own Ralph Renick was one of the first reporters to interview Castro and report that all was not as it seemed in sunny Havana. To every young person in southern Florida who dreamed about being a reporter someday, Ralph Renick was our idol.

And now, here he was, in the lobby of the Americana. Be cool, I thought, giving him a slight smile as I headed toward the check-in desk. Remarkably, he smiled back.

"Are you Betsy Carter?" he asked.

My mind got cluttered. This was Ralph Renick, for Christ's sake, say something clever.

"Ummm, could be," I said.

"Hi," he said, smoother than guava jelly. "I'm Ralph Renick. I'm your date for tonight."

Only Sherry Lee could have devised such a brilliant homecoming. As we walked into the ballroom of the Americana—me and Ralph Renick, that is—I saw heads turn. People whispered. That night, I was cooler than cool—Honoria and prom queen all balled into one.

He was the perfect date. We bopped, we slow danced, we did the twist. He told Gail Sweeney and Jim Fisher how happy he was to meet them, and how much I had told him about them. When Sherry Lee told him about the Poo-bah Club and gave him the handshake, Ralph Renick gave it right back. And when it came time to get our picture taken together under the artificial rose trellis at the end of "Memory Lane," he smiled warmly and put his massive arm around me.

· · ·

It's easy to feel constrained by your own parameters. You look at your parents and the house in which you grew up and think, that's it: These are the things that define my life, why bother to try and break out of them. That night, Ralph Renick taught me that life is as big or small as I would let it be, and that there were people in the world, beyond Julius Singer, who could make me feel as alive and attractive as I'd ever felt.

Twenty

Being alone on Saturday afternoons was harder than any other time of the week. That's when families did chores together and when the promise of a weekend stretched before me. I tried to fill those afternoons with shopping for groceries (more chicken for the freezer), going to museums, picking up dry cleaning, but inevitably, I found myself alone again in that slip of late afternoon, just before the sun sets.

That's when I'd fall into a thicket of self-pity and depression. I'd go over all of it again: being childless, the fire, Malcolm, the accident. Now I couldn't even see Nicky anymore. It was probably best for him. Then I'd really wallow in it. God did hate me. Phoebe was right. I was being punished for my past life.

On one of those bleak Saturday afternoons, I was walking home from Bloomingdale's, where I'd passed the time by trying out all the mattresses in the bed department. There was the other side of the afternoon to get through, and Saturday night and all of Sunday. If you could see or do anything you wanted to right now, what would it be, I asked myself. Nicky. I'd go see

Nicky. By the time I got home, nothing was going to stop me.
I'd call Julius's ex-wife, Nina, and ask to see her son. What could
she say that could hurt me? The worst that would happen was
that she'd hang up on me. I had nothing left to lose.

Nina Singer was listed in the phone book at the address
where we'd dropped Nicky on Sunday nights. I'd never met her;
I'd only heard stories. She was temperamental, too independent.
Her big crime, according to Julius, was that she presented herself as someone who would be obedient and turned out to be
completely the opposite. *Really crazy*, he'd say. *So irrational.* I
punched in the numbers. *But Nicky adored her. How bad could
she be?* The phone rang. A woman answered. "Hello Nina, this
is Betsy Carter." I heard my voice tremble. "I just broke up with
your ex-husband, and I miss your kid so much." It had been
over a month since I'd seen him. Maybe he'd forgotten me;
maybe he didn't care enough to ever want to see me again. My
heart was pounding.

"Well, he misses you, too. Come up here right now." Nina's
voice was more girlish than I'd imagined. There was a trace of
humor in it and I couldn't tell whether or not she was kidding.
I didn't wait to find out. I got on a subway and headed uptown
to Nina's apartment as fast as I could.

When she opened the door, Nicky was standing next to her.
They had identical broad, almost zany smiles. Seeing them together was the most natural thing in the world. Every time I'd
been with Nicky, no matter where we were, I could sense how
anxious he was about being away from his mother. Now I saw
him looking totally relaxed. Clearly, she was the piece that had
been missing.

The three of us stood awkwardly at the door; Nicky was the

reason we were all here, and he was only seven and a half. Now what were we supposed to do? Nina laughed. "This is pretty wild, isn't it? Come on in, we can talk about ex-husbands and lovers."

It was a gracious way of saying, "I know this is absurd, but we're in it together," and I liked her immediately. We spent the next two hours talking about our lives while Nicky played in his room. Every now and then he called me in to show me his train set or to play a game. I felt strangely at home there. That afternoon marked the beginning of a new family for me. I guess you could call it husband swapping, only I got the wife and the kid and neither of us got a husband.

When I told my mother that I was dating again at forty-two, I could hear a heavy sigh at the other end of the phone. She didn't say what I knew was on the tip of her tongue: "This isn't going to be easy. After all, you're no spring chicken anymore." She just warned me: "Whatever you do, don't tell anybody everything at once." My mother had always been keener than I about keeping her secrets to herself. Still, I was grateful for the advice, and even more so for the clarity of the thought. She'd recently been diagnosed with an inoperable benign brain tumor—a misnomer if ever there was one. It was an unstoppable mass that had been growing for nearly ten years.

By this time, she had begun to lose her words. Those headaches she'd been waking up with every morning got worse. The sight in her left eye was fading.

There is a jellyfish called the lion's mane. It looks like a translucent mushroom cap and has 150 tentacles attached to it, each about five feet long—thus its name. The stinging ten-tacles dance around its body like streamers. Each one of them shoots off toxins that can be fatal. That's what I envisioned floating around inside my mother's head.

When I called the doctor who had diagnosed her, he told me not to worry: "She'll be doing laps in the pool until she is eighty-five," he said in a patronizing voice. She was seventy-four, eleven years away from eighty-five. The tumor had already claimed the sight in her left eye, now it was working on her right. This thing wouldn't wait for eighty-five.

"Everything's going," she said on the phone one day, after telling me that she had no smell or taste left. "I'm no good anymore."

"Of course you are. Besides, I need you to be at your best. How else am I going to make it through dating?"

I embellished a story about how the night before, I tried to jump out a bathroom window at a restaurant to escape my latest bad date. She brightened up.

"Oh honey, I wish I could have been there."

Over the next six and a half years, the creature, as I came to call her brain tumor, would tortuously and insidiously poison her laughter, and then her balance. Eventually it would destroy her speech, making her words nearly unintelligible.

My trips to Miami became more frequent. Each time, I would go through old pictures with her, letters, birthday cards—anything to try and coax back the mother I knew and still needed. On one visit, I found a poem in my twelve-year-old handwriting called, "Going to Work."

Who knows where I'll be or what I'll do,
But when I grow up I want to be just like you.

234

I remembered the morning I wrote it, while watching my mother put on her red-and-white-checked sleeveless blouse and navy-blue tailored skirt. She looked so trim and beautiful as she pulled out of the driveway in her silver Buick. At the time, she was the comptroller of a printing plant in Hialeah. We had just moved into our own house in Miami and my father had a steady job. She never said it, but I'm betting this was her prime.

Often I'd watch her sitting at her dressing table, rouging her cheeks and curling her eyelashes. Sometimes, I'd catch my father's eye in the mirror and he would say to my reflected image, "Not bad for a woman her age, eh?" She was fifty. On the rare times we'd go to Collins Avenue on Miami Beach, she'd stare at the old people walking with canes or in wheelchairs and always say the same thing: "You can take me out and shoot me before I become an old lady living in a condo on Miami Beach. Not me, not for all the tea in China." When you're in your prime, it's hard to imagine you'll ever be anywhere else.

The words *Miami Beach* conjured up everything she loathed—everything pretentious and beyond our reach: the ladies who clacked across Collins Avenue in their high heels, tight shorts, and way too much jewelry; the big Cadillacs whose drivers seemed headless because they were so short; the gaudy houses whose chandeliers shimmered through the large bay windows facing Alton Road. Was it any wonder that, years later, I could never see my place in Julius Singer's world?

When my parents were both in their late sixties, I won my lawsuit from the cab accident and used it to help them buy a condo in Miami Beach. They couldn't stop making jokes about it. "The next thing you know, your mother will dye her hair blue," my father would say. Secretly, I think they delighted in having made it. Their bedroom faced onto the ocean. Often when I'd be on the phone with my mother, she'd say, "I can't believe it. I can hear the water from my bed. Listen!" And I'd picture her holding the phone to the window so I could hear the sound of the crashing waves.

Now she rarely left that bedroom. Trips home became sadder. With each visit, the apartment smelled more like a hospital: rubbing alcohol, disinfectant, it added up. My father was handling it the best way he could, continuing to talk to her as if nothing were amiss. He held her hand and stroked her head as she lay on the couch. He filled the refrigerator with orange juice and apples and her favorite kinds of cheese in an effort to get her to eat, and fed her when she was too tired to do it for herself. He told her jokes and asked her questions about old boyfriends and reminisced about trips the two of them took together—anything to keep her mind going.

He'd promised her he'd never put her in a nursing home, and now he was honoring that promise. When we sat together in the living room, he urged me with his eyes to keep talking, to ask her advice. Sometimes she would say something and we'd lean in close to try to decipher her words. Other times she squeezed my hand or stroked my face. As each visit drew to a close, I packed my bags and tried not to think about how I might never see her again, or that if I did, she might not even recognize me. Instead, I busied myself by arranging for a cab or making sure the plane was on time.

On one of those visits, when she was still able to walk, she made her way into the kitchen about an hour before I was to leave. Later, as I put my suitcase in front of the door, she came over to me and pressed a brown paper bag into my hand. "Something for the plane," she said.

I thanked her and tucked it into my bookbag. Once on the plane, I held the bag in my lap. Somewhere over the black skies of Norfolk, Virginia, I took it into the bathroom and locked the door. I reached inside it and pulled out something soft wrapped in silver foil. A sandwich, I guessed. As I peeled back the aluminum, I recognized the smell right away. Cervelat—the garlicky salami that my grandfather used to import from Germany. Cervelat on white bread with butter—the same sandwich that my mother had packed in my lunch box every day for thirteen years. I ate the sandwich slowly knowing that this was the beginning of our saying good-bye.

Twenty-One

Sometimes a figure in the news moves into your head and starts to have a bearing on your day-to-day moods. In the spring of 1988, a forty-three-year-old man named Walter Hudson slipped and fell in the passageway between his bathroom and bedroom, and—because he weighed nearly 1,400 pounds—couldn't get up. The police were called in to help. At that time, his waist was more than nine feet around and each of his legs was fifty-six inches in diameter.

When he was fifteen, and only 350 pounds, Hudson declared that his legs could no longer carry him, so he stopped going out of his house. For the next twenty-eight years, he stayed in bed—naked—draped only in a sheet, getting out of bed once, when his family moved from a housing project in Brooklyn to a small house in Hempstead Village, Long Island. There he remained, living with relatives, including his sister, a registered nurse who might have noticed that he usually started his day by eating two pounds of bacon, thirty-two sausages, a dozen eggs, a loaf of bread, jam, and coffee.

Then he fell and all hell broke lose. *Newsday*, the local newspaper, responded to the police call and reported on the elaborate tactics that the police used to hoist Walter Hudson onto his feet. The New York tabloids followed. With his beatific smile and Cherokee braids, Hudson fascinated reporters, who turned poetic to describe him: "Like a fantastic Buddha carved out of dark granite," one wrote, "each breast wells out like a saddle bag, and comes to rest at his waist." Dick Gregory, the comedian turned health nut, contacted Hudson and offered to bring him to his weight-loss clinic in the Bahamas. When Hudson still refused to leave home, Gregory put him on his Bahamian powder diet, and his entourage camped out on Hudson's couch to insure that he wasn't sneaking food. The diet worked: he got down to 600 pounds. Hudson became something of a celebrity. He started Walter Hudson Ventures, a fashion line for overweight people, and he even got engaged.

After a while Gregory got fed up with being stuck in Hempstead Village and dropped Walter as a client. Hudson immediately gained back most of the weight, and on Christmas Eve 1991, four years after he first made the news, he died of heart failure. He was buried in a specially built 800-pound casket that was towed on a trailer and lowered into the ground by a crane.

My fascination with Walter Hudson wasn't about weight. It was about how he had slipped into the morass of excess and, to put it mildly, had a run of tough luck—all in public. I felt a surge of optimism when I read that he'd dropped to 600 pounds, and I cried with Kathie Lee the first day he walked out his front door and onto the *Live! with Regis and Kathie Lee* show.

During the summer of Walter Hudson, I rented a small

house in Sag Harbor, Long Island. It was a tiny mock Victorian with paper-thin walls and metal doorknobs that fell off the doors each time they slammed. But the house was close to the bay and tennis courts and was surrounded by the short piney shrubs indigenous to that part of the Island. It was a perfect weekend getaway, where I could ride my bike, play tennis, and hope that if I kept busy, no one will notice that I was carrying around nearly 1,400 pounds of loneliness on my five-foot five-inch frame.

The past months had been filled with various men who wanted to be my friend and others who disappeared after a few dates. I even made dinner for one of them, despite my usual lackluster performance in the kitchen. Roasted chicken. Finally, one made it out of the freezer and into the oven. I cooked it in a glass dish that I thought was oven-proof, and when the dish blew up splattering glass and chicken fat all over the oven, I realized it wasn't. It was too late to do much about it, so I washed off as many of the shards as I could, put it in another pan, then stuck it back in the oven. When I served it later that night, my guest was gracious—even funny. "Chicken under Glass," he called it, carefully spitting fragments of glass into his napkin. That was our last dinner together.

One morning I played tennis with a man I had met at a dinner party. He was also divorced and we talked about ex-spouses and renting houses in Sag Harbor. When we finished playing (he won), I asked if he would like to come back to my house for some lunch. "Oh, no," he answered quickly, "I have to go to a meeting this afternoon." So I went home, made a tuna fish sandwich, put on my bathing suit, and walked over to the bay. As I got closer to the shore, I saw a familiar form running in and out of the water in chase of someone else. It was my tennis partner, and he was running after a young blond in a yellow bikini.

I stood transfixed, my face flushed with embarrassment as they played in the waves together. "If you get my hair wet, I swear I'll kill you," she teased. He splashed her. She giggled, careful to keep her head high above the water. I backed away from the beach hoping no one had seen me. Then I ran as fast as I could, the hot sand burning the soles of my feet. Once inside the house, I slammed the door hard behind me. All I heard was the sound of six metal doorknobs hitting the hardwood floor. The dating thing wasn't working out so well.

One weekend, I drove out to Sag Harbor with my friend Pucci, who was also single. The talk turned to men and our stories inevitably sounded the same sad notes: unfeeling, cold, remote, deceitful.

Just as I'd told Bruce and Stan, I told Pucci, "I need to meet one of my own."

"Wait a minute," she said, her eyes widening. "My friend Bob has a weekend guest staying with him. He's very tall, funny, smart, around our age—"

"Sounds great."

"Only thing is, he recently got divorced and he's, um, a little depressed."

"Whoa. No, thank you. I've gone out with every depressed guy in New York. I think not."

Later that evening, I got a phone call from Pucci. "Bob would like us to come over for a drink. We won't stay more than a half an hour, I promise."

The air was so heavy that night, even the mosquitoes flew

low to the ground. Inside Bob's house, the smell of wine mingled in the sticky air. The light was dim. I was vaguely aware of
empty glasses on the floor and bare feet parked on the wood-
stained coffee table: the end of a sweaty, inebriated evening.
How soon could I get out of there?

Through the dull light, I glimpsed a large man. He had black
hair and a beard the same color, and he was wearing a black
shirt unbuttoned enough to reveal a thicket of dark hair on his
chest. He was seated in the middle of a couch, his outstretched
arms draped over the back so that fingertip to fingertip, the span
of his arms covered one end of the couch to the other. He
seemed to be staring through the darkness straight at me.

Clearly, this was Gary, the guy Pucci had mentioned in the
car: tall, around my age. I heard him laugh with Bob in a throaty
har, har way. Later, after Pucci introduced us, he laughed with
me, a sweeter, less boisterous laugh. We talked briefly about
Bob—whom I'd only met three minutes ago—and where we
each lived in the city. It didn't take me long to turn the conversation to what was foremost on my mind.

"So, have you been following this story about the guy in
Long Island who couldn't leave his house for twenty-eight years
because he weighed fourteen hundred pounds?"

"Have I been following it?" he answered emphatically. "I've
been living it. Walter Hudson and I, we're like this." He held
up his two thumbs side by side.

He was an editor at *Newsday*, the newspaper that first broke
the Hudson story, and had been involved in its continuing cov-
erage. We discussed Walter Hudson's diet, his sister, the nurse,
and speculated what the inside of his bedroom might look like

and what he kept in his closet. "Can you imagine how the old *Life* magazine would have played this story?" Gary asked.

I told him that, growing up, *Life* was the only magazine at our house. "I knew more about Elizabeth Taylor and Nicky Hilton than about my own parents," I said. He told me how his photograph appeared in *Life* when they did a piece about his first grade class. We talked about his parents, Austrian Jews who came to Washington Heights during the war. Now he lived only four blocks from me in the city. "Nice man," I said to Pucci as we left. "Smart. I'll bet we become good friends."

It didn't occur to me then that Gary might also be someone fun to date. When it came to men, I was used to difficult and remote; the darker the better. I particularly sought out men whom I could never reach; I seemed to like that a lot. But Gary—he was handsome, we came from similar backgrounds, we were in the same profession; he was charming and totally accessible. Why on earth would I ever go out with him?

That night, long after I'd stopped thinking about him, I slipped into my queen-sized bed in my otherwise empty bedroom in Sag Harbor. Unbidden, the image of the man on the couch flashed through my mind. "He'd fill this room nicely," I thought, before falling into a deep sleep.

Months later, Gary told me that the moment I walked into Bob's house that night, he felt a warm light spilling off of me.

"That's because I was wearing a yellow blouse with palm trees on it."

"No," he said, "it was more like sunshine."

After I left, he called the two people we knew in common: my old friend Kit Taylor, from *Esquire,* and her husband, Jack.

"She's the one," Jack told him. "We've had our eye on fixing the two of you up for years. Kit told her about you right after she and her husband split up."

What Jack told him next would have queered the deal for most men: "There's something about her that's a magnet for bad luck. She's had quite a run of it lately. Boom, boom, boom. One thing right after the other. It's too bad."

When I asked Gary if he had found Jack's words discouraging, he shook his head. "It just made me feel sad," he said.

The Monday after we met at Bob's house, an envelope arrived on my desk. Inside was all the copy on Walter Hudson since the story had first broken. Clipped on top of it was a note in jagged inverted handwriting: "I thought you'd want these for your files. Great to meet you Friday night, Gary."

When I called to thank him, we made a plan to go and see Laura Nyro at The Bottom Line. He wore Canoe cologne from what was surely a very old bottle. I worried that he hadn't found his dating legs yet, but when he put his arm around me during the concert, it felt warm and sheltering and like that was where I wanted to be. The weekend after Laura Nyro, he came out to visit Bob again in Sag Harbor. On Saturday morning we met for a bike ride.

Until I met Gary, I'd only been with men of average size: men I could have carried if I'd needed to; men whose clothes I could wear comfortably. But at six feet, four inches, Gary was way out of that range. His head alone looked to be a fifty-pounder. He crouched atop Bob's bike, his long athletic legs bent nearly up to his chin. He gripped the handlebars from underneath, and not surprisingly, the bike wobbled a bit once he got going.

It was a beautiful late summer's day. Roadside stands were filled with jars of dahlias the size of headlights and Popsicle colored zinnias. Gary stopped at one stand and bought me a bunch of flowers. "They go perfectly with your outfit," he said, smiling at my lemon shorts and orange top.

As we rode on, we talked and laughed like two old friends We counted the number of black Porsches and BMWs that rode by. We talked about how money didn't seem to make people in this part of the world any happier. "Just higher quality FMs." I said.

"What's an FM?" he shouted.

"Fashion Mistakes. You know, like men with pastel sweaters tied over their shoulders. Leather pants and bare midriffs."

"Oh, you mean like the Spandex bike outfits, and those silly symbols on golf shirts."

"What about guys at the beach in thongs? Eww."

As we yelled back and forth it occurred to me that I had laughed more in the past two hours than I had in the last two years and how I ought to pay attention to that.

By this time, we were riding single file on the long stretch of highway that runs between Sag Harbor and East Hampton. The highway was smooth with shiny black spots where fresh tar had just been poured. It wasn't the kind of road, or day, that would harbor a pothole. But that's what Gary's front tire hit. I watched as his bike crumbled and he was pitched to the side of the road, but I was following so closely behind, there was no time to slow down. My front tire hit his body and I flew five feet into the air. Shit, I thought. Which body part will it be this time? Miraculously, I didn't crash into the ground. Instead, Gary held out his left arm and caught me, breaking my fall. We lay there in the spoon position: Bob's flattened bicycle with zinnias and dahlias strewn around us. When we caught our breath, I was the first to speak.

"You know, there's this black cloud—but I didn't think it would catch up this fast." He was too stunned to answer.

It took nearly ten weeks for Gary's bruised spleen to recover. By that time he had already moved in with me.

Twenty-Two

I didn't tell Gary everything at once. Over time, we exchanged the fragile pieces of our lives. Sometimes, we played Russian roulette with our trust, telling each other things that were scary and intimate. Then we'd catch ourselves, and one of us would ask the other, "Do you still like me?" Reassured, we'd act out our deepest insecurities, testing each other in unspoken ways. He thought I didn't love him enough. I thought he harbored some black unspeakable secret. I knew that if my ex-shrink, Phoebe Slom, were still around, she'd reassure me: "Of course you have reason to worry that he has a dark spot. Everyone does, you know. You've just been unfortunate in finding out too late."

If anything, Gary was too emotionally accessible. He could brilliantly articulate his own defenses and neuroses, and had no trouble intuiting mine. Sometimes his thoughts—complicated and neatly soldered together—spilled out of him so quickly I could hardly keep up. After several months with him, it was hard to believe there was anything I hadn't heard or didn't know.

In the name of noticing things before it was too late, I kept score. Silently, I piled up evidence: a paper he'd written in the ninth grade about a lonely boy—the loneliest boy in the world— who finally killed himself because he had no friends. The melancholy music he composed and played on the guitar. The way tears welled up in his eyes when he talked about his dead dog, Willis, or his dead cat, Shere Khan. The bolts of anger that flashed across his eyes whenever the subject of golf came up. I was watching; I was listening. "Is there anything you see about Gary that you should tell me now?" I asked Miriam, who had never stopped reminding me that she knew Malcolm was gay from the moment she met him.

"Well, yes," she said, choosing her words carefully. "He appears to be moody."

On the first long weekend Gary and I spent together, we rented a small house in Vermont. We made love in a giant four-poster bed, hiked around a crystalline lake, played Ping-Pong, made popcorn, and watched old movies. Gary sang "We Are the World" and did a perfect imitation of everyone in the song— including Cyndi Lauper and Ray Charles. Weekends don't get more perfect than that one. On the way home, we stopped for an early dinner at an old inn on the New York-Connecticut border. I sat across from him, watching his warm face bathed in the candlelight, and smiled at the wonder that this time I might get it right. Here was a man who was smart and so funny, a sympathetic soul, a comfort. One of my own.

It was a lovely moment; one I wish would have lasted longer. Lost in my own bliss, I hadn't noticed Gary's complete digression.

Now his voice had deepened and he was gesturing with both hands, using words like *valence* and *Socratic method*. The passion of his own anger fueled him as his face flushed and his speech got faster. I tried to understand what he was talking about—something about private schools, I thought, but realized I'd missed that train minutes earlier.

A horrible feeling, the bottom falling out of a bag of garbage, swept over me. My brain went into full alert, and I heaved a sorry sigh. Oh, God, I thought. I can't believe it. I knew what his secret was.

When he finished railing, I tried to smile supportively—an insincere upward turn of the lips, no teeth—and reached my hand across the table to stroke his broad cheek. "I know, I know," I kept repeating. He smiled back.

"It's okay, it really is."

By now I was rubbing his cheek so hard, his skin was starting to turn red. "I know, I know."

Gary's smile faded into bewilderment. "What? What is it that you know?"

I leaned forward. "I think you've been institutionalized."

He leaned forward. "What?"

"I think you've been institutionalized," I said.

"I don't know what you're talking about," he said.

"It's okay, it is. Everyone goes through hard times. It's great that you actually did something about it."

"*What the hell are you talking about?*"

"You know, it doesn't bother me at all." My voice was soothing, if a little brittle. "I love you for who you are now." All I could think about was getting back to the city unharmed. "What's in the past is in the past."—and getting his stuff out of my apartment—"Isn't it great how open we can be with each other?"—without inciting a psychotic episode.

We rode back to New York mostly in silence. Every now and then we exchanged clipped conversation. "How's your week going to be?" "Busy. And yours?" "Same." It was hard to believe that we were the same two people who, earlier that weekend, had made love for hours and laughed through *Taxi* reruns at three in the morning. Gary later said that after the conversation in the restaurant, he worried I might be far crazier than I had ever imagined he was. By the time we got home his steely anger and resolve had me pretty convinced that he was telling the truth; that he never had been institutionalized. I tucked my doubts away under, "Things to Keep an Eye On."

Being in love with Gary rounded my edges. *Miracle . . . reclaim*. The words did happy cartwheels in my head. With the insurance money from the fire, we bought a house that needed total redoing. It was on a beautiful spot on Long Island, atop a bluff overlooking Gardiner's Bay. We planted tulips, roses and an assortment of wild beach grasses, and painted the trim and deck a Miami sea green. We rebuilt the house so that the rooms were airy and filled with the smell and reflection of the water. At night, the sun dipped into the bay, filling the sky outside our windows with showy splashes of color. It was a happy house, and spoke to the dreams and giddiness of two people newly in love.

Life danced along to a ballad for a while, the only dissonance being my mother's illness. All my life my mother had tried to pull me away from danger, even breaking up with bad boyfriends for me when she had to. Now I was with someone who was good to me, who made me feel happy, and it was important to me that she meet Gary and understand that, while there was still time.

· · ·

Because it was the day before Christmas, the DC-10 to Fort Lauderdale was packed like a jar of herring. We were in the last row where Gary, and an even larger man reading *Model Railroader*, flanked me like Great Danes. Back there in the belly of the plane, the constant rumbling and groaning made conversation impossible.

As the plane began its descent, my eardrums felt as if they might burst. I swallowed, I yawned, I pulled my mouth back into a death-mask grimace, hoping to turn down the pain. Nothing. Then I realized I'd gone completely deaf.

"Ahh, my ears," I said, cupping them with my hands. Gary handed me a stick of Juicy Fruit and made exaggerated chewing motions as if, in my deafness, I'd forgotten what to do with gum. The other guy gave me a lemon sourball.

"Thanks," I screamed, sucking and chewing at the same time.

Suddenly, the churning stopped and everything went still. We dropped onto Fort Lauderdale as gently as a coconut to the beach. My ears popped, and normal sounds jetted through my head. The stewardess pulled open the doors, and we stepped out of the plane.

"Do you smell mildew, you know, like damp towels?" Gary asked.

"Yup," I answered. "Home sweet home."

At the gate, I looked around and hoped against hope that someone would be there, waving and laughing when they spotted us. But of course, that wasn't possible now. As we walked impatiently behind rows of visiting grandchildren, and made our way to the cab line, I got lost thinking about past reunions at this airport—coming back from Ann Arbor, bringing Malcolm home for the first time. It was easy to forget the present whenever I came to this place. Gary grabbed my hand in a gesture that reminded me that we were here and this was now.

The cab driver took us the longest way around. His long brown fingers tapped the steering wheel in time to a Tito Puente song playing on the radio. I didn't feel like breaking his concentration. Besides, it felt strange and awkward bringing Gary to Miami—like bringing a date home to meet my parents, even though this date was the man I planned to marry—and I wasn't in any hurry.

An antiseptic smell greeted us as we stepped out of the elevator in my parents' building. I knew immediately it was coming from their apartment. We followed the salmon-colored rug with its palm-leaf border to Apartment 10-C, where the door was slightly ajar. Inside, my father was seated in the wooden armchair wearing the same coffee-brown pants he had worn during my last three visits. My mother was lying on the couch in a freshly pressed pink-and-white checked robe. She was wearing lipstick that ran slightly askew on her face. It struck me that they had been sitting this way for hours. As soon as he saw Gary, my father jumped to attention and put his hand over his eyebrows as if he were about to salute. Then he threw back his head in an exaggerated gesture of looking at the sky.

"You must be Gary," he said, standing on tiptoes.

"I'm not *that* tall," said Gary, smiling and shaking my father's hand. He was plenty versed in big-guy jokes. "But I am Gary."

Then Gary sat down next to my mother on the couch. "I'm

so happy to meet you," he said, placing his hand on her shoulder. "I've heard so much about you." She rolled her eyes as if to say, "I can only imagine what she's told you."

Over the next few days, Gary stayed by my mother's side. Sometimes they talked; other times, he read while she slept. By now, we didn't dare leave my mother alone in the apartment. At night, a nurse slept next to her in bed; my father had moved to the couch. Often he and I went out together, leaving Gary to watch over my mother. I wanted him to get to know the mother who read voraciously and could size up the measure of a man in a heartbeat. "I can see that in her eyes," he told me.

Every once in a while, she looked at Gary, then said to me, "Very big. Very big." That wasn't enough. I wanted to know that she saw more.

One afternoon, we both sat by her bedside and showed her our photographs. Most of them were pictures of the new house, but there were also some of a nearby restaurant that looked out onto sailboats in the sunset. "That's where we're going to get married," I said. I pointed to a spot on the terrace overlooking the water. "See, right there." It was hard to know what my mother understood these days.

She studied the pictures of the house, then looked again at the ones of the restaurant on the bay. She pointed to the gold ring on her left hand. "Married?" she asked.

"Yeah, Mom, Gary and I are going to get married."

Her eyes filled with tears—maybe because she knew she wouldn't be able to make it to the wedding, or maybe because she was just happy for us. Her eyes filled with tears a lot these days, and maybe it had nothing to do with anything except her own memories and their private connections. Gary bent down and kissed her on the cheek. "I promise you that I'll take good care of your daughter," he said.

She patted his hand, then squeezed it. "Kind man," she said staring up at me.

"I know," I said, relieved that she understood.

If only my mother had made it to the wedding, she'd have met the characters that have populated our phone calls over the past years. Pete, Helen, Phillip, Nina and Nicky, Bruce and his kids and his sisters and nieces, the *New York Woman* gang—all the people who filled in the spaces where my own family left off. When I heard my father speak in German to Gary's mother, I expected to hear my mother's voice answer. Miriam, her son Jonathan, my father and I posed for family pictures. We all stood with our hands dangling at our sides, like there was something we should be holding on to that was missing.

The morning after the wedding, I called home. Sonia, the nurse, answered. "She wants to know everything," Sonia said. I told her about the sunset, how after the ceremony, I was so emotional I nearly stopped breathing. I talked about the funny toasts and how we danced until I collapsed on a couch at 1:30. When I told Sonia that Gary carried me out of the restaurant just as they were bringing out the garbage, she repeated it slowly and in a loud voice to my mother. "I wish you could see her face," Sonia said. "She's laughing with you."

Twenty-Three

By this time, I should have understood that it's all a matter of filling in the space between now and the next time you get clobbered. But during that one week between my wedding and the fifth anniversary party for *New York Woman,* life was giving me a smooth ride.

A recession was chewing up New York, and I'd had to make drastic cuts in the magazine's budget. The issues were getting thinner, the advertising more scarce. I had to lay off two people in the fashion department, and I had a bad feeling there was more to come. We noticed that the American Express executives had stopped dropping by. Several magazines in the city had already shut down. It was a nervous time for publishing. But I kept telling myself that any time was a nervous time for people in publishing.

On the night of the party, it was easy to drown out any concerns I might have had. Kit McClure and the All Girl Band filled every corner of Larabelle's with loud, danceable music. There were celebrities everywhere and photographers desperate to photograph them. American Express executives kissed me on the cheek while their wives told me how much they liked the magazine. Even the mayor showed up for a brief time. How could a magazine that gave a party like this be in any kind of trouble? I kept asking myself. Then I thought, Why do you keep asking the same question?

The next morning, the staff straggled into work still groggy with last night's euphoria. As we gossiped about The Guerilla Girls' outfits, Tom's assistant, Lisa, called me. "Some party, can you believe the turnout?" I started to chat.

She was uncharacteristically abrupt. "Tom wants to have lunch with you today. Can you meet him at Zen Palate at one?"

What an odd choice for a restaurant, I thought. Zen Palate was strictly vegetarian; Tom was a meat-and-potatoes guy. I remembered how Tom stood back and watched all of us dancing the night before without saying a word. I hung up and continued to share in the gossip about the party, though it kept gnawing at me that he'd chosen Zen Palate for lunch.

Every piece I'd ever read about breaking up advises you to do it in a public place; ideally, a restaurant. As restaurants go, Zen Palate was as soothing as a spa. The lighting was low; there were large pots of rubber tree plants, and the music playing sounded airy, as if it were being blown through bamboo stalks. It was the last place anyone would want to make a scene. We sat down, and I waited for Tom to ask his usual provocative questions: "So tell me everything about the honeymoon. How's the big guy?" But he didn't say any of it. He ordered tofu; now I was really worried. I ordered a rice and mushroom casserole. Tom's jaw was fixed as if he were trying to keep his face from falling. He picked up his chopsticks and started rubbing them together. "This recession," he began, "it's a bitch. Your numbers are killing you. Your circulation is in the toilet, advertising's awful. I have to tell you, American Express is rethinking their commitment to its city magazines."

The food came. I still hadn't thought of anything to say, and he wasn't leaving me much space in which to say it. "Betsy. . . ." he said, poking at his tofu as if it were a dead mouse. I knew I was in for it. "Frankly, we've tried to find a buyer for *New York Woman* and we couldn't. So it's up to you, if you want to give it a try . . ."

He didn't finish his thought. I understood what this meant. If I couldn't find someone to put up money for the magazine, they were going to fold it. My face got hot and I could feel the mushrooms backing up on me. But we were in Zen Palate, centered, relaxing Zen Palate—how could I make a fuss? He told me for the time being I should keep this information to myself. Neither of us finished our food.

That afternoon, I was supposed to go with the staff to a sale in Danbury, Connecticut. Just before we boarded the train, I thought about calling Gary from a pay phone at Grand Central. We'd only been back from our honeymoon for two days. Should I start dumping my world on him so soon? But I needed to hear his voice, so I picked up the phone, and told him what Tom had told me. There was a pause, he was probably biting on his finger, something I knew he did when he got nervous. Then he said all the right things, that he was sorry, but that he had faith that whatever happened, I would be fine. "I love you, honey," he said. "Be brave." The word *brave* sounded sad and heavy to me and my eyes filled with tears. I didn't want to be *brave*. I just wanted my magazine to survive.

Wanting something so badly made me feverish. It filled me with a furious drive that was irrational, and bordered on obsession. For the next three months, I ran around town making presentations to media companies and independent moguls, hoping somebody would buy my magazine. Once again, my friend Bruce offered me help. There was this guy, Lou, who worked in his investment banking firm and did all their media deals. Lou would help me for as long as I needed.

I was racing against the clock: I had until the new year, only three months, to find a buyer. We continued to work on the magazine, filled with hope against hope that we would keep publishing. Most nights, I met Lou at his office. We made lists and plotted strategy. As long as there were lists and strategies, there was hope. Each night I came home and told Gary what Lou said and whom I was going to see the next day. "There's this company in St. Louis that owns paper mills," I told him, my voice trilling with excitement. "They may be looking to get into the magazine business. We'd be a perfect way in for them."

One night Lou told me that he thought we'd made a good connection. "Sid Farber's the number two guy in a major publishing organization," he said, "They're ambitious to grow the company, and he wants to meet with you tomorrow." That night at dinner, I told Gary about Sid. "I feel optimistic about this one," I said, knowing full well about Sid's awful reputation.

"I don't," said Gary, who by this time had started up his own magazine about the media. "Guy's a scumbag. He's an old newspaper man, a real son of a bitch." I'd seen pictures of Sid in the papers. Fat and balding, he always had a young beauty on his arm. He smoked cigars and looked smug, like he believed women actually liked him for his personality. Exactly the kind of man Gary hated.

The next morning I showed up early for my meeting with Farber. He kept me waiting in his office long enough for me to study his photgraphs showing him with famous people. There he was with Cheryl Tiegs and with Magic Johnson; there was even a picture of him, in uniform, at baseball fantasy camp. There was a hard hat hanging on the door. It seemed as if he was trying awfully hard to be one of the guys. When he finally came in, he was smoking his famous cigar. "Tell me what you've got," he said, sitting on his couch, his legs spread apart. I gave my presentation in as sunny a manner as I could muster; I couldn't tell if he was paying attention. "Let me ask you something," he interrupted. "Why would you think I'd be interested in a magazine that has no circulation and is dying on the vine? It's not like I *need* a fucking women's magazine." He looked at his watch.

"Sorry to waste your time," I said.

"Yeah, well, whatever." He smiled. "Good luck, you'll need it."

I felt as if I'd been exposed and taunted just to satisfy one man's need for cruel pleasures. That night, when Gary asked me how it went, I was too humiliated to tell him the truth.

In the meantime, I had to keep the staff busy and hope that too many people wouldn't jump ship in case we found another buyer. American Express said they would continue to pay us but they wouldn't publish another issue until there was the promise of a sale, so each day we showed up for work and watched *Guys and Dolls*, and *Casablanca*, and took long lunches. A friend sent me an African violet with a note saying she was sorry this was happening. Wrapped in purple foil, the plant sat on the side of my desk and never produced a single blossom.

The art department was empty and the computers were shut down. Writers didn't visit our offices anymore; the phones hardly rang. There was no reason to have meetings, no one needed to close my door and have an urgent discussion about anything. It was too sad to watch the slow dismantling of it all, so I lost myself in making presentations and setting up more meetings, even if, in my heart, I knew they were futile.

By Christmas, Lou was out of suggestions. Whenever the subject of the sale came up, Gary looked away and talked about other things. One night he snapped at me, "Give it up already. You're not going to win this one."

Over Christmas, I developed a high fever. For the first time in my life, I got laryngitis. One afternoon Pete called. I croaked: "I've lost my voice. I think that's a pretty blatant metaphor, don't you?"

"You know, you haven't been a whole lot of fun lately," he said. "Maybe you should think about getting a bird."

After the Christmas break, it was hard to face work—or not work—again. The routine of watching movies at the office and killing time felt pathetic. Every couple of days, someone showed up in an Ann Taylor suit. Job interview! Who could blame them? On the first Monday back, Gary asked me to meet him for lunch at a nearby diner. I looked forward to it as a break in the day; it was the first time we'd met for lunch since getting married. I slid into the booth beside him and he gave me a weak smile, not a kiss or a hug. His voice was cold and he struggled for words. "What's wrong?" I kept prodding. Finally he answered.

"I can't stand this anymore. This *New York Woman* thing has taken over your life. We just got married. You're never home and when you are, all you talk about is the sale of the magazine. I'm not sure this is going to work out."

I assumed he was talking about the magazine. "I know it might not work out, but don't you think I have to try everything before I give up?"

He shook his head. His face shut down and dark clouds moved in. "I'm not talking about the magazine," he said. "I'm talking about our marriage. I'm not sure it's going to work."

I was incredulous. All the indignation from the last few months welled up inside me.

"I come back from getting married, find out that my magazine might be about to go out of business unless I can find someone to buy it, and you're telling me that because I find this upsetting, and because I'm trying to save the magazine I started and have been running for five and a half years, that our marriage might not work out?" I was practically shouting.

Hadn't we just spelled out "for better or worse" in front of everyone we knew? Wasn't this a little early to bail out because of "worse"? Secretly, I thought I should have followed my instincts; of course he'd been institutionalized; he was probably a psychopath, a commitment-phobe, a—who knows what else. And here I'd gone and married him.

"It's just that I think the magic is gone," he said.

Until you've heard the phrase, "the magic is gone" come out of the mouth of someone you love, it's hard to imagine how apt the cliché "cut my heart out with a knife" can be. The words left me frozen. Suddenly, I couldn't stand to be in the same room with him. I squeezed out of the booth and ran into the street. "As soon as this mess is over," I vowed to myself, "I will pack my bags, move to LA, and get away from him and this whole awful business of magazines."

Later that afternoon, I called Gary from a phone booth. Our voices were tender; clearly we'd both been shaken by our earlier conversation. He apologized for his strong use of language. He explained that he needed to say something startling so that I would understand how fed up he was with what he believed to be my futile attempt to sell the magazine. He loved me, he said. I told him I loved him too. "We'll have chicken for dinner," I said.

"And baked potatoes," he added.

"Pinkies," I said.

"Pinkies."

For the moment we retreated into domestic snugness. Still, the dreaded words *the magic is gone,* stayed with me.

The following night, Tom called me into his office. His eyes wouldn't meet mine. "This is it," he said. "We're out of time and potential buyers. Tomorrow we pull the plug." By this point, I was almost relieved. I began to make a mental list of whom I would call to try and help the staff get new jobs. Tom and I decided that I would gather them in my office in the morning, then he'd come downstairs and deliver the news. "It's important that neither of us cry," he said. "I know this is hard for you, Betsy, but try to be brave." It was the second time in three months that someone had told me to be brave. By now it seemed beside the point.

The next morning everyone met in my office and waited for Tom. No one said anything. We all knew why we were there. Pale, angry faces greeted him as he walked over to my desk and stood beside me. True to my word, I was dry-eyed. I stared at the floor and waited for him to speak. There were no sounds. I looked up and saw Tom open and close his mouth like a marionette. His face turned red and his eyes filled with tears. "I didn't want this day to ever happen," he cried. "I am so sad, so very very sad."

The next day, we held a wake. Writers, photographers, friends and relatives wandered in and out of the halls drinking wine and eating popcorn. We talked and reminisced, and mostly we cried. We were passionate about this magazine—the possibilities of ideas, the thrill of creating something so smart and original that we were sure it could change the world—and now it would be gone. I hated the capriciousness of the business and the way magazine owners could give and take at a whim. I swore to myself that I would never so desperately want something that was ultimately in the hands of someone else.

Before I left the office that night, I went into Helen's office. Ann Kwong was there; she was four months pregnant. Helen was packing up pictures of her son, Toby; Ann was making plans for our first reunion dinner. I took the sterile African violet and dumped it into Helen's trash. "Well, so much for that," I said, trying to sound lighthearted. "Now what shall we do?" We each offered up a stricken smile, none of us saying what was obvious: that *New York Woman* was already slipping into our past.

Twenty-Four

As a consolation prize, American Express sent me to something called an outplacement center. It was really an expensive day care center for burnt-out former executives. "It will help you think about where you want to go from here," the woman in Human Resources assured me. Her statement begged many questions, none of which I bothered to voice out loud.

I had my first appointment at the center on the day after the magazine closed. I was wearing a blue sweater. I remember the blue sweater because when I started crying, my counselor, Bernice, handed me a tissue and noted how perfectly it matched my sweater. I heard concern in her voice and that made me cry. Behind Bernice's desk was a beautiful photograph of an empty beach right after a wave had crashed to the shore. The picture made me cry. Being at the outplacement center with the other displaced executives—mostly men who shuffled around in cardigans or sat in the lounge reading the want ads for hours at a time—made me cry. Bernice sat with her hands folded in her lap as I blew my nose.

Then, as if we'd already started talking, I said: "I failed. Not only that, but I brought everyone down with me. I don't think you understand; I have nothing to fall back on."

Bernice moved to the edge of her chair and flipped the edge of her scarf behind her head. Then she stabbed her finger at my résumé. "No, you don't understand," she said, her voice deepening. "You have everything to fall back on, you just don't know that yet. You feel bereft now, and your grief is very appropriate." She stared at the picture of the waves. "You're still out there somewhere," she said, pointing to the blue water in the background. "You're not even close to shore."

I cried even harder. She scribbled notes onto her legal pad, then added, "It's so wonderful how in touch with your feelings you are. You're doing so well."

As part of the program, I took a battery of aptitude tests. The results were not startling: I scored high in enthusiasm, bossiness and the need to be noticed, and low in orderliness, planning, and social conformity. They told me I had the most in common with photographers and musicians and the least in common with emergency medical technicians and Air Force enlisted personnel.

At our third meeting, Bernice drew a diagram of a rectangle divided by a diagonal line to form two triangles. The upper triangle was labeled "Old situation"; the lower one, "New situation." The diagonal was called "Transition." "Transition is a cold, swift current," she said. "You have no choice but to dive into the cold water and start gasping and swimming." She turned to the photograph on her wall, pointed to a dot in the middle of the water, and said, "You're about here."

"Figuratively, I'm nowhere then," I said, straining to see how far off shore I was.

She handed me a tissue. "Sometimes the best thing to do after a situation like this is get out of town," she said. "Get away from the place where it all happened and go somewhere you've never been. Can you do that?"

When I told Gary about Bernice's suggestion, his eyes brightened. "Sounds like the right idea," he said. In the week since the magazine folded, he worked late every night and I split my days between talking on the phone to ex–*New York Woman* staffers and reading the condolence mail I was getting about the magazine. Nothing had happened to bring the magic back and though neither of us admitted it, we both knew that a break was exactly what we needed.

I used some of my severance money to go to a spa in Arizona. I'd never been to a spa, but it sounded like a place where I could lie down and people would take care of me. I bought spandex shorts and a matching bra and, by the time I came home, Gary had made the airplane reservations using our frequent flier miles. First thing the next morning, I left for Arizona.

There was something about this spa that naturally separated the people who were there to have a good time from those who were there to recover from something awful. They must have pegged me as a charter member of the something awful group, because I was assigned to a windowless bungalow at the end of the service driveway, where the sound of laundry trucks on the gravel road was the last thing I heard as I fell asleep at night.

On my first morning, I took a tennis lesson. My backhand was wildly out of control, and I kept hitting high lobs over my instructor's head. Finally, he called me to the net.

"You're strung tighter than a cat in heat," he said, white

teeth gleaming against his tan. "What kind of job do you have, lady?"

He meant this to be a light remark, something to relax me, I knew that, but my words still bubbled with tears.

"I don't have any job," I said. "The magazine I edited just went out of business."

"Well, fine then. More time to pay attention to your foot-work." It was clear he'd heard it all before.

That afternoon I went for a massage. The masseuse tried to be discreet about the tension he felt in my back and neck. "Jim-miny Cricket," he said, kneading his fingers into the knots under my shoulder blades. "You might want to check out our yoga classes." I lay on the table and tried to relax into the music. The music: it sounded awfully familiar. "Adagio for Strings," by Sam-uel Barber. The theme to *Platoon*.

That night, and for the next three nights after that, I found myself at the sad table for dinner, the one for those of us who sneaked away into our bungalows during the day to cry. We were the guests who'd come alone and naturally gravitated to one another. We spooned clumps full of spaghetti squash and carrot and raisin salad onto our plates, and talked about the grievous events that had brought us to the Arizona desert.

On the first night, a woman from Philadelphia with dark half-moon circles under her eyes told us that she'd just found out her husband had another wife and two children in London. A woman with short red curls and a baby voice told us that she'd recently been operated on for uterine cancer and would be starting chemotherapy when she went home to Atlanta. The woman with the cheating husband threw her arms around the woman with cancer and started to cry. "Does it ever end?" she sobbed. I stayed quiet, realizing how lucky I was. That night, I went to bed grateful for the lullaby of laundry trucks.

On my final night at the spa, there was a newcomer to the sad table: Kirsten from Austin, Texas. Kirsten from Austin seemed like someone who was meant to always be cheerful. She had laugh lines around her mouth and delivered her sentences like someone used to having an audience. Even as she told the story of her husband, Larry the low-life, as she called him, she couldn't help being funny. "Here I am in Texas, teaching Bible school, no less, while Mr. Low-Life is traveling the world for IBM and doing the Lord's work in California." Turned out, Larry had a wife and three kids in Pasadena. It seemed a trend was developing. I made a mental note to call my friend Ellen at *Redbook* when I got home. Bernice was right. Getting away was the best thing I could have done. I was actually starting to feel blessed that all I had to worry about was losing a job and having a husband who didn't like me anymore.

Back home, I had to face life without a title. This was the first time in my adult life that I'd been out of work. I wasn't "Betsy Carter from *Newsweek*," or "Betsy Carter from *Esquire*" or "Betsy Carter from *New York Woman*." I was trying to build a résumé of a different sort. I took up squash; my teacher started calling me Tiger. I wrote freelance articles and did consulting work for magazine companies. Mail started coming to my house addressed to "Betsy Carter, Media Consultant." Gary and I were getting along better, though there was a polite distance between us. I was sure the magic still wasn't back. By

early spring, the exhaustion of winter wore away and I felt excited about the future. I even started to write a book. Bernice
was big on seizing the moment. "Most people get on one track
their whole lives and stay there," she said. "You've been kicked
off yours. Second chances don't come along all the time." I was
beginning to feel that maybe mine had come.

Twenty-Five

This was not how I chose to spend July Fourth. It's my favorite holiday. Picnics, Malcolm's blueberry crumb cake, barbecued chicken, fireworks at the beach with Gary. And here I was in a hospital, taped and stitched and dragging bottles and tubes behind me like one of those Mama Duck–Baby Ducks pull toys.

One month earlier, on my birthday no less, I'd gone to see my gynecologist for a routine checkup. It was my first birthday since *New York Woman* folded five months earlier, and I spent it alone—no cake, peonies, or colleagues to sing "Happy Birthday to you." Even Gary was out of town.

The doctor greeted me that morning with a large smile. "Wow, you look great," he said. "I'm sure the rest of you is doing just as well." Anyone with even a modicum of superstition would have heard that sentence, knocked wood, and spit over her shoulder, but it went right by me. He chatted as he checked my breasts. Suddenly, his fingers stopped at a spot under my left arm and the smile went out of his voice. "There's something here," he said. "I'm sure it's nothing, a cyst maybe. But you should get a mammogram as soon as possible."

That night, Gary came home in time for us to go out to dinner. "I don't feel very festive," I said. "The way he said 'as soon as possible. . . .'" I never finished that sentence.

The next day after my mammogram, the technician held my X ray up to the light and pointed to something that looked like a snowball under my left arm. "Look at that," she said. "Pretty big. I'll send it over to your doctor this afternoon." Late that same day I got a call from my gynecologist. He'd already made an appointment for me to see a breast surgeon the following morning.

When I called the surgeon's office to try and postpone the appointment, the receptionist said, "I don't think that's a good idea." I tried telling her that I had a meeting at the same time, some important project I was working on. "I really don't think that's a good idea," she repeated.

"Oh boy," I said.

The next morning, Gary came with me. The surgeon looked kind, but he also looked like someone who was used to delivering bad news. He studied my X ray, then palpated the lump under my left arm. "I don't like this," he said. He did a needle aspiration, withdrawing fluid from the lump, which he would test to see whether or not the growth was malignant. "I'll have the results this afternoon," he said. "Come back at three."

Gary and I went home. We opened the fold-out couch in the living room and lay down, pretending we were watching television. We held hands and didn't talk. What was there to say? There was no diagnosis, just possibilities, one more awful than the next. When we came back at three, the doctor called us into his office right away. A doctor who doesn't make you wait is a bad sign. He didn't even bother with euphemisms. "It's a tumor, a big one," he said. I watched Gary's face sag and his mouth hang open. "You know, malignant," he repeated in case we'd missed it the first time. "Go get a second opinion if you want, but I think you need a mastectomy and chemotherapy, and I wouldn't waste time."

When we left his office, Gary and I hugged each other and cried.

"The only way we're going to get through this," I said, "is if we tell each other everything that's on our minds."

"Okay, I'm afraid you're going to die."

I pushed his arms off of me and said, "That is totally un- acceptable. Don't ever say that again." Especially since that was exactly what was on my mind.

I called nearly everyone I knew. I told my friend Susan that I'd either end up divorced or married more than ever by the time this was over. She told me, "Remember this is not a death sentence."

In the next days, no one bothered to tell me to be brave— do whatever you need to, was what everyone said. But nothing could quiet the ruckus in my head. Helen called all the *New York Woman* staff; my friends Susan, Susan, and Victoria came over at night and ordered in pizza with us. Miriam told me about all of my mother's friends who lived fifteen and twenty years after having mastectomies. I couldn't stand the sorrowful tone in people's voices when they spoke to me. I couldn't face what had suddenly become routine—going back to the hospital for yet another test. The hope was that the malignancy was contained in one place, but we wouldn't know that for certain until after the surgery. If Gary thought that the magic was gone four months earlier, what would he think when I was minus a breast? We had been married for nine months, nine rocky months. This latest news overwhelmed us both and we asked the surgeon to give us the name of a therapist.

He called that afternoon. "Her name's Greta Friedman," he said. "She specializes in cancer patients and their families." *Greta Friedman,* I wrote. The letters up and did a fandango then settled down as *am great friend.* As omens went, this was the only sliver of hope I had.

The next afternoon I took a cab to Greta's office, where I was going to meet Gary. I thought I was holding myself together pretty well until the cab pulled up in front of her building. I paid the driver then opened the door to get out. The next thing I remember was a man in his early twenties with a Mickey Mouse watch and shoulder-length curly hair helping me to my feet and giving me a handkerchief for my bleeding arm. Somehow, I don't know how, I fell out of the cab and into the gutter.

"Good heavens, what happened to you?" asked Greta, as she opened the door.

"I fell out of a cab. My arm, it's bleeding. I don't remember what happened."

She went into the bathroom and came out with a wet towel. "Here, this should help."

When Greta wasn't being a psychologist, she was an artist. Her putty-colored walls were filled with collages she'd created. She built small boxes and filled them with scraps of egg cartons, fragments of shells, hunks of rope, half-burnt matchbook covers, nubby fabric swatches, scraps of metal all pieced together in odd shapes and pleasing colors. They looked like what you might see if you opened a child's cigar box of treasures. They were mesmerizing. I supposed the message she was trying to communicate by having them all around her office was that Greta saw art in everything.

For the month that led up to the surgery, Greta took us gently through the language of cancer: Chemo, mouth sores, nausea, reconstruction. "What will you think when Betsy goes bald?" she asked Gary.

He rubbed his own saucer-sized bald spot. "That I have a comrade," he answered.

Greta frowned. "This is no time to be evasive."

"How can he possibly know how he'll feel about it?" I jumped to his defense while imagining the worst.

"The hair will come out in clumps," she persisted. "It will fall out in the shower and on your pillow, and for a while you'll look thatchy and then you'll be bald." It was important to get fitted for the wig now, while I still had my hair. "The chemo. You'll feel flulike all the time. The oddest smells and tastes will make you nauseous."

"Let's talk about breasts," she began one session two weeks before the surgery.

"Fine," I said. "But before we get started, I have a question for you?"

"What is it?"

"I need to find an exorcist. Can you help me?"

"An exorcist? Why on earth would you need to find an exorcist?"

I explained about Phoebe and my past life.

"I must say, I've been hit with everything before. But an

exorcist? This is a new one. Everything is so out of control for you right now, but an exorcist won't make the cancer go away."

"Yes, but if I'm being punished for a past life, maybe this is the only way to stop it."

"Yes but. . . ."

We went back and forth that way for four sessions. The question never got resolved, it just got pushed aside by other distractions. There were CAT scans, bone scans, a colonoscopy, countless blood tests, trips to Ralph the chatty wig-maker, who told me that he put aside his work for the Orthodox women whenever a "sick emergency" (that would be me) came along. Every minute was filled with a reminder that from this time forward, the texture of my days would never be the same, and that the promise of time ahead was something I would never take for granted.

Those days are a blur, even now, ten years later. Tins of popcorn arrived at the house; someone sent a juicer. Cards came from people I barely knew saying that they'd heard the news and they were praying for me; one friend sent earrings because she didn't know what else to do. I remember Gary sitting in countless waiting rooms fidgeting in chairs that were always too small for him. "Men get freaked by this kind of stuff," Greta had warned. "It won't be smooth."

But that part went more smoothly than I could have imagined. Because I was so anxious, I didn't remember anything that any doctor said to me. Gary sat next to me during each appointment. He carried a notepad and wrote everything down. He started a file in the computer called "Betsy Stuff," where he wrote down what each doctor said.

Two days before the surgery, my father called. "Your mother

wants to talk to you. I don't know how much she knows, so be careful what you say."

By now, it had become impossible to talk with her on the phone. "Hi, Mom," I said, trying to sound cheerful. "How are you feeling?"

There was silence on her end, and I could tell she was straining to say something. "Ma—le—vo—lent," she said, carefully unfolding the word. "Ma—le—vo—lent."

I knew exactly what she meant. "Yes," I said, "I have a malignant breast tumor. I'm going to be fine, but I promise I'll answer any question you have." She had no questions. It was the last time we ever talked about it.

The night before I went into the hospital, I overheard Gary on the phone. "We'll be in for a week, and three weeks later we start chemo." Horrible words, yet the "we" laid to rest my worst fears about him.

After the surgery, I had a tube coming out of my back where they took tissue for the reconstruction. The front of me felt like a train wreck, like I had a wooden breast. The first two days, I was in a drug/pain fog. I remember being wheeled back into my room after surgery and seeing Ron standing next to Gary. I saw the concern in their faces and tried to say, "It's so nice to see you," but I don't know if they heard. The only other thing I remember from those first two days was a woman with scuffed shoes and brown hair falling in her face sitting at the edge of my bed. She told me that her name was Dr. Julia Smith and that she was going to be my oncologist. She told me the tumor was out and that I wasn't going to die. "We'll ride this out together," she said. She had kind eyes. I had no more tumor. Did you know that an anagram for *no more tumor* is *me room to run*? Later Greta Friedman agreed that I had finally had the exorcism.

By July Fourth, three days after the surgery, I was walking around and starting to have company. Lucky for me, my room at New York University Hospital was on a high floor; I'd have a front row seat for the fleet of tall ships that would go down the East River and, later, for the fireworks.

I asked a doctor on my floor why most New York hospitals overlook either the Hudson River or the East River. "This would make tossing out toxic wastes or dumping dead bodies into the river convenient," he said. Was that meant to be some kind of a doctor joke? I never found out.

Early that morning Gary called to say he'd be there by 8:00. "I'd better start fixing my hair—while I still have it," I said. We'd been making a lot of hair jokes lately, trying to make the inevitable seem like something we'd actually planned. I put on lipstick, and sat in a chair by the window waiting for him. We were careful with each other, like people on a second date. Same questions, different context. How would it be to have sex with him? What would he think when he saw me naked? We had new secrets now, but unlike when we were dating and telling each other everything, we kept these to ourselves.

"You look great today," he said, bending over to kiss me. He put his arm around my right shoulder as we watched the tall ships, surrounded by a team of tug boats and police boats, chugging down the river. Just like me and Gary and my friends. Flanked so close, they weren't going to let me sink.

Someone gasped behind me: Ellen. She'd walked into the middle of this tableau—my back, Gary's tanned arm, the ships. "It's too much," she said, near tears as the needy orchid in her arms started to tremble. Later that afternoon, Ron, Miriam, Susan, and Victoria showed up. They brought barbecued chicken, fruit, potato chips, popcorn, cookies, and orange soda, my favorite. Nina came with dark circles under her eyes. She and her boyfriend Larry had broken up the night before. She hadn't slept a wink, but managed to drag a coffeemaker through the subway for Gary, who hated the coffee at the hospital. I could see from how Lisa was sweating as she lugged her guitar behind her that it was hot and humid outside. Gary, my sister, my friends, they were spilling out the door of my hospital room. We sang Beatles songs, folksongs, sad love songs. Lisa played a few chords of "Yesterday," and sad-eyed Nina climbed into bed with me. I saw them watch me. Their smiles were too bright; I knew they were scared for me. I was scared for me, too.

Pete called in the middle of the party. "I'm downstairs," he said. "Can I come up?"

I told him there was a big crowd. "Can you wait about a half an hour?" I asked.

"Yeah, sure," And then, "Do you know a good place around here for a guy in a clown suit to hang out for a half hour?"

After the party, I fell into a dark tight sleep dreaming that I was dancing *Swan Lake* in a packed concert hall. I was so tired, but I couldn't stop dancing or I'd ruin the production. Greta had warned me about the exhaustion. "You'll have to learn to tell people when you're tired, so they'll leave you alone," she had said. At nine, the nurse came in to wake me: "If you want to see the fireworks, room 1213 is empty. Front-row seat!"

I shuffled off. Room 1213 was filling up with people from all walks of oncology. There was a sparrow-thin lady in a wheelchair, a girl with her face swaddled in bandages, a guy sucking oxygen from a tube, and me, the uni-breasted lady, all clapping and hollering as fireworks tore up the sky.

Having the mastectomy and reconstruction was merely the initiation, as it turned out. Afterward, I would get to spend quality time with my cancer. With the chemo came a demanding nausea. All I knew was that walking by a Chinese restaurant or looking at a pool of melted mozzarella on a slice of pizza could ruin an afternoon. On the third week after my first round of chemo, hair dendrites started showing up on my pillow and clogging the drain in the shower. Then, like dead flowers in the garden, I just plucked out the rest of it.

Dr. Smith got the lab reports back and told us that the tumor was big, and the node involvement was extensive. This was not a light case of breast cancer. How could the words she was saying have anything to do with me? "You'll have chemotherapy. We'll bring out the big guns." Although my cell structure and general health were on my side, she warned that the chemo would be rough. "I can always tell who will do well with it and who won't. You'll get through with flying colors." She looked me in the eye when she talked and I decided to believe her. She told us how she hated this disease, but that, paradoxically, sometimes people came out more alive at the other end. "You understand that you will die. That can be a gift." So live your life like you mean it, is what I took away from that. Doctors don't strike me as brave, but this one did. Let the games begin,

I thought to myself. It was me against me, and I was determined to win. I became the peppiest and most eager chemo patient ever. Dr. Smith even sent other cancer patients to me for cheering up.

Often Dr. Smith's waiting room was so packed that people were forced to sit on the floor in the hallway until she could see them. "Packed house," we would joke with each other. On one of those days, I was sitting on Dr. Smith's examining table right before my third chemo treatment. "Everything's healing so well," she said, running her fingers across the scar that circled half my back.

"Looks like someone tried to open me with a can opener," I said lightly. Then, without knowing exactly why, my body started to contract with sobs. Until then, she had only seen me resolute and cheerful. She pushed her hair out of her face and kept her hand on the back of her head. "Well, thank God this finally happened. You couldn't go on the way you were."

For the next forty-five minutes, we talked about dying, about her children, about how she could tolerate this job and for how long, about what it felt like for me to hear my name and the word *cancer* in the same sentence. We talked until I was calmer and until the row of people sitting in the hallway ran halfway to the elevator. No one complained, I guess, because at some time or another, they'd all had their turn.

I tried to act like a person leading a normal life, but the fact that my body had become a bloated toxic waste dump was never far from my mind. The wig came to symbolize how alone I

felt. Friends pretended not to notice, but to me it was as sub-
tle as a hair shirt. If we went out to dinner with a small
group, no one mentioned cancer, but as soon as I got up to
go to the ladies' room, I could see the heads at the table come
together in a huddle as someone asked Gary, "How's she doing?" I was never not different. Sometimes I made heartfelt
attempts to play tennis. Just wearing the shorts and holding
the racket in my hand made me feel as if I was still in the
game, but I could barely make it through a set without having
to sit down and rest.

I continued doing the freelance work I started after *New
York Woman,* but the din of anxiety was often all that really
filled my head. During the times when panic or fatigue most
got me down, I called Miriam, and she'd leave work to come
and be with me. She'd pat my head as I lay on the couch. In
a perfect imitation of the German accents we'd grown up
with, she'd tell me funny stories about our childhood: about
Mrs. Ruttleheimer and her plumed hats—*hunting hats* she
called them—or the time my grandmother yelled at her friend
Emmy, "You are a meshuggener noodle!" Nina sat through a
chemo session with me, and had all of the patients laughing
as she did a dramatic reading of the personal ads in *New York*
magazine.

One morning I heard Gary whisper on the phone to his
dentist's receptionist: "She's bad today, I have to reschedule."
He never said he was watching that closely, but often he
brought work home so I wouldn't have to be alone. He came
with me to my appointments with Dr. Smith. Sometimes a well-
meaning note—"I know how you feel, my brother died of kidney

cancer last year"—strangled whatever optimism I'd manage to bring into the day. That's when Gary would open his "Betsy Stuff" file. "A garden variety tumor," he'd read in a triumphant voice. "Dr. Smith says, 'I'm not worried.' "

Then one day, right before Christmas, I had my last chemo session. Just like that it was over. A month later, hair buds, like the first crocuses of spring, began to sprout on my shiny head. I bit into a Macintosh apple. The skin cracked beneath my teeth and a burst of sweet pure apple nectar filled my mouth. There was no metallic aftertaste and I didn't worry about whether it would make me gag. Food was back.

Gradually I stopped waking up to a thundering heart and the acrid taste of fear. Friends were less solicitous and started talking about their own problems again. Gary and I made plans for the future. Things that never seemed possible now were. Gary loves animals and had been talking about our getting one. I'd never had a pet before and with my asthma, it seemed unlikely that I ever would. Lately we'd heard about dogs that didn't shed; hypoallergenic dogs like Tibetan and Wheaten terriers. Cancer had become the fifth wheel in our marriage. Now that it had moved out, replacing it with something benign and living seemed a perfect idea. We'd name the dog Lou as a gesture of appreciation for the Lou who tried to help me sell *New York Woman*.

A few weeks later, we drove to northern Connecticut and picked out a Tibetan terrier puppy. She was white with a cinnamon stripe around her middle and a pink nose. Since she wasn't a Lou at all, we called her Lucy. In the kennel, she'd been living in a crate with her four other siblings. Her shaggy mom watched patiently as they scrambled over one another to get to her teats and suckle. The woman who owned the kennel had had breast cancer three years earlier. "This one's good luck," she said, placing Lucy in my arms along with a piece of sheepskin she'd slept on and a purple-and-red stuffed doll she liked to chew. It felt awfully cruel, wrenching this tiny creature away from her family like that. On the long drive home through Sunday traffic, little Lucy sat in the palm of my hand and howled in a piercing high pitch. I stroked her with my finger and cried too. Why was I taking on this responsibility now? How would I know what to do?

She scared me, in the beginning, the way she bit my fingers and gnawed at the furniture. It crossed my mind to give her back. Then little things happened. On a chilly December morning, Nat King Cole was singing, "Chestnuts roasting on an open fire," on the radio. I sang along—spirited, but painfully off-key. Lucy looked up at me, her head cocked, in the same incredulous way as anyone else who has ever heard me sing has done. She liked to sit near me and have some part of her body touching me. I began having conversations with her and making up songs about her. (Maybe it was time for me to get a full-time job.) I gave names to all her toys: there was Adventure Man, Becky Bird, and Irma the Duck. Gary's cousins came to visit from Sweden. Six-year-old Clara pulled at Lucy's fur and lugged her around like a stuffed animal, but Lucy never complained. Then on a rainy afternoon, as I was leaving the house to meet an editor for lunch, the phone rang. It was bad news. A friend who'd had breast cancer four years earlier learned she'd had a recurrence. Gary was out of town; there was no one to call. I sat pinned to the couch with misery. Lucy sat next to me. What could she have known? That I was making snuffling noises? That my voice had gotten stiff? She reached up and started licking my tears.

Twenty-Six

[ver since the afternoon of the diagnosis, Gary and I had planned a trip to Hawaii. It was Dr. Smith's idea: light at the end of the tunnel, and all that. Hawaii would be the transition back to real life. When we came home, we would replace the couch that Lucy had chewed her way through. Maybe we'd look for a new apartment; I'd find a job at a magazine. Lately I'd been compulsively trimming the wig. By now it had lost its will and no longer even resembled hair—a Chihuahua, maybe.

Going to Hawaii became the metaphor for coming into the sun. Often Gary would sit with me during chemo and we'd study the Hawaii brochures: pictures of crescent-shaped beaches with palm trees and moonlight, red volcanic cliffs, lush pineapple fields. We daydreamed ourselves into those pictures—the luau buffet, the king-sized beds, the thick terry cloth robes—never believing it could be that good.

The white sand, the smell of Norfolk pines, the garden of unearthly giant black stones, it was more perfect than a brochure could possibly capture. We went snorkeling, and walked on the beach and drank champagne and did all the things we promised we would do during the chemo months. It was whale-mating season in Lanai and from the tennis courts, high above Hulopo'e Beach, we watched the whales heave themselves out of the sea like great metal tanks appearing on the horizon of a hill. On one of those afternoons, the wind picked up and sucked the raggedy wig off my head. It blew around the court and we chased after it. No doubt it wanted to get away from me as much as I from it.

As we gave chase, I kept my hands over my naked head. Imagine what the people next to us must have thought: a bald woman and a man in size thirteen tennis shoes chasing an aberrant Chihuahua around the court. We laughed as we ran. We couldn't stop—we were doubled over, tears running down our cheeks. We finally wrestled the wig to the ground; by then, only a few spidery hairs remained. I had no choice. From now on I'd have to go bald. I had thought I would burn the wig in some kind of cleansing ritual. Instead, I dumped it into the trash with the used water cups and dead tennis balls, and served the next point.

We made it to the end of a set without me having to sit down and rest. Tennis was back.

That night, as we dressed to go to dinner at a fancy restaurant overlooking the ocean, I thought about what all the books had said about how to accessorize a bald head. Wear big earrings; make sure your eye makeup is dramatic. Have a positive attitude. If you feel comfortable presenting yourself to the world, everyone else will follow. My eager eyes stared back at me in the mirror. For the past six months my face had been the color of old newspaper. Now my cheeks were pink, my freckles were back. I looked healthy.

At the restaurant, I smiled at the maître' d' and made jokes with the waitress. They seemed blasé about my shiny head and all the eyeliner. After dinner, I went to the ladies' room. When I came back, Gary told me that a pleasant looking older couple had come over to the table. The woman pointed to my empty chair and said, "That was that Irish singer, wasn't it? You know, Sinead O'Connor?" The husband nodded as if to say his wife was always right about these things.

"I told them yes, you were Sinead O'Connor. I mean why not?"

I searched his face to see if he was kidding. Gary hooked his finger into mine. "Pinkies," he said.

Pinkies.

ACKNOWLEDGMENTS

I am indebted to Kathy Robbins, my extraordinary friend, adviser, and agent.

With her enthusiasm and keen eye, Leigh Haber at Hyperion made this a better book in every way.

Pete Dexter's suggestions were as smart and honest as he is, and I am so grateful to him.

Helen Rogan and Lisa Grunwald read an early version of this manuscript and were always there when the going got tough.

Special thanks to Malcom Carter for his generosity and support; to Miriam Brumer, Ron Rosenbaum, Jenifer Schweitzer, Samantha Schweitzer, Victoria Skurnick, Jeanie Seligmann, Nancy Kramer, Susan Kamil, Susan Moldow, Valerie Salambier, Ellen Levine, and Kathy Rich for cheering me on; and to Cassie Mayer at Hyperion and David Halpern at the Robbins Office, whose friendship and help were invaluable.

Gary Hoenig lived this book—on and off the page. I can never repay him for his uncompromising love, kindness, and gift for editing.